Liana Mistry is a pseudonym. The author lives and writes in Mumbai, India. This is her first book.

My World Without Jehan

Surviving a Brother's Suicide

Liana Mistry

SPEAKING TIGER

SPEAKING TIGER BOOKS LLP
125A, Ground Floor, Shahpur Jat, near Asiad Village,
New Delhi 110049

First published by Speaking Tiger Books 2023

ISBN: 978-93-5447-557-3
eISBN: 978-93-5447-561-0

10 9 8 7 6 5 4 3 2 1

Typeset in EB Garamond by SŪRYA, New Delhi
Printed at HT Media Ltd, Greater Noida

For my brother

CONTENTS

Author's Note

This book is written from my memory. It tells a story seen through my eyes. I have tried to be as truthful as possible and to respect the essence of the events as they happened. Some events and characters have been amalgamated for creative reasons. Any errors in remembering these events are my own. There is no intent to hurt or to offend.

I hope to reach out, through this book, to people who share my experience—those of us who have lost a loved one to suicide; we who struggle every day to find answers and to understand why; the ones who grieve in silence because the stigma and pressures that accompany the act of suicide are so overpowering and overwhelming even today.

My father has agreed to publishing this book under the condition that I use a pseudonym.

I wish to acknowledge and thank *Tehelka* magazine, in which certain short excerpts from this book were published anonymously.

Prologue

I WAS FOURTEEN when my brother killed himself. The four of us that remained went our separate ways, grieving in secret, never meeting each other's eyes. There was no attempt to sit down together and process this enormous loss. It seemed easier to bury the pain, ignore the guilt and carry on with the business of living. Sometimes it felt that he had lived only in my dreams.

It took thirty-four years and the writing of this book to even have a short conversation about that distant event with my surviving brother and my father, the gist of which was: Why are you writing this? Why now? Why can't you just leave it alone? I was told that I had been too young: to remember, to grieve; that I did not know what had really happened: the people who did know had not felt the need to talk to me about it; that I had lived a happy and therefore seemingly unaffected life. My mother was dead by the time I wrote this book or she too would have strenuously resisted any attempt to speak or write about those days long past.

The writing has happened in short bursts, with long

intervals in between. I was in the throes of post-partum blues after my second son was born when I wrote two or three essays that referred to my brother's suicide, directly or indirectly. I published only one piece anonymously in *Tehelka* magazine, the others stayed hidden in my computer. That was sixteen years after the fact and I had only just begun to recognize the resentment I harboured inside. Those pieces of writing constituted the first time I acknowledged a need to tell his story and mine. It brought a certain relief burdened with guilt, but when I was done, I closed the file and tried to get on with life. It was too overwhelming a feeling to acknowledge to myself, let alone to the world.

Then, some years ago, in 2018, my mother died of old age and cancer. The anger that came roaring up was frightening; it overpowered me easily. It took a while and the wisdom of old friends for me to acknowledge that this rage was the result of years of banked emotions, from the time my brother killed himself, complicated by more recent losses. (I lose people in clusters. With my mother, too, I lost some people I loved—to hurt and the blame game. But that is another story.)

A few months after my mother died, I wrote my first serious essay after a gap of fifteen years. It told my brother's story, his life and his death. This time, instead of saving it on my hard drive, I sent it out into cyberspace. The response was immediate and overwhelming. Memories, emotions, love came back to me in the form of messages and phone calls and photographs. Something ancient inside me, hard and bitter, finally found an adversary worthy of its mettle. It's hard to write this—I like to think of myself as a rational being—but the love that came pouring into my inbox turned that inner hardness into something far more malleable. Something I could finally take out and examine, even discard in part. The response to that piece loosened old inhibitions and anxieties about what the family would say or think. The words were clamouring to be written and this time—older, braver, angrier than I'd ever been in my life—it was easier to write from the gut, about the things that mattered very much, that had always mattered.

I had spent all those years silently mourning my brother, unable to speak of him freely, partly because I'd been too frightened of the emotions it might unleash, and partly because my immediate family had erased him from our collective consciousness. It had never occurred to me that there had been others mourning his loss, who needed to speak of him too and who hesitated because I never indicated my need to do so.

It's been several years of writing since then. At first, I exhausted myself with the need to get the words out. I wrote hungrily, draining myself of all feeling. My sleep was, as always, troubled by night terrors, but these were not the old familiar ones. I would awake having dreamt new dreams, with new ideas raging to be let out.

It's enough, I told myself. To get the words out. To write. It's enough for now.

Hometown, 1962–1976

I WAS CONCEIVED in Switzerland, where my parents were spending, by all accounts, an ecstatic second honeymoon after a separation of eighteen months. For years afterwards, my dad, Eruch (pronounced Ayruch, the sharp ch of China) Chinoy, would call me his little Swiss Miss, in a nudge-nudge, wink-wink sort of manner that elicited much groaning and eye-rolling from my older brothers. Eruch would smile into his moustache, looking mighty pleased with himself. He blushed a fiery crimson and never mentioned it again when I finally told him, aged around sixteen, that I knew what the reference to Swiss Miss meant.

Honey, my mother, had been a college lecturer in our hometown's university for a few years when she was awarded a Ford Foundation scholarship to complete her PhD in Food Science at Iowa State University. She was married, she had two sons, Fali, who was six, and Jehan, who was five, but she went anyway. Eruch kept the home fires burning and looked after the children. In this, he had the eager cooperation of his mother (Mamma), his aunt (Mamiji) and his sister-in-law, our Roshan Kaki. All three women were vindicated in their firm conviction that Honey was a no-good, spoilt rich brat with no maternal instincts to speak of. Why else would a young Parsi woman, living in a joint family circa 1969 in a small town in Gujarat, with a besotted husband to boot, leave not only her mother-in-law and husband but her two young sons to fend for themselves while she waltzed off to further education in a foreign country? (It was even worse because my father was a college dropout.)

The first thing Honey did on arrival in Des Moines, Iowa was to cut off her waist-long hair. Of her many acts of rebellion, that was one Eruch never forgave. There is a photograph of my mother, taken shortly after her arrival in the USA, wearing a leather miniskirt, knee-high boots and dark glasses sweeping back the blunt cut. 'Wow, Liana! Who's that honey?' my seventeen-year-old boyfriend had exclaimed involuntarily when he first saw it. Honey overheard and I caught a fleeting look of pleasure on her face before she tightened her mouth in well-rehearsed disapproval. She'd spent a lifetime honing that skill.

Honey came from a relatively well-known local family. Nariman, her prosperous dentist father, looked like an overweight, blustery Adolf Hitler.

'*Tahné to goli ma bandook bhari ne maarus!* (I'll load a gun in this bullet and shoot you!)' incoherent with rage he once threatened Eruch, who had come a-wooing.

Nariman was well known in the little university town for his volatile temper and his generous nature. (Honey's mother

Dinamai had also qualified as a dentist, though she never practised.) After seven stillborn sons, my grandmother finally gave birth to Honey. She survived, and by some fratricidal sorcery, imbibed the strength of all seven unfortunate brothers. Her very existence was reason enough for her to be pampered rotten by her father. The neighbours and the retinue of household staff, humble folk living in the centre of Mandwi, the old part of town, shortened her far too exotic name, Helaine (a minor Greek goddess), to Honey. Her younger brother, Rustom, completed their family. Honey grew up in a haveli (one of the many stately homes originally built to house the former king's harem, and then rented out in more democratic times to respectable citizens like my grandfather), surrounded by doting retainers, chauffeur-driven cars and a love for the limelight that never quite faded. In comparison, her brother was content to live a more grounded life.

So when Honey decided, at the age of thirteen, to bestow her affections on her Holy Name High School classmate Eruch Chinoy, aged fourteen, the poor boy was naturally bedazzled.

Hidden behind a tree in the school yard, he had once pointed her out to his best friend and solemnly declared, 'That's the girl I'm going to marry.'

It turned out to be a prophetic statement; Honey and Eruch were to live happily and acrimoniously together for the next seventy years.

Melodrama ruled Eruch's life from a tender age. He was the elder son of a young widow. His father worked in a cloth mill in 1930s Bombay. Cycling home one monsoon night, he was knocked off the cycle, hit his head on the pavement and bled to death. He left behind a pregnant wife, Aloo Chinoy and six-year-old Eruch.

Aloo moved in with her elder brother, Dorab, and his wife, who lived in a small provincial town. There she gave birth to her second child, Firdaus (forever after called Fredoo). Dorab and wife became the children's guardians and looked after the little family till the boys were grown men. Eruch naturally hero-worshipped his mama although he was, by some accounts, a bully. To this day, Eruch will not hear a word said against three people: his Dorab Mama, his boss and his dead son, Jehan.

The classroom romance begun on the grounds of Holy Name High School flourished well into college. By then, it was obvious to everyone that Eruch was destined for greater things than a college degree. Accordingly, he dropped out after his second year and went to work in the textile mill where his Dorab Mama was a foreman.

Honey went on to complete two master's degrees in Home Science, and by the time they married, she had started her career as a university professor. Their union was a clash of two social classes and two opposing temperaments. She came from a wealthy, highly educated and progressive family. She had always had her way in all things, and would expect the same deferential treatment from her in-laws. But the long-standing romance had given them many years to prepare for the arrival of their headstrong daughter-in-law. Defensive barriers had already been laid down in the Chinoy household.

Honey entered a marital home rife with undercurrents and conflicting loyalties. Eruch was torn between blind worshipful loyalty to his Dorab Mama and familial ties to his mother and brother. He had spent his childhood trying to emulate his hero, who was only too human, with strengths but also flaws.

Dorab was an only son born into a family of women, a man accustomed to rule over his household, which now consisted of his wife, his sister and her two boys. With no children from his own marriage, he was both a loving patriarch, and a petty dictator within the family. A doting and indulgent head of the house for the world to see, but no member of the family dared oppose him in any matter, great or small.

Eruch probably came to this realization as he grew older and became a father himself. Unable to let go of the lifelong worship of a man who had, after all, rescued him from a poverty-stricken childhood, he chose to remain oblivious to reality. Needless to say, Honey had little time to waste on Dorab Mama, his wife or Eruch's mother.

Honey was never cut out to be the bridge over troubled waters. She was an oddity to her in-laws: highly educated in a family where no one had aspired to higher education, a career woman in a family whose home-bound women were cowed by their men. Fredoo's wife, Roshan, who joined the family a year later, might have become a comrade and ally but the two young women disliked each other almost from the start.

Honey and Eruch conceived quickly. My older brother Fali was born a year and a half after their honeymoon. The first grandchild and grandson, much was made of him. He was a fat baby. And he loved to eat. He once crawled under a low bed and got stuck there. The household turned itself inside out to locate the baby. Fredoo had to slide himself in and pull Fali out.

Jehan was born just over a year later. It's funny that all my memories and stories of my hometown involve Fali and few that I can recall are about Jehan. There is no doubt that he too was much loved. A vivacious, extroverted child, kind-hearted and very affectionate, everyone had a good word for him. His quirky behaviour would be met every so often with an indulgent 'Oh that Jehan...' and a tender shake of the head. Nonetheless, he grew up in Fali's shadow, at least until Honey left them to study in the US.

Her departure in October 1969 must have left a huge hole in their lives. At thirty-four, Eruch was as unable to cope with her absence as his little boys—well, at least one of them. He was a loving but traditional dad, happy to leave the day-to-day care of the children to the three women of the house who coddled the boys. At first, the pampering in the absence of a strict mummy must have been very welcome. But the months passed and it gradually dawned on the two young boys that their mother was not coming back any time soon. Fali was phlegmatic at worst, and by all accounts, he was stoic about his mother's absence. Plus, he was still Grandson Number One, the little prince who could do no wrong. Did he feel abandoned? I cannot say. These events predated my arrival into our happy family. Also, this topic was never discussed openly, even in later years, except on one faraway day in a future I could not have imagined. As I write, I imagine myself in Fali's shoes. I know that *I* would have nursed a severe and lifelong abandonment complex, a grudge, an uncertainty that ate away at the heart of my most subliminal relationship—that with my own mother. I would never have forgiven her. But that's me. Fali and I are very different people. I have no idea what goes on in my brother's mind, any more than he knows what goes on in mine.

Jehan was another matter altogether. Vulnerable and volatile, he simply fell apart when he realized that Honey, who had been away almost a year, was not expected back home for yet another. Unlike Fali, he was flamboyant in his grief and had a breakdown of sorts. He stopped eating for a while, losing alarming amounts of weight. By all accounts, his frightening withdrawal and depression were the aces the family played to convince Honey to return home, before completing her PhD.

It was also entirely likely that her pilot project wasn't up to the required standards and she had to confront failure for the first time in her sparkling life. Perhaps she even knew that a premature return was inevitable. But the family story persisted about Jehan missing his mother so much that she abandoned her studies to rush back home. Although 'rush' may be an exaggeration. Eruch wangled an assignment in the UK from his indulgent boss, ostensibly touring textile factories to learn new techniques and order state-of-the-art machinery. He timed it so that they could have a leisurely reunion on the Continent before returning home in April 1971, laden with gifts and a pregnancy. The Swiss Alps had lived up to their reputation for rekindling romance!

I was born on a bitter January morning in 1972. The cold turned my lips and fingers blue, and the family doctor ordered me to be rushed to the terrace. There, the weak winter sun revived me and I let out a wail. Honey and Eruch named me Liana, and the family promptly nicknamed me Linu.

~

The family home was ugly and cold, a squat cement bungalow. Ten shallow steps led up to the deep porch. Inside, it was dark and clammy, a warren of awkwardly shaped rooms, a short flight of stairs leading down to an even darker kitchen, a long, steep wooden staircase disappearing upwards to the first floor. The rather more cheerful and sunny bedrooms were situated here, one shared by the two old ladies, one for Eruch and Honey and I imagine one for the younger couple. Where the boys slept I don't remember. Leading off from these rooms was a large terrace, overhung by flowering trees. An unkempt lawn spread out from the front porch towards the gate; here, a beautiful neem tree stood sentinel.

The part of the house I remember best was the terrace. On summer evenings, after the blast of the sun's furnace, the stuffed cotton mattresses, lumpy yet firm, were dragged out and laid down in a line on the still hot stone floor. By the time the family was ready for bed, the sun had long set and the sudden drop in temperature had caused the dew to dampen the mattresses. Now they were cool receptacles for our heat-exhausted bodies. There we lay, nine in a row, chattering and catching up, all animosity laid aside, with the cool scent of night jasmine filling the air. On full moon nights, Roshan and the old ladies would cook flattened rice in thickened sweet milk to be scooped up with hot puris. This was a traditional way to greet the month's full moon. I sat on Roshan's lap, being fed the treat, before snuggling up with her for a dreamless sleep.

Eruch and Honey were social creatures. They were part of a group of young people who had known each other since childhood. They met most evenings to play badminton. An outdoor court and net was laid out in the garden of our family bungalow, complete with floodlights, and Raju, our house help, served drinks and snacks sent out from the kitchen by the ladies of the house. Honey was a former university badminton champion and her place was on the court, not in the kitchen. On days when the weather didn't permit outdoor play, they trooped off to a local club. Eruch would ride his Lambretta scooter, Honey would sit pillion and the two boys would squeeze into the sidecar.

Once I came along, I was only occasionally included in these evening outings. Most of the time, I was handed over to Roshan and Fredoo and I spent the evening either at her parents' home (I called them Kaki Pappa and Kaki Mamma) or at the local botanical gardens. I became their surrogate baby, the one they both longed for and could not have. Kaki potty-trained me, sang me to sleep and fed me. I have no memory of my mother caring for me in the first three years of my life. No mundane motherhood chores for Honey. But she read to me. She bought books for me and taught me the alphabet of my mother tongue. She crocheted a pair of amazing bellbottom trousers so that I could channel my first crush, Rishi Kapoor. She taught me to dance the garba. She whistled Beatles songs to me. In a sense, Honey got me started early on all the passions that make me happy.

Except for one.

Roshan, my Kaki, gave me my love for food and cooking and feeding the people I love. Roshan also channelled her creativity through me, or, to be more precise, through my participation in local fancy dress competitions. I hated those, being shy in public, but walked away with the laurels because of her brilliantly conceived costumes and a heavily biased jury, usually comprising my mother's university colleagues or my nursery school teachers.

The four years I spent in that old rambling bungalow are naturally blurry, mostly images and sounds: The little room under the steep wooden stairs where Fredoo and Eruch tinkered with electronics and watches. The sound of Engelbert Humperdinck and three or four accompanying whistles, all in perfect pitch. Harmonicas playing lazily on beaten-up rexine upholstered sofas sagging in awkward places. Honey's dressing table, lined with cut glass perfume bottles and her trinkets.

I imagine I remember some things because the stories were told to me so often and by so many story tellers.

I grew up with stories of the fabled Julie—the best, most beautiful dark brown German shepherd that had ever lived. A departing sailor had, in last-minute panic, discovered he couldn't take his dog on board with him and handed her over to my grand uncle, who brought her home. She was Eruch's first dog, and the reason we always chose to bring home a female dog ever after.

'More loyal,' pronounced Eruch, 'less likely to misbehave.' This with a perfect absence of irony.

When I joined the family, Maggie, another German shepherd, impeccably pedigreed, was already an adult. Maggie was patient with us as babies. As she had done with my older brothers, she would carefully stand still and allow baby me to be placed on her back. I would clutch the thick fur on her neck and get wildly excited as my uncle Fredoo egged me on for the 'horsey ride'. She really did seem as big as a horse.

In the sooty black and smoke-filled kitchen in the basement, my Kaki would hand me crunchy fresh vegetables to munch on—raw okra/lady's finger and French beans were my favourites. I also held court to a patient Roshan on the red plastic potty I had. Honey barely held back her frustration at a daughter who was far better at talking than at being toilet trained.

Fali was once home from school for a long time with nephritis and a near brush with kidney failure. I would crawl through thin muslin curtains towards the bed on which my sick elder brother lay, calling out his name, 'Falu'. Eruch would recount, with tears in his eyes, how his Fali had withered away in that year, and his love for food was diminished on a diet of salt-less boiled food. Eruch's heart broke the day Fali asked if he could please eat his meals in his room instead of at the dining table, because it was too difficult to watch us all eat regular, tasty food. This story has stayed with me, though I was only a one-year-old myself—so powerful was Eruch's telling of it.

All this, but no memories of Jehan. None.

There are old sepia photos in my childhood album, in which I see that he was the one who played with me and clowned around for my entertainment, the one who smiled the widest, perfect white teeth gleaming in a sweet face. And yet, try as I might, I have no memory of him from those early years.

Home by the Sea, 1976–1980

I WAS FOUR years old when we moved to a little seaside town in South India. To call it a lightning bolt would be trite. But the trite is often closer to the truth than we care to admit. Honey's sojourn in the Land of the Free was bound to have a fallout. (In fact, there were many.) In the years after her return, she was clearly the Star—she was not shy about showing off her achievements or laying down her rules. She and Eruch were equal partners in their relationship. When she returned from her stay abroad, he was happy to let her make the important decisions, financial and otherwise; to navigate the family ship Chinoy through the shoals and currents of life.

Were there inklings of a mild lifelong restlessness in Honey? Or of a hidden insecurity in Eruch? Would she stay this time? Honey's love was always a somewhat detached creature. Her sons lived with the spectre of her abandonment for the rest of their lives. Her in-laws resented her flight of freedom and resultant independence even more fervently than before. The only conciliatory gesture she made to the family was to give birth to me. I say this with no pride, having had no say in the matter. But after two boys and a gap of seven years, a granddaughter was greeted with much excitement. Things might have improved for a while but Eruch needed a change from his humdrum existence. Honey had had her moment in the sun—now it was his time to shine.

Fate, in the form of his beloved boss, stepped in. This man, owner of a successful textile mill and other businesses, was persuaded by his son to set up a luxury yacht-making company in the Deep South, where the best carpenters and craftsmen were to be found. The son had in turn been swayed by American collaborators who swore that there was a ready market for fibreglass ocean-going yachts with hand-crafted wooden interiors. The boss and his son had never set foot in South India. They decided to promote Eruch and send him on the adventure of a lifetime. Eruch was to be General Manager of a company making luxury yachts—about which he knew nothing. The boss was confident that Eruch would learn on the job and make a success of the operation.

The news broke over the family like a tidal wave. Honey was still traditional enough to realize that she couldn't argue or bluster herself out of this one. A flourishing university career of seventeen years couldn't win against a husband's prospects and his self-esteem. Besides, her return from the US had not been triumphant. All was not hunky-dory at work after her abortive PhD attempt. Her colleagues were being promoted over her and she was caught off-guard at a moment of frustration and personal angst. She gave in and almost immediately regretted it. She was throwing away her numero uno status, her financial independence. She would now have to learn to play second fiddle for the first time in her life and in her marriage. And worst of all, I think she was convinced that given the chance, she had the brains, the financial acumen and the managerial chops to set up this company and run it effortlessly. Instead, she would now be the happy housewife and social butterfly. I think too, that the first kernels of bitterness took root in Honey around this time and were secretly nurtured until they emerged, a lifetime later, a flourishing forest of spite and anger, with a thick undergrowth of discontent.

And Eruch? Eruch was suddenly transformed. He went rushing off, galvanized by his boss' declaration of faith in his latent abilities, to discover the unknown. He supervised the construction of the factory on the backwaters of the Arabian Sea, found a house in a fashionable part of town, and sought admission for the boys in the only decent English-medium school there. All this took over a year to accomplish. Finally, it was time for the rest of us to join him. That was really when life changed for us all. The school had a place for Jehan in standard five. It was newly established and only added one higher class each year. There was no standard seven yet and therefore no place for Fali. The other schools taught classes in the local language and hence were not an option.

Fali was thirteen years old. He loved his world and his place in it. He had friends and cousins, an extended family that doted on him. The bombshell that turned our lives upside down apparently had no effect on the stoic of the family. In true impulsive teenage style, he declared that if the seaside town didn't want him, then he didn't want it either. He was going to stay in his hometown. In fact, he would stay with Eruch's cousin, Soli, who had recently returned home from the USA with my aunt Chitra and their two sons a few months older and younger to Fali. This beloved aunt of mine had come back armed with a PhD and set out on a stellar career at the same university that Honey was now bidding a farewell to. (When they had landed at the airport, her mother-in-law, straining her old eyes to see, had thought my aunt was carrying a third child, a baby in her arms. The old lady clutched at Eruch, who had accompanied her to the airport, muttering imprecations at unruly sons and disobedient daughters-in-law who didn't think it fit to inform the matriarch of the family of her latest grandchild. The grandchild turned out to be a big blonde teddy bear, a gift for the niece they had never met. That bear was almost as large as two-year-old me and remained my faithful companion, witnessing my life with glassy button eyes until I got married twenty-one years later. He never uttered a word of reproach either.)

Meeting close cousins every single day, running in and out of their homes, is one thing; living with them is quite another. Perhaps there were rules to be followed now. Fali would no longer be kingpin and spoilt darling of the house. Instead, he would be one of three boys, all treated with the same tough love my aunt and uncle meted out. The cousins had grown up smart and talented and independent. They did household chores, cleaned up after themselves. It was an American-as-apple-pie household into which Fali was convinced he would fit in just fine.

A kid who had never lifted a finger in his life, bolstered by fulsome praise from all sides, and suddenly bereft of his own family, was now going to be living in a strange new environment, admittedly in the same town he loved and called home, but far from his mother. Those were days when you booked a trunk call and were connected only after hours of waiting, sometimes not at all, by the operators who were always ladies and who spoke with a certain dryness in their voices, possibly wearied by long hours of denying human communication. There was no internet, no Skype, and no cell phone. There were only letters written by a young boy trying hard to be grown up and independent.

Eruch and Honey made that call to leave Fali behind with the best of intentions. Certainly, our cousins treated him as one of their own. But he now became a visitor during the holidays, still part of the family but apart in some indefinable way. Even if this realization had hit him then, that this separation would be as much of the mind as of the body, it would have been too late to do anything to resolve it. Eruch was settled in his important new job. How could thirteen-year-old Fali beg them to return? But this is conjecture on my part. Fali neither begged nor in any way indicated that he was anything but a happy teenager, living life on his own terms, the umbilicus stretched thin by distance and absence.

Ironically, it was Jehan, now the centre of our truncated family, who remained insecure and haunted by Honey's first abandonment. Fali, separated twice now in his short life from that beautiful, wilful, intelligent woman he called mummy, weathered the storm in quite a different manner.

He came to us during summer vacations (each time I thought a cousin was visiting), and of course there were the letters and those pesky trunk calls and regular updates from Soli and Chitra Kaki. One summer, Jehan and I were vacationing back home. Fali and our cousin Rushad had gone trekking to Kashmir. They returned just before the end of our holidays, lugging a huge crate of cherries and a little yak hair purse for me. It was my first purse, a cute yak face with black eyes and a red tongue, and very special, because Fali had given it to me. But for all that, he was a distant thought for most of the year. Soon, in our strange new town, his memory waned in my mind and Jehan's presence took centre stage.

~

At four years of age, I spoke only my mother tongue and a little Hindi. The local languages were incomprehensible to me. I missed Roshan and the old ladies. But there was also plenty to distract a toddler. A new house, white and sunny and airy, filled with an amazing new fragrance I couldn't identify. A sunny, well-kept garden, a garage with a *car*. We'd never sat in a car in my memory and now we had two at our disposal: big, bumbling Ambassadors, each with a driver. The garden walls were only waist high, making it easy to explore the neighbourhood of more such bungalows. And other children! For the first time in my life, I had friends who lived down the same street, some of whom went to the same school as Jehan. I would join them in the coming year.

That new fragrance that I remember so well? It turned out to be the salty tang of the sea, with notes of coconut and fresh fish always tantalizing the senses. I took one look at the blue backwaters framed by the dark green coconut trees and fell in love with this piece of heaven by the ocean. We landlubbers were quickly transformed into seafarers and ocean islanders. Our backyard neighbours were the Norwegian Fisheries, with a retail outlet redolent of fresh seafood. The fisherwomen came around daily, bearing leaky bamboo baskets filled with pearl spot, crabs, prawns and mussels. The neighbour ladies helped translate the haggling at first, and soon enough, Honey was trying out a pidgin version to loud choruses of approval.

My mother was in her element once she came to terms with her new set of circumstances. She had left her college professor avatar (slinky saris and armfuls of oxidized silver bangles) behind. Now Madam would wear dark glasses and denim skirts, chiffon saris or tie-and-dye kurtas; she would swish into the backseat of the chauffeured car and be whisked off to garden parties or funfair openings, or more prosaically, to the market or the dentist.

Leaving behind exam papers and lesson plans also seemed to give space to her latent creativity. She lavished attention on the house and the garden. She returned triumphant from a shopping expedition one day, laden down with canvas, paints and charcoal, and books to teach herself painting. She dabbled with watercolours, oils and crayons. Her art was tentative at first, and many years later, I was still opening a book or a magazine and finding a scrap of paper with a finely etched lily or canna done in soft pastels. As her confidence grew so did the scope of the projects. An easel was the next buy and she painted some watercolours of the natural landscapes that were our view from any window of the house. She must have lost interest after a while because the next time she picked up her paint brushes was almost ten years later. That last phase of her art produced some very enigmatic portraits of old men and women, and the colour palette too was far more sombre, all olive greens and mustard browns. She had experienced the finality of life in those ten years, and she seems to have poured all her despair and anger into the lines on those old faces.

Our neighbourhood, Backwater Estate, was in a 'nice' part of town. At the end of our street was the promenade along the backwater and The Fine Arts Hall. Our little colony of six bungalows all belonged to a traditional matriarch. She had built the five bungalows for each of her married daughters and lived in the sixth one herself. Eruch, always charming and friendly, completely bowled over his landlady. We were quite exotic for the Deep South of the mid-1970s. Fair skin was to be coveted in a land of the darkest velvet. The Syrian Christian and Jewish communities could also dazzle with their light skin and striking features. Freckles, bright carrot hair and the bluest of blue eyes made the handful of Jews left in the fortified inner town very distinctive. But while they were exotic birds, we Parsis were the stuff of legend and fantasy. What made us truly unique was our religion. We were quizzed repeatedly about its antecedents. Not Hindu or Muslim, not Christian either—what were we?

When we arrived in town, there was only one other elderly Parsi couple there, who lived quiet lives alongside their Jewish neighbours. A handful of Parsis came and went in the five years we spent there, mostly young naval officers and their glamorous spouses. Consequently, we attended the funerals of many old folk settled in plantation country in far-flung and isolated parts of South India. There was no one else, so we went. To pray and to comfort, to bury and to mourn. Eruch would come over all sentimental, and before he could expound on the loneliness of expatriates far from home, Honey would be packing sandwiches for lunch and instructing Jehan to fill the water jug for the drive.

I remember one such event: a misty afternoon, a shabby house clinging to a wind-swept hillside, Eruch reading the funeral prayers from a prayer book. The deceased being a dour, uncommunicative man, his widow had lapsed into talking to her own reflection in a cracked and cobwebbed mirror, the loneliest of habits in a country where no one spoke her own language. That gloomy house frightened me as much as the old lady, who showed no sign that she knew that her husband was dead.

Eruch surprised no one more than himself by falling passionately in love with his new job. The American collaborators were given short shrift by him. He was the pukka Ubbha Parsi (Ramrod Straight, or morally upright, the reader may choose) cast in the British mould, and had little patience for their bluster and red-faced arrogance. The rest of us were more welcoming, especially (in my case) when they came laden with shiny pink-and-gold tins of Almond Roca (a cheap candy that was my first taste of imported anything and remains a craving forty-five years later) and amazing long-playing records which they generously left behind for Jehan when they fled home to Texas. I grew to love The Beatles (on a double album), the Eagles and Herb Alpert, playing the records on Eruch's little turntable when he wasn't around. After treating the Americans most uncivilly, Eruch proceeded to take umbrage when they upped and left. But he decided that he was going to get this boatyard up and running. And he did. The local engineers, shipwrights and craftsmen were more than capable, and soon, the little yard on the backwater began to produce elegant, ocean-going yachts.

When a yacht was ready for export, we would take the day off to celebrate. The yacht would be launched off the ramp leading into the channel and Eruch would proudly and carefully steer it to the port where a huge cargo ship waited. The yacht would be loaded into the ship, Eruch supervising every detail obsessively. It must have felt like saying goodbye to a kid heading off to college! Meanwhile, Honey, Jehan, Fali (if he was with us) and I would be entertained by the ship's captain, loaded down with all kinds of contraband goodies and generally made much of. At the end of a long, exhilarating day, Eruch and Honey would hug each other as we walked to the car and we would go home, only to repeat the experience three or four months later.

Jehan entered Gurukul Vidyalaya in the top class and quickly became the golden boy. I was enrolled in the little nursery school run on the Naval Base. The first couple of months were very frightening because the young teachers and my fellow students spoke English which I did not. I knew that Honey waited outside for the couple of hours I was in school. Any chance I got, I made a run for it, opening the little latched gate and bolting for the safety of Honey's arms. The teachers would come chasing, to soothe and to persuade a very angry and scared toddler to return to school. And then, just like that, I was fluent in English and there was no looking back. I moved to Gurukul Vidyalaya soon after.

First standard meant new classmates and a new teacher. Rama Miss was a fresh graduate from teacher training college. She spoke the most beautiful English—her diction was clear, her enunciation perfect. Listening to her speak, I fell in love with the language. She sang to us too. She had a guitar, covered in stickers, and it seemed the most delightful thing to my eyes.

One day, she said to us, 'Read something every day. Just read.'

Her word was law. I misinterpreted her advice to mean read one book every day. And I did. I have. Ever since. I read everything I could lay my hands on, simply because my teacher had told me to. I read encyclopaedias and dictionaries when I ran out of Enid Blytons and Frank Richards. One morning, I stood up in class to refute her story of storks bringing babies to hopeful parents. I proceeded to give a garbled version of the biological truth to my bewildered classmates. That evening, Honey had an interesting telephone conversation, which she later narrated to us, chuckling as she did so:

'Mrs C, what has that child been reading?'

'Hello, Rama, why, whatever's the matter?'

'Oh, not much—she's just got my class of seven-year-olds in a tizzy about where babies come from! I say, Mrs C, it's one thing to encourage the girl to read, but how on earth did she get her hands on medical textbooks?'

'Oh, ha ha, those were my father's. I didn't know she'd been looking them up. Thanks, Rama, I'll sort it out.'

I was Rama Miss' favourite student. Or perhaps it was her personal brand of teacherly magic that made every child feel the chosen one. She spoke to us about all kinds of things we had never thought about or experienced, and showed us by example to be kind, funny and sensitive to others. She stuck to her principles, even when intimidated by management. She taught us to stand up to bullies in the nicest way possible—lovingly yet firmly. When the school decided to switch her class and give us another teacher, we barricaded ourselves in our classroom and defied (with quaking hearts) our strict principal until she agreed to let our class teacher continue with us. She was our class teacher from standard one to three and these were magical years of singing on the school terrace, class projects on food, creating our own theatre group, and concerts of great organization and ingenuity.

Rama Miss became a close friend of our family. Her uninhibited laughter rang often in our home. She was irreverent, often making my dad blush with her wisecracks. He adopted her as a younger sister and thought nothing of reading her a lecture or two. My mother saw in her an untrammelled version of her younger self: a carefree, young teacher, enthusiastic and innovative, and loved her for it.

~

Was I jealous? Did I think she loved Rama or Jehan more than me? But then, *did* she love me? I suppose Honey did. After two boys, she was going to make sure I lived her dream. She was ambitious and even ruthless, in the nicest way possible. The family was fairly united in those early years on one thing: it was best to leave Honey alone to rule her little world with no opposition, no rebellion. This kept the peace.

I was six years old when she decided that cultural education was the first step on the ladder to social success. A classical dance class was offered in school to the girls. The venue was a dank and musty shed. The head teacher was a gruff old man (actually, he might have been any age between thirty and sixty), sprouting white hairs from ears and nose, with enormous eyebrows that had a complete social life of their own. He did not speak any language I understood and vice versa. Our guru–shishya relationship was doomed from the start and I could have told Honey that, except she took a cursory look around, decided that her daughter would make an excellent exponent of the ancient dance form and...left.

I made it through three classes of sheer terror, the catatonic kind that accompanies incomprehension. Slowly, it dawned on me that all I had to do was to imitate the movements of people around me. I still remember a couple of hand mudras and the positioning of the feet in basic posture as demonstrated by the rather nice young ladies. My confidence seemed to come back, and I told myself that can do this. I can learn to dance and pick up a language too—one stone, two birds!

The best-laid plans of mice and men...

Class Number Four: The old teacher deigned to show us young 'uns the art of the eyebrow waggle. He stood, arms akimbo, and let loose with first one, then the other, and finally both eyebrows doing complicated calisthenics independent of each other. He bent down to show each of us the sheer artistry at close quarters. He eyeballed an already terror-stricken six-year-old and her bladder gave up the unequal struggle. I simply let go. Later, a chastised mother crept away from that hall of ancient Indian culture, a soggy daughter clutched in her arms.

While I wet my pants and failed to become the danseuse of Honey's dreams, Jehan became the leader of the Backwater Estate gang. Six or seven of us walked to school, wading through monsoon rain water that was knee-high, at least for me, the shortest of the bunch. The lane we walked along was bordered by touch-me-not bushes. On drier days, we would walk, arms outstretched, furling the delicate leaves as we brushed past them.

School was an imposing modern building three or four floors high. Arriving late for the morning bell remained an on-going nightmare because latecomers lined up and got a swish of the principal's cane across their outstretched palms. Jehan regularly dawdled and paid the price. The one time I was late, I dissolved into tears and escaped with a gentler than usual cut.

I was growing into a timid, often frightened girl. The oddest things turned me to jelly: the beetling eyebrows of a dance master; the sound of my principal's high heels as she patrolled the corridors; invitations to playdates at friends' homes. Still, I enjoyed school. Learning came easily. I had wonderful teachers and even having to study the still incomprehensible local tongue as well as Sanskrit didn't detract from the anticipation of a brand new adventure. Jehan was not enthusiastic academically, to put it gently. He shone at all kinds of cultural activities, and was very popular with the girls. He didn't pay me much mind in school and I barely noticed him either.

At home, though, we were inseparable for the first few years. We bickered and quarrelled all the time. I acknowledged his leadership and usually gave in before his caustic tongue reduced me to tears. For all that, he was a caring brother, allowing me to tag along on all kinds of adventures. In the early months, we explored our neighbourhood with the other kids. We brought home little fish from a tiny stream that flowed in a lane behind The Fine Arts Hall, persuading Honey to buy us an aquarium. We kept parrots in cages, but after the second or third bird died of overeating, Eruch put his foot down and no more parrots suffered at our hands. We had lovebirds too, prone to depositing large splashes of doodah on unsuspecting heads. They regularly escaped from the house and could be spotted plaintively chirping in the trees for a couple of days before the neighbourhood cats killed them for their sport.

We missed Maggie but Honey soon rescued a puppy and brought her home. Badly mistreated and neglected by our former neighbours (Honey would snarl when she spoke of them even years afterwards), this little white puppy was left chained to their gate, no matter the weather. Their children liked to chain her to the back of a bicycle and ram it into the garden wall. When they decided to move back up north, they simply abandoned her. My mother marched over, picked her up and brought her home. She had been named Tommy by her previous family and we called her the closest female name we could think of: Tina. She had had an English sheepdog dam and a street dog sire. At first, she would hide under the sofa and snap at everyone, but especially me. I think I reminded her of the girl next door. It took a while and a few scares to gain her confidence. She turned into a sweet natured dog who adored Honey. We could hear her toenails clicking along as she pattered after her from one room to another, never letting her out of her sight. Tina accompanied us on all our travels. We discovered early on that both she and Jehan got car sick. They would sit, one at each rear window, heads hanging out, while Honey hung on to the belt of one and I to the collar of the other.

Jehan discovered his talent for showmanship around this time. We all loved music but only he had inherited an ear for pitch from Eruch and Honey, who both played the harmonica and whistled all day long. Honey had brought back a treasure of long-playing records from her stay abroad: Harry Belafonte, James Last, Paul Mauriat, 50 Guitars. They had added to this collection steadily: Hindi film music, Hindustani classical, opera, Strauss and Beethoven, Rachmaninoff and Ravel, Ravi Shankar and Parveen Sultana. Music roamed free in that white house by the sea. Jehan began to sing, first for school concerts, then, as his confidence grew, on stage outside school. He bullied and cajoled a few of his friends to back him up and formed what may have been one of the earliest rock and pop acts in those parts. He was only thirteen and they didn't get paid but it was all very serious. They even booked a couple of gigs in other little towns, travelling by train to perform 'Hotel California', 'Feelings' and 'Bohemian Rhapsody'. He persuaded Honey and Eruch to buy him a pair of knee-high leather boots and a leather waistcoat. He fronted that amateur band with amazing flair. They jammed in the garage, and I was allowed to hang around, secretly nursing a crush the drummer. Our neighbours were at first aghast, then cautiously appreciative of this family who alternately scandalized and entertained them. We must have seemed like aliens to them, the forty something couple, she in short skirts; he, fair and pink cheeked and charming; kids who were allowed to play in the mud, and play precious records until they scratched them. Our youngest friend Nitish was especially enamoured of our complexions. He simply could not understand how we had achieved that most precious goal of his—white skin.

'Tell no, Jehan, please tell, I want to be like you.'

Jehan solemnly informed him that there was a simple enough trick.

'See, Nitish, just don't dry your face in the morning after your bath. Then the talcum powder sticks better and you'll be white like me.'

Hero worshipping my wicked brother, he insisted on following the instructions to the letter, much to the confusion of his mother and the amusement of all us friends. Many, many years later, I came back to the seaside town and met Nitish, now an unrecognizable stranger. He had tears in his eyes as he recounted this story to me.

It may sound like a happening place and time, but in reality, it was a sleepy backwater town and there were long stretches when my mom and brother were bored to tears. Having reluctantly sacrificed her career, and making the best of a bad move, Honey initially poured her formidable intellect and energy—besides her fleeting interest in painting—into her garden. She quickly figured out the art of cross-breeding and artificial pollination, and soon her roses were her pride and joy. The next goal was of course the grand prize for best roses at the Annual Horticultural Society Show. The annual winner of that prize had thus far been a matronly local socialite who just happened to have a little girl about my age—a beautiful, rosy cheeked, lisping angel. That year, it was apparently not enough for the organizers to provide our little community with an eventful weekend of feuds and death threats masquerading as blue ribbon and Top of the Show. No, some dimwit had the bright idea to end the Horticultural Show weekend with a bang: a beauty pageant for local children was announced as the final event of the Show.

The buzz among the coconut palms was that the little girl I mentioned earlier, she of the toothy lisp and rosy cheeks, was a shoo-in for first prize. Had her mother not demurely and deliberately acknowledged this eventuality on the morning of the rose show, I would still have been safe and home free. But the universe conspired in many little ways to mess with my happiness. Not only did the rival win first prize for her roses, she then graciously invited the loser (Honey's gnashing of teeth was audible) to attend the evening's beauty pageant and watch as the rival mother and daughter team swept the day's prizes.

My mother and brother stomped home after the flower show, raging.

'Mummy,' Jehan cried, 'are we going to let that woman get away with this? Just let me get on that stage! I'll show her!'

'Jehan, it's a beauty pageant. You can't possibly...'

'Oh, really? Should we just kidnap that shiny little brat? We can give her back after the show.'

'Jehan, now really, no, that's too drastic. Though you know...it does sound workable... NO. No, Jehan, we are not kidnapping any child.'

Fortunately, they simmered down and discarded these crazy ideas. Only to hatch an even crazier, almost diabolical plan. They were going to use their secret weapon!

'What,' I innocently enquired, 'is a secret weapon?'

They did not deign to answer, and now that I think of it, refused to meet my eyes either. They rooted around in Honey's cupboard, emerging triumphant with an old length of jersey fabric she had brought back from her sojourn in the US. It was slinky and shimmery and a little bit psychedelic, paying homage to the sixties. I got the first inkling of the Cinderella–Fairy Godmother situation developing when I was told to stand still for dress measurements. I was then ordered off to wash and blow dry my waist-long poker straight hair. As I obediently stood under the shower, I could hear the clickety-clack of the sewing machine. It seemed merely minutes later that a floor-length dress hung ready for me to slip on.

Then it dawned on me.

I was the secret weapon!

Two more unlikely fairy godmothers had rarely been seen.

Mother and son cackled and rubbed their hands together at the sight of Cinders. No mouse or pumpkin dared to come to my rescue. Their true colours revealed, the witches of Backwater Estate were on a warpath, carried away by thoughts of revenge for cut noses and suchlike.

Much later that evening, I came home with my haul of cardboard crown, satin sash (bearing the legend Little Miss Angel 1977), a wilting sceptre and the only prize worth the double perfidy of mother and brother: a huge, multi-layered sponge cake from the best bakery in town, each layer sandwiched with a different flavour of Kissan jam. I stoically ate my way through the damned thing and tuned out a vindicated and exultant family.

~

One memorable evening, Honey sat at the dining table, shelling green peas. Jehan and I sat with her too, and Jehan's devilry suddenly triggered an outburst of teasing directed at me. I was a whiny kid, and sure enough, it wasn't long before the waterworks started. Honey warned Jehan once, then again, but he ignored her and continued teasing me. And then suddenly, the plastic colander of green peas was flying across the table, aimed with the accuracy of a past carrom champion at Jehan's head. The stunned silence that followed was three pronged: my tears dried up in amazement. I had never witnessed one of the legendary disciplinary measures meted out at regular intervals to the boys; these always happened behind closed doors. Jehan was left mouth open mid-teasing, air whooshing out of his lungs at the deadly throw. He sat there, peas decorating his hair and lap. Honey looked on, a bit dazed at her own actions. By the time Eruch came home from work, the three of us had worked ourselves up into hysterics, embellishing the little incident into the stuff of family legend.

The summer vacation was when Honey paid her annual dues, the fine for having escaped being a full-time daughter-in-law. The old ladies demanded that our family host them a few months each year. Eruch and Honey guiltily accepted that Fredoo and Roshan too deserved some time alone, and so, every year, summer vacations meant two things: the arrival of Fali at the start of the vacation, and then, halfway through, the return of Honey and the kids to our hometown. Here, we left Fali and brought the old ladies back with us. Or sometimes, Fali turned around and came right back with us, if managing the whole bunch was proving too much for Honey to handle on her own. Eruch was far too important a personage at his place of work to accompany us on these long sojourns. Instead, he wangled a couple of short work trips every year to visit the family back home.

Tickets for a first class compartment were booked three months in advance. Here, Eruch and his nitpicky ways came into their own. Anyone would be mistaken in thinking he was setting off for a picnic on the appointed morning, with such anticipation did he plan his siege of the booking office. The coveted first class compartment, the one closest to the loos, was reserved. It slept six, and Tina curled up at Honey's feet. Oh yes, in those halcyon days of train travel, the family dog travelled with you, as long as the entire first class compartment had been reserved for your use. The trip from our arid hometown to the home by the sea involved a switchover in Bombay, at Dadar Terminus, of not only train but platform as well. It was one thing to manage on the way in, with three mostly obedient children wary of their mother's short temper and one bag per person. It exploded into chaos on the way back, with two arthritic and recalcitrant old women, determined to give their wayward daughter-in-law as hard a time as they could get away with, and their accompanying luggage.

The luggage! Two large and battered tin trunks, one doughty cabin trunk that had survived some ancestor's adventures overseas, cloth bags stuffed full of non-perishable foodstuff (they didn't quite trust the cuisine of the South), a hamper with more of the same, and additionally, plates and cutlery and glasses, a water carrier, canvas bedrolls and walking sticks—it would not have amazed anyone if a polly parrot had accompanied them as well. All of this, plus six humans and one dog, were disgorged at Dadar Terminus usually around mid-day. By then, Honey's temper was riding high in the hot summer sky. There'd be perhaps an hour between trains, a scant hour in which to make our way over a couple of foot bridges and switch platforms. Honey's eagle eye would scout out the most amenable looking luggage porters, usually buff men from UP or Bihar, with paan-stained mustachios and jolly of face, and the platoon would set forth, Honey leading the way with Tina at her heels, trailed by me, and then the boys each in charge of a little old lady. A couple of porters formed the vanguard, and a couple brought up the rear in our stately, seething progress along the platform, huffing up one bridge, puffing down another, to arrive finally at the first class compartment of our long-distance train. The ladies would be installed first, cumbersome pieces of luggage carefully stashed away, more necessary items left on the lower bunks, and the porters would salaam Honey's handsome tips and hop off the train just as the guard blew his whistle. Tina would bark with excitement, and Honey's hands would stop trembling from nerves as she would take up her spot at one end of the lower bunk, determinedly ignoring the two women on the one opposite fussing around with our first meal of omelette sandwiches or cutlets stuffed into chapattis. The boys would take one window each, Jehan making space for me, and we were on our way.

Vada pav at Karjat, chikki at Lonavala, cousins waving and beaming at Poona station, loading us down with still more biscuits from Kayani's or bhakarwadi from Chitale's, egg and chicken biryani at Renigunta, the amazing thali served by the railways on prior order, late night tea at sleepy stations with no name—these marked our progression via Maharashtra, the border of Karnataka, and onwards till we reached the Arabian Sea around thirty-six hours later. (It was recently point out to me that I had railway stations confused in my memory. Renigunta is from future train trips to Bay City on the other side of the country. Some memories get hazy with time, but the essence remains truthful. All such errors are my own, just as this story is my own, from my memory.)

Eruch would be waiting for us at the station, beaming his good-hearted smile at his mother and aunt. He would then be withered by a look from Honey, who would stalk past him, nose in the air, and seat herself, arms folded, in the front passenger seat of the Ambassador. Eruch would sigh in anticipation of weeks of warfare and we would go home, tired and truculent. The only one of us who emerged, tail wagging and spirits intact, from this annual journey, was Tina.

~

Once we left for South India, Roshan Kaki became the backbone of the family. Her father, Kaki Pappa, built for her and Fredoo a beautiful new house, very modern, full of angles and interesting corners. They left behind their grey existence in that old grey house and moved into this sparkling white, light-filled home set in a beautiful manicured garden. I did the grihapravesh (housewarming ceremony) for that house. It seemed like a fairy tale castle to my child's eyes, white on the outside, white on the inside—white walls, white swing, furniture painted white, airy white curtains—ruled by my elegant Roshan Kaki.

Summer vacations were now spent in Roshan's queendom. The afternoons inside the white house were deathly silent. The dry heat was furious but the house, cleverly built with deep balconies and curious overhangs, kept the worst of it at bay. Curtains made of vetiver were doused with water and the rooms stayed cool and fragrant. It was here that Roshan Kaki taught me the basics of cooking—to roll out round chapattis, to pickle fish roe and make elaborate dar ni pori (sweet lentil pie). She was an expert in making the large, intricate designs in chalk powder with which we decorated our entrances on festival days. She had taken this hobby to a fine art. The courtyard in front of her house was especially laid with light grey stone so that her beautiful designs, glowing in white with little highlights of colour, would stand out. On the morning of my navjote (initiation ceremony into the Zoroastrian religion), she covered every inch of that space, large enough for two cars to park side by side, with chalk designs. I remember her sitting on a low stool, the chalk boxes on a thali next to her, each with a design of a fish or flowers or hearts cut out in the base of the metal dish. The chalk powder would fall through the tiny holes that formed the pattern when the box was tapped smartly. If done right, a clear figure would be left on the floor. She would take a tiny pinch of red or green or whichever colour was appropriate and dribble it into the centre of a flower or the eye of a fish. Then she would press down with her forefinger to flatten the tiny heap of coloured powder into a perfect circle.

Roshan Kaki was a beautiful young woman who loved children. She lavished all her maternal love on her nephews and most of all on her only niece. She was not sophisticated about it—she once told seven-year-old me that I was actually her child and my parents had snatched me from her and taken me away. Jehan and I had been sent on holiday with the family by ourselves that summer. I ran crying to Jehan, terrified that she would not send me back, insisting that he call Honey immediately. But I couldn't articulate the horrible thought to my mother. All I could say was that I wanted to come home right away—right away. Roshan Kaki never mentioned it again; nor did I.

Behind those billowing curtains and tall ceilings though, there was the vague unhappiness that comes from frustration. Fredoo dealt with the small failures of his life by continuing to live out an extended adolescence. Roshan flatly refused to pander to his wild ways and kept him on a short leash. Eruch took her side and Fredoo was left to manage wife, mother and aunt without even the support of his adored big brother. He still worked at the same company where Eruch had started his career, but they did not share the same idea of fidelity. While Eruch was determined to finish his career with these revered bosses who had given him his first start in life, Fredoo had no such intentions. In an impulsive move, he resigned from his job, caught up as he was in a dream of starting his own business, which earned him Eruch's lifelong scorn and wrath. My Fredoo Kaka is a wonderful human being, but he has retained a childlike naiveté into adulthood. He was quickly marked by unscrupulous associates as an easy target. The business failed, the losses piled up. The beautiful princess of the white castle girded herself in steel armour and showed us all, her sister-in-law Honey especially, just what her mettle was. She took on two jobs, ran a crèche out of her empty garage and took catering orders for all kinds of delicacies to keep the castle running.

Once, Honey asked her where her precious red gara was.

'I sold it, to pay Fredoo's debts,' Roshan Kaki replied, in a quiet voice.

Honey pursed up her mouth. 'You should have offered it to me, Roshan. We are family, after all, and we could have helped out.'

And Roshan had her little moment of triumph. 'Oh, Honey, you and Eruch couldn't possibly have afforded it. Never mind, my cousin gave me a very good price for it.'

For once, Honey was left speechless.

Life in our hometown soon left us travellers behind, until we felt like visitors and guests in the old familiar places.

~

When Fali came down for his vacations, fresh tensions would break out. He would arrive, and proceed to push Jehan and me around as was his right as the eldest sibling. I was a fussy and spoilt child, pampered silly by Eruch. I had developed a cool little strategy for when Honey made vegetables I didn't care to eat. While Jehan held court and unwittingly distracted the others, I would quietly stuff my cheeks full of the offending vegetable, then excuse myself, having an empty plate to show as evidence. In a matter of seconds, I'd be in the ground floor bathroom, hop on the hot-water pipes running at knee level parallel to the floor and spit the mouthful out the window. I could justify my actions by persuading myself that Honey's roses flourished underneath that window due to my regular dispersal of nutrients into their bed. She was none the wiser, because the gardener watered away the evidence early every morning. What I hadn't bargained for was Fali. This big, quiet boy, even less inclined to draw attention to himself than I, was an enigma to me. Here was a relation of sorts who visited us twice a year, didn't pay me much attention and left after a few weeks. He sat watching as I played out my chipmunk routine for a few days. Then, one fateful night, when the vegetable du jour was broad beans cooked with potatoes, a combination I particularly gagged on, he left the dining table at the same time as me. Except, he made his way into the garden and stood watching the little bathroom window. The mouthful of vegetables was spat out on the grateful roses soon enough.

Fali came back to the table and ratted me out: 'Do you both know what this little brat has been doing? No wonder your roses are doing so well, mummy. She's been throwing up her dinner in them.'

That was possibly one of the very few times in my life that I caught a whaling from both doting parents. Fali sat there, looking unconcerned, while I dissolved in tears, and Jehan prattled on, completely ignoring recent events.

With Jehan, Fali was far more visceral, kicks and punches being handed out freely by our guest. Physically weaker, Jehan was not above sneaky retaliation. Fali's favourite sneakers would go missing or his current favourite record would mysteriously develop a scratch. These are vague memories and readers should know I am embellishing them from clearer memories of a few years fast forwarded. One summer, Fali fell down the stairs leading from our second-floor terrace to the bedrooms. He sprained his arm rather badly and spent a few weeks in a sling. I remember Honey rushing to the stairs and the note of panic in her voice as she held Fali in her arms. And I dimly wondered why she was so worried about this boy who would soon go away again.

~

Jehan had formed a close group of friends within a year of arriving in our new home. Three of these boys, Paul, Joshua and Manoj, were his band mates as well. The lead guitarist, Paul, was a tall, strapping boy, with a mop of curly black hair and enormous liquid black eyes. He was Jehan's best friend. He teased me and I kept away from him, though I had a secret childish crush on Josh, the drummer, who was quiet and gentle. Jehan and Paul were inseparable for the first few years. They hung out mostly in the open garage shed, sitting on the low white wall, propping their feet on the fender of the car. Here they would spend hours chatting, playing music and eating gooseberries from the tree overhanging the garage. Then, and the exact time is vague in my memory, Jehan and Paul had a falling out. It was probably soon after they returned triumphant from their tour of the tiny neighbouring towns. The dynamic of their little group was forever altered. Josh and Manoj still came around, but it was clear their loyalties were torn between the two boys. It seemed Paul had confided to them his reasons for fighting with Jehan and they were inclined to take his word against Jehan's. It was all very confusing. What could Jehan have said and done that Paul would go so far as to tell stories behind his back? Sara and Angelica, the two older girls in our neighbourhood gang, whispered about it but refused to let me in on the secret. I was too young, they dismissed me. And I was also Jehan's sister. It took a while before Jehan's formerly undisputed position as leader of our gang was re-established. He had to work all his charm on the girls, who had a soft spot for him anyway, and they, in turn, persuaded the rest to accept him back. Paul never joined our escapades again, nor did he play guitar for the band any more. Jehan refused to tell Honey what had happened, but he was clearly deeply upset, taking his hurt and anger out on the family by snapping at us and acting even more volatile than usual.

Sometime after Paul disappeared from our lives, a quiet afternoon was shattered by alarmed cries from neighbours who had seen smoke billowing from the bathroom ventilator on the first floor of our house. I recall a locked bathroom, Honey banging on the door and shouting to the driver and houseboy for help, not allowing me to peek in through the door when a solid kick from our driver finally opened it. And finally, Jehan, limp, being carried out.

'I fainted,' he said. 'It's nothing, don't worry.'

It's such a hazy memory, this one, as if I've tried

unsuccessfully to blot it out. Did Honey block it out too? And Eruch? Did they remember that panicky afternoon on the day that came to haunt us all eight years or so later? Like all such doubts in my head, it will stay unasked and unanswered. In uncanny heralding of future days of panic, Fali was conspicuously absent for this first one too.

When I bugged Jehan once too often about Paul's sudden absence from our circle of friends, he snarled at me to shut up and leave him alone. That evening, I couldn't find my teddy. This one was small and brown, having been brought all the way from Germany by Eruch's best friend for my second birthday. He was my best friend, my Paul, and I loved him; he sits in a corner of my cupboard even today. But that evening, I simply couldn't find him. The house was turned upside down but teddy had disappeared. I cried myself to sleep that night, my arms missing the familiar bundle. The next day came and went. I was distraught when I returned home from school—still no sign of teddy. Then Anthony, our driver, came running. He was holding a very sorry looking bear, dirty, one ear hanging by a thread, a deep gash in his stomach from where the stuffing oozed out white and fluffy and both red button eyes missing. Anthony had found him lying among the dried leaves behind the garage. Honey gave him a bath, sewed up the ear and the gaping wound but I refused to let her stitch on new eyes for teddy. He remains blind to this day. The upheaval in my life over, I was happy again, paying no more attention to Jehan who was acting uncharacteristically kind to me. He was even willing to play silly games and didn't treat me to the sharp side of his tongue for quite a while. It never occurred to me to wonder why. On his birthday, he gave me a small teddy bear. The smallest one in my family of bears yet, this one was all plush velvet and came with a growly voice when you squeezed him around the middle. Though he was by far the nicest teddy I'd ever had, I still took my old battered boy to bed. Jehan's attempts to get me to favour the new bear never did succeed.

~

Our four years living by the Arabian Sea are like snapshots in my head, most involving either friends or travel. Some are Naval Base stories, of young lieutenants who came to stay on short assignments. Often newly married, they found friends and mentors in Eruch and Honey. They would ride over to our bungalow on Sunday mornings, laden with ice cold beer from the defence canteen. Lawn chairs were arranged under the shade of the trees, Jehan was deputed as DJ, and I was happy to sit and giggle over the antics of our guests. Honey would lay out a spread of fried fish, mutton kababs and dhansaak, guaranteed to send the eaters into post-prandial somnolence. Eruch presided, his voice getting louder, the smile on his face growing broader and the stories more elaborate as the afternoon wore on. He loved company and entertaining people. Moving away from his hometown really set him free from inhibitions he may have had in the past.

Once, Usha Uthup was to perform at The Fine Arts Hall.

The hall doors and windows were left wide open to catch the evening sea breeze. Sitting on our lawn, chilled drinks and snacks in hand, we listened to the entire concert as if she were performing on our porch.

Then there are memories of our neighbour (Anisha and Nitish's mother) calling from her house next door on Sunday morning:

'Jehan moné, Liana molé, come and eat.'

Off we ran, a little shy of our friends' father, glowering into his morning tot of rum, and gasping at the sight of a breakfast feast laid out as a matter of course after Sunday morning church: fluffy appams, duck curry, egg roast, idiappams, kootu, semiya payasam. We would stagger back home, describing to an envious Eruch and Honey the unctuousness of that most un-breakfast like food.

One night, I woke up to hear Eruch and Honey whispering urgently to one another and the phone ringing. Labour unrest had arrived in our forgotten little corner of the world and some friends of ours were trapped in their house, held hostage by a gang of angry workmen. The man was the manager of their factory and his frightened wife and small children were huddled with him inside. Eruch set out to their rescue. He narrated the exciting adventure to us the next morning. He had called them just in time and prepared an escape plan before the mob cut the telephone line. Having driven down the back alley, he killed the headlights but left the car engine running. He crept to the back door and knocked softly. The family was waiting, a suitcase packed and ready. They tiptoed out in the middle of the night and Eruch drove them to our home, where they lived very quietly for the next few days until they could leave town. Many months later, the labour strikes were broken ruthlessly (although the Emergency had been lifted) and the family could return to close up their house and mark an end to their life there.

On weekends, we would pack the car with hampers of food, thermos flasks and ice coolers. Tina would jump in, followed by the four of us and we would set off—no maps, just helpful directions given verbally by friends and confirmed along the way by the gentle and courteous villagers. We found a magical waterfall once, at the top of which was a natural pool. Set beside it was a little government lodge which anyone could use for the day. There was fishing, and an enthusiastic friend once brought along his tackle, determined to catch us our dinner. Sure enough, we returned home that evening with large rainbow trout. Honey prepared a whole fish for grilling, anticipating a delicious dinner. But the phone rang, just as the fish was about to be popped in the oven. It was our fisherman's wife on the line, alternately apoplectic and apologetic.

'Have you cooked that dratted fish? Throw it away, Honey!'

He had wrongly identified the fish. No rainbow trout, this, but the notorious parrot fish, with deadly trident shaped bones.

'Whatever you do, don't let the children eat it!' she pleaded. And that was the end of the rainbow trout dinner.

Perhaps we opened cans of sardines instead. This was possibly the trigger for Eruch's lifelong fascination with tinned food. A frugal childhood had left him with a need to always see a full larder, and what better than cans of seemingly imperishable food stuff to fill the storage to bursting? I have sometimes raised the subject of possible botulism, but Eruch continues to merrily stock up tins of every description, opening one every now and again and replacing it with two more at the earliest available opportunity.

~

Our time here was like a dream, sheltered by the blue sky next to a blue sea. Then it was over. The market for luxury yachts nosedived, the company was wound up and Eruch was promoted to a middle manager position in his boss' flagship company, a textile mill in Bay City, on the opposite side of the country's coastline.

This little unassuming town had been our Xanadu, our Shangri-La. Here, Eruch had finally found himself, and broken free from his lifelong indebtedness to his uncle, his childhood guilt for letting his mother and brother depend on charity. He had expanded his mind, and his stomach too. The whip-thin, athletic man who had arrived in 1975 left five years later, a portly, indolent, good-humoured man, with hidden health issues, but full of self-confidence, and finally, really and truly, the head of his family.

And Honey? She had loved her life in this new environment, the social whirl, the elevation to memsahib, the freedom from the in-laws. But she couldn't have it all.

She had had to give up financial independence, which was probably the most precious aspect of her life up until then. Along with the dependence on Eruch came the shift in authority too. Her focus now switched to her husband, his health, his career, his welfare. If she had to depend on him for *her* security, then she would make it her business to ensure he didn't screw up. I think she could never bring herself to acknowledge this weaker persona of herself, at least not in front of her sons. To them, she continued to be the woman whose love for them was never quite unconditional. But the Honey I have a clearer memory of was not the rebellious, abrasive and independent woman that has been described to me. My mother became gentler, kinder, more invested in my life, after we left our hometown and Roshan Kaki behind. The mother I knew ceded first place and the choicest pieces of chicken to her husband. Honey had settled for suburbia and it showed. The rage simmering underneath was so well hidden that it frightened even her on the rare occasions it boiled over.

In our last year by the sea, Jehan, almost fifteen years old, was elected Head Boy of Gurukul Vidyalaya, almost single-handedly running the clubs and cultural activities he had initiated. By now, his talent and charm were the stuff of local legend. He could talk up a storm, knowing exactly what to say and how to say it. He was embarrassingly generous—he thought nothing of baking through the night so that he could take cupcakes or brownies for his entire class the next morning. Or on a whim, creating beautiful candles and cards as gifts for our neighbours—for no reason at all. When Angelica, our neighbourhood friend, fell ill with chicken pox, Jehan spent hours serenading her with her favourite songs outside her bedroom window. Jehan could do no wrong—he was sweet, charming, loving, all the positive adjectives you could think of.

At home, though, the early signs of trouble ahead were starting to show. The charm would switch on, then off, and when it was off, a cruel streak showed up, at first only to his family. It was as if a battle was being waged between two different Jehans.

'Mummy, I need new boots!'

'Jehan, your boots are fine—what do you need a new pair for?'

'These old things? I need new ones for the next concert!'

'Jehan, beta, you know we can't order such an expensive pair again. A bit of polish and these will look fine...'

'No, they won't! I'm telling you, I NEED new boots!'

'JEHAN! No boots!'

'I hate you! You never listen to anything I say!'

And five minutes later...

'It's okay, mummy, I'll manage with my old boots...will you help me polish them?'

The fight over, all was forgiven. Things would quiet down. But then the next day, or the day after, he would have his little revenge.

'Are you wearing that skirt again, mummy? It's too tight on you...you really should eat less at your age.'

'Jehan, really! Don't be mean...'

And the demand for boots would be renewed.

Or he would confide in Honey's friends—little intimate conversations that carefully left Honey out. He was not above letting drop some little shortcoming of Honey's in the most innocent way possible.

'Aunty, your nails are so pretty. Mummy tries and tries, but she's so clumsy. Poor mummy, I have to help her with her manicure.'

Sometimes he wasn't even punishing her for a recent admonition or punishment. This was just what he did: played people off against one another, whilst keeping his own nose clean. Gradually, this behaviour began to infect his outer world as well. He would take sides in a little spat between two friends, making sure neither knew that he was actually fuelling the quarrel. These little power games seemed to satisfy a need in him, to be wanted, to be indispensable. Jehan thrived on confrontations, meltdowns and reconciliations. He was quick to take offence, not so quick to forget. He claimed to forgive perceived slights but always found ways to return the hurt in spades. He was easily hurt and flaunted it for all to see. He would pout and sulk, refuse to meet the offending friend, or write long, tearful letters to common friends, narrating a completely biased version of events. This would go on and on until someone played peacemaker, and in bewilderment, the offender ended up apologizing to Jehan, often without ever understanding why.

The pattern repeated itself—a cycle of confrontation–

resolution which progressed to a more concerning absence of any filters at all. He had no sense of self-preservation or inner fortitude. He allowed everything, everyone to affect him intensely, deeply, personally. He loved and hated with all of himself, holding nothing in reserve, unable to hide any emotion from the world. The frustration lay in his own expectations—that everyone he loved would respond in the same high-voltage, intense manner. But no matter how much he was loved and wanted, the emotion simply never measured up to his own unrealistic standards. As this conflict intensified, I think he truly felt unloved...or unlovable. No one could love him enough to stem the doubts in his own mind. The more popular he was, the more he was loved and surrounded by family and friends, the more he felt neglected or unappreciated or just not loved enough. Left unaddressed, his conviction that he was not loved/was unlovable would become the overriding factor in his life, a prism through which all actions, emotions and people were judged. And found wanting.

This was Jehan at fifteen. He was about to discover one more key facet of himself in the big city, and resolutely ignore it, just as the rest of us preferred to do.

When Jehan left the Arabian Sea behind, he left as a star that could only shine brighter. A star that had risen in the little neighbourhood he ruled with charm and caprice. He had found his personality, however much it confused him and confounded others, in the four years spent out of Fali's shadow. He looked at our move to Bay City as a fresh challenge. Also, the new city had plenty of schools and there would be no more separation for our family. For Fali was coming home to us. We reassured each other that we had missed him, he was an important part of our family and that we looked forward to having him back in our lives. None of us could tell whether Fali felt the same way we did.

What each of us thought in the dark of those last nights, scented by the sea breeze, was left unarticulated. What Fali felt about leaving the only town he had ever known, his school, his friends, remains a mystery to me. Once, after I was grown and my mother was dead, Chitra Kaki, our aunt who was his surrogate mom for four years, mentioned a small insignificant incident to me. She related how Fali had vehemently told her many years ago: 'I will never marry a Parsi girl.'

My aunt was taken aback at the fervour in Fali's voice. The wounds were not going to heal just by bringing him back to live with us again.

As for me, still unaware of the tensions and currents that flowed right under the skin of my family, I only knew that I hated the thought of leaving my friends and school behind. It wasn't easy for me to make friends. I was shy and stuck-up at the same time, very prim, to the point of childish paranoia as to what constituted good manners. The thought of Bay City was overwhelming. The night before we left Backwater Estate for the final time, I cried inconsolably. My life as I knew it, with its magical memories of our home by the sea, was ending.

Bay City, 1980–1985

WE ARRIVED IN Bay City in 1980. We spent the first three months living in cramped and basic accommodations at the quaint Parsi Dharamsala in the old part of town. This gave us all an opportunity to learn to be a family of five again. Every day, the three of us took a long and (for Jehan and me) frightening ride on the public bus to school and back. There was no Honey to drop us off in a chauffeured car. Fali herded us along, keeping up a muttered litany about spoilt brats who had never used public transportation before.

It was a relief when we moved into an apartment building within walking distance of school. The boys shared one room, the parents another, and I was the lone occupant of the third bedroom. This was a first for me, a privilege I had fought for and won over Jehan's impassioned pleas that he needed his own space. It was clear that sharing a room with Fali was going to be difficult on many levels: Fali didn't think twice about dropping muddy socks on the floor, Jehan liked to keep his space scented and clean. Close proximity also meant more physical confrontations that Jehan was keen to avoid.

Even their choice in music clashed: Cream and Pink Floyd versus BeeGees and Boney M.

But Eruch had decreed that as the only girl, I deserved a room of my own, and the boys would just have to learn to share. It never occurred to me that sleeping without the comforting presence of my mom and dad would be a lonely and frightening experience. The shadows frightened me, night noises made me jump and it wasn't long before I regretted the fight I had put up to have my own space.

I grew to love my school, Wayland Manor. This was the first time my brothers and I were enrolled in the same school—Fali in standard eleven, Jehan in standard ten and I in standard four. I had a pretty inflated sense of my own importance, fostered by virtue of being the youngest child and only daughter at home as well as a teacher's pet at school. Consequently, I wasn't the most liked girl in my new school, but I had my little group of friends and two of them were very popular. So I got along. I was usually the first to arrive at school, since I lived close by. As I grew older, I came to cherish that feeling of peace and secluded quietness under the rain trees that shaded our school grounds.

Our school must have had less than five hundred students, all the way from lower kindergarten to standard twelve. We were a mixed bag: diplomats' kids who didn't speak a word of English, children with all manner of disabilities, troubled kids thrown out of other schools. We had our share of the good-lookers, the heart breakers, the serial boyfriend material, the Malaysians, the Sri Lankan Tamils (refugees from the

Tamil–Eelam conflict), the druggies. It was a little microcosm of the world, our school, with an eccentric Australian as our principal/dictator.

Mrs Klugerman or Head Miss had washed up on the shores of Bay City possibly in the 1960s. Divorced and remarried to a desiccated wisp of a husband of Swiss nationality, this strapping, brawny woman took conservative Bay City society head on and gave the gossips plenty to talk about. She wore dresses, belted and flared. Her hair was short and jet black. She whipped the senior boys at tennis every evening, taught us glorious music and was the despair of senior school teachers racing to complete the syllabus. She would stand in the assembly hall, hands on her hips, like a sailor weathering a storm, throw her head back and routinely bellow in the middle of another Physics or French lesson—'Standard Ten, report for music class!' And we would abandon theorems and grammar rules to sing our hearts out, never understanding then that she had figured out the perfect way to de-stress us in the middle of a public exam year. Assembly every morning ended with us marching out to the tune of 'Colonel Bogey's March', thumped out by Mrs Klugerman. We had endless concert practices, spending magical afternoons riding our bikes through the shady avenues of the city before reporting back to rehearse for *Merchant of Venice* or *Joseph and his Technicolor Dreamcoat*. We were mostly happy in Wayland Manor. All of us learnt quickly to live with and like each other or Head Miss would want to know why.

We had fierce inter-house sports and cultural competitions,

learnt the meaning of fair play (our school motto was 'Play the Game') and grew up in beautiful white-washed colonial bungalows that housed our classrooms. A gorgeous shocking pink bougainvillea shaded our assembly hall and huge rain trees hung over the basketball and tennis courts. We Waylanders were the bad boys of the city. We were reputed to be the mavericks, the crazies, the supposed druggies and of loose morals, led by our eccentric, much loved and feared Head Miss. In truth, we were simply the misfits, castoffs and kids from progressive families. We shared two walls with Boys' Academy, the big rough and tough boys' school and the other wall with another branch of Gurukul Vidyalaya, an austere school of solemn children who, it seemed to us, rarely laughed out loud.

Those first years in the big city were good years. At home, we were around forty kids running in a pack up and down the three floors of our apartment buildings, staking out the common terraces and water tanks as our hideouts. There were rivalries and feuds, secret clubs and intrigue. An old lady living in a second-floor apartment taught many of us the rudiments of piano playing. I managed for about six months but then gave up; mine was always a lazy love of music. There were other interesting neighbours. The Rajmata (Queen Mother) of some erstwhile north-eastern princely state lived one floor below us and took a shine to Honey. They had long conversations over cups of tea served by a faithful retainer, often about career women and their frustrations, sometimes about our hometown's royal family, to whom the old lady traced some distant connections. The Princess Royal of our hometown had been Honey's friend and mentor in university. One day, the Rajmata presented Honey with some Ondori books. These were Japanese cross-stitch pattern books, much prized in the pre-internet days. Along with the books came a roll of the most exquisite French material, soft and white, with very fine squares. Honey fell in love. It filled the vacuum left by the knitting and crochet she'd given up in the sultry weather of coastal South India.

She went out and bought the best quality rolls of canvas available locally, very rough and with large, uneven squares. Anchor threads were carefully matched to the designs and Honey started on her first cross-stitch project, a bunch of red roses and smaller violet flowers against a black backdrop. The large squares meant that Honey had to use star stitches and the full six strands of floss in order to cover the canvas adequately. (A star stitch, for those who may not know, is done over nine squares—a plus sign overlaid by a cross-stitch—instead of the usual four, and uses all six strands of threads as against the usual two. At least, that's how Honey interpreted it for me, roping me in to cover the background with the endless black stitches. That's how I learnt to cross-stitch.) Consequently, the finished project was enlarged several times over the original delicate design in the Ondori book. It hangs in Eruch's dining room to this day. The white material was carefully wrapped in muslin and put away for a special project. It finally became a beautiful sari border of multi-coloured roses, and Honey proudly wore it on Fali's wedding day many years later.

It took a while for the family to adjust to living together. Fali had grown up in his parents' absence, and he had no intention of submitting to their authority again. I was eight years old and I watched this new family dynamic with a wary fascination. This big boy, quiet and calm, was very different from the only brother I had known for the past four years. Fali was seventeen years old, and an enigma to me. Not for him the loud declarations or emotional outbursts that Jehan specialized in. But he was as watchful as I was, though I wasn't in his radar as much as he was in mine. Was he happy to be reunited with us, or just confused if the loss of his independence and friends back in our hometown was really worth it? I know I felt very deeply for him, once I figured out that he really was my brother, just as much as Jehan was. The soft spot in my heart was always reserved for the underdog, the scrapper, and that is what Fali became in my mind in those early years together.

His teenage rebellion and angst did not sit well with Eruch, who decided, a bit late in the day, to play aggrieved and traditional patriarch to the hilt. There was one occasion though when asserting his authority backfired very badly on Eruch. In the large apartment complex, we had each found a group of friends. Fali took to hanging out with a group of young people downstairs. He was handsome and liked the girls as much as they liked him. Jehan, who baked cakes and taught anyone who asked nicely the latest dance steps, who gossiped with the girls and gave tips on wooing them to the boys, was adored by everyone. But Fali was clearly the catch of the little community we lived in.

I had made friends too, and one of them came from a conservative Catholic family. They were three sisters; the middle one, Helen, was my friend. Her older sister was madly in teenage love with Fali, and he simply wouldn't give her any attention. When her parents questioned her about the unusual amount of time spent loitering downstairs on the way home from school or the grocery store, she naturally painted herself into a lily-white corner. That her parents fell for this fantasy she wove so adroitly was abundantly clear. The father was a parochial individual with patriarchal notions and the accompanying frail ego. He was convinced that Fali and his friends were ogling his princess as she walked past them in the evenings. The princess, thwarted in her attempts to woo Fali, fuelled this belief.

One night, things came to a head and the outraged father came storming up to our house to complain.

'This rascal boy of yours, he stares at my innocent girl. He makes eyes at her. Whistles! What he means by this, Mr *Sinoy*, please explain.'

Fali flatly denied corrupting his daughter's virtue. He was so affronted by the accusations that for once, he opened his mouth.

'Dad, have you seen her? She's not my type at all. And Mr D, sorry to say this but I don't need to whistle, she comes running anyway.'

This minor incident might have been the end of the matter but I do have a hazy memory of Eruch and Fali having a showdown, a confusing recollection of some altercation,

Honey raising her voice, and even some talk of Fali in some kind of trouble with the police. I was never a part of these grown-up moments, but that didn't stop me from watching and squirrelling away the particularly memorable or traumatic bits in my brain. Honey was furious, and seemed to be restraining herself from punching the outraged father's lights out that night. Which father she was aiming for remains debatable—possibly both. It was all very exciting and provided fodder for the apartment building's gossip machine for many days afterwards.

We were never very close after that incident, Helen and I.

~

Eruch, brought up in a patriarchal and somewhat authoritarian environment himself, was often embarrassed by such refusal to cow to authority, or in Jehan's case, by the flouting of social dictates. He would bluster and bluff his way through arguments with his sons. His daughter, the apple of his eye, was never subjected to his mild wrath. I was sheltered, the quintessential youngest, the baby, the daughter, and the three men of my family had an unspoken pact to keep me cocooned in this swaddle of protective ignorance. Honey looked on in ironic amusement, the derisive look in her eyes a warning of the inevitable metamorphosis coming my way: there would be no cocoon, no protective family men, she seemed to be saying. You'll be on your own, adrift; make sure you know enough to figure it out by then. Honey had no intention of guiding my way. She always favoured the sink or swim approach to raising her girl child.

Eruch's most endearing characteristic was that he loved women. Not in a sexual way; he simply admired and adored them. All this and yet Honey never felt a moment's discomfiture. His heart had been handed over to her all those years ago, and in her tight grip it would stay. After the incident with Mr D, he proceeded to play peacemaker between the two families by praising Mrs D's heady homemade red wine, and easily inveigled the recipe out of her in the process. He mastered the art of home brewing and was soon pouring out thimbles-full of the stuff for all my underage friends. We knocked it back under his watchful eye, and if we got too giggly, he would calmly drive everyone home and tell the amazed parents that it was all his fault.

'The children asked for a sip, just a tiny sip, of my homemade grape juice, you know. It might have fermented a wee bit in this heat. So sorry. Just let her sleep it off. Good night now.'

Fali certainly made up for his earlier absence in those first years of reunion. I would dissolve into tears disappointingly soon in a teasing session, and he was a bit wary of Honey's sharp tongue when it came to defending her youngest. Not so with Jehan. Fali was a tough, scrappy fellow, and his idea of a good evening's entertainment was a bloody nose earned in a football match. He had no idea what to do with a brother happiest pottering around the kitchen, either baking up a storm or creating beautiful frosted candles. Their fights were casual, low-key but constant. I suppose these were no more than the rub and stress of sibling contact, but as the youngest by seven and eight years, the fights took on dramatic proportions in my eyes. My early childhood in the seaside town had been free of any such daily conflict.

The brothers couldn't have been more different. Jehan with his distinctive and flamboyant tastes, the histrionics, flaunting his differences for everyone to see, and Fali, always keeping out of sight, circumspect, almost boring in his staid clothes. They were only two years apart in a very small school where no one could keep any secrets. While Jehan headlined every social occasion in school, and thought nothing of volunteering to apply make-up expertly in the green room or demonstrating the correct way to catwalk to a roomful of giggly girls, Fali managed to stay well under the radar, finishing his two years in Wayland Manor without leaving behind any impression.

Jehan was everyone's darling. He was the guy every girl crushed on. He let them down gently, then turned into best friend and confidante. He loved the attention, any attention, and so he played along while he continued to search out his own nature. The old obsession with the limelight, of being universally needed and loved, had tipped over into a more adult need—Jehan needed to find someone who would love him with the same ferocious intensity with which he was prepared to hand over his own heart. He was desperate to find that one person who would be everything to him and vice versa. And he was quickly realizing that his tastes did not run to the female gender. In the conservative, traditional 1980s City by the Bay, finding this elusive person was a big ask.

Still, he was as popular and charming as ever—that hadn't changed. He was the first one to start the dancing at every social and sang his heart out at every jam session with no persuasion required. Jehan had something positive to say to everyone, and everyone knew that for all the mood swings, he was a gentle soul and a kind heart. Though he lashed out often and unfairly, he was quick to turn contrite and apologize as well. No one really held a grudge against Jehan, outside of the family. The more everyone gushed over him and his wonderful nature, the more Fali ignored him in those early years. And Jehan gave it back almost as much, sniping and bitching, until the overt rivalry dwindled into a guarded and stilted relationship at home, and a formal fraternal one outside. That equation changed not long after, with Fali taking on the role of protector and confidant to an increasingly troubled Jehan. But the early days were fraught with little bursts of strife and tension, or so it appeared to me.

Fali didn't quite know what to do about me either. I was mostly beneath his notice in those early years though one evening remains etched in my memory as a standout event of our fledgling relationship. Honey, Eruch and Jehan were all going out. Fali hadn't been quick enough to make his plans and so he was deputed to babysit eight-year-old me. The evening started out innocently enough, but then the devilry became too tempting. He emerged from the kitchen, holding Honey's huge iron cleaver, used to hack through mutton bones.

'Linu,' he said musingly, lovingly fingering the edge of the cleaver, 'Mum hasn't left enough dinner for the both of us. So, I think...'

I looked at him with no inkling of what was to come.

'I think...I'LL JUST CHOP YOU INTO LITTLE PIECES AND COOK ME SOME CURRY!'

This was followed by him chasing me around the house, brandishing the cleaver, whooping and yelling for all he was worth. I became hysterical. This boy I barely knew seemed to have murderous intent fully backed up with a plan and I was all alone in the house with him. Screaming, I ran into my bedroom and dived into my cupboard. By now, even Fali had begun to realize that the joke had not gone down as intended. How was he supposed to have guessed that this silly little girl would take him at his word? Abandoning the cleaver, he begged and pleaded with me to come out of the cupboard.

'Linu, I was joking. C'mon, Linu, stop crying. LIANA! IT WAS A JOKE!' setting off further hysterics.

Honey and Eruch returned home to find reigning pandemonium. I was coaxed out of my hiding place by a very sympathetic Eruch while Fali got the tongue-lashing of his life from Honey, with choice asides for the rest of us. It was likely the entire apartment building heard it as well. Her well-rounded diatribe included references to her moronic children (all three included in a spirit of fairness), a snappy order to me to stop the wailing, and lamentations for the misuse of her good cleaver.

Fali was grounded for weeks afterwards, and the end result was that I learnt to keep a very healthy distance from this new addition to our family.

~

The one time of year when all disputes and bickering were laid aside was the weeks before Christmas. Many of our neighbours, including Helen, were Christians, and the kids, at least, needed no excuse to impart the Christmas spirit to all the residents. Trees were decorated, stars hung on every landing, and rehearsals got underway for carol singing on the night of the twenty-third of December. This was the highlight for all us kids who were not going for midnight mass on Christmas Eve. We set out in a large group at around 8 pm, making the rounds of the neighbourhood. We sang carols at each door, and I don't recall a single home that did not welcome us with homemade sweets, or a cool glass of sherbet or even just smiles and clapping. This might be nostalgia. No doubt there were hurt egos or bruised pride to contend with in an undertaking of this sort, but all I remember is the sweetness of that evening of song. Jehan joined us as the star performer; we were all in awe of his stage career. Fali and the older boys accompanied us ostensibly to keep an eye on us little ones, but usually lost interest at the first cigarette and tea stall.

Cigarette smoking was a huge point of abrasion between Eruch and his eldest son. Soli, Eruch's cousin who had given Fali a home for four years, chain-smoked. Eruch blamed

Soli for Fali's habit. The family knew Eruch's little speech by heart:

'That Soli, smoking like a chimney in front of the children. And *my* son had to pick up the dirty habit! His own sons don't touch the stuff. Why couldn't you leave cigarettes alone, Fali? Never indulge in gambling and smoking, and all those drugs and things—haven't we taught you this? You'll always be a slave to these habits, my boy!'

Fali continued to puff away, barely acknowledging Eruch's words.

My brothers were satellites orbiting each other, never quite touching but unable to get away from each other. Fali's friends overlapped with Jehan's. In fact, it was Fali who introduced Jehan and me to the large and motley crowd that hung around in the compound of our apartment complex in the evenings. Bablu and his younger sister Ziya. An older guy, Siddharth, or Sid as we all knew him. Sid lived in a complicated joint family on the ground floor. He in turn introduced Jehan to his neighbourhood pals, Hari and Prashant.

Soon, my brothers, Sid, Hari and Prashant became a little gang, riding around town on Fali, Sid and Prashant's bikes. The older boys took Jehan under their wing, and over time, became fiercely protective of this strange and sensitive kid. They kept him safe from his own moods, jollied him out of the blues and shielded him the best they could from the ups and downs that he seemed to take to heart far more intensely than they could imagine. Jehan's mood swings were dramatic and no one, least of all him, seemed to know what would trigger the high or the low. When the mood took him, he would spoil his friends and us silly—baking goodies, buying gifts—the love he felt pouring out in every act. Just as suddenly, the good times would disappear. A thoughtless word, a misinterpreted gesture, things his friends brushed aside, affected him far too much. When the mood changed, everyone knew it—he wasn't shy of letting his depression show. He would withdraw behind his bedroom door, or slouch moodily out of the house, often not bothering to tell Honey where he was going or when he'd be back. Hari or Sid would go hunting, finding him on the beach or in some other favourite haunt. Sometimes, he would not eat for a couple of days, or eat when everyone else was sleeping. These friends probably found his roller coaster hard to ride, and yet they cajoled and coaxed him out of the dumps and back to some semblance of normalcy. Everyone would sigh with relief, Jehan would smile again, and life would go on.

~

Prashant lived down the lane, and seemed to have an unhappy family life. He was a portly, dishevelled guy, living an aimless life after college. He minded his family's silversmith shop during the day and schlepped around the tea stall in bathroom chappals after work. Jehan developed a feverish affection for Prashant. Unpolished and very rough at the edges, he was the oddest person to appeal to a fashion conscious and fastidious

Jehan. He had little charm, almost no conversation, and yet soon, we heard nothing but this boy's name on Jehan's lips. I think he found in Prashant that one special person he had been searching for. Paul had been an unconscious choice—Jehan was probably too young back then to understand or even articulate what had drawn him to Paul, and Paul had instinctively pulled away when Jehan became obsessive in his friendship. There was no such ambiguity in Jehan's mind about Prashant. Jehan was growing up, and only too aware that this attraction he felt for another man would probably never be reciprocated. He also knew that if he did shout it from the rooftops, as was his nature, he would quickly find himself in trouble, starting with rejection by Prashant and his own family. That did not discourage him. Jehan threw himself into a quasi-romantic, completely one-sided relationship with Prashant, who laughed it away and indulged his friend's eccentricity. But the more Jehan wanted to be everything to Prashant, as Prashant was obviously to him, the more Prashant kept him at bay. It was apparent that Jehan was far too flamboyant and open in his affections to be introduced to Prashant's conservative family as a friend—it would have raised eyebrows and been misconstrued right away.

Prashant had plenty to deal with himself, without this added stress. Constantly nagged by his father to do better at work and in their conservative social circles, he was having a rough time at home. Then came news that Prashant was to be married off to a country belle from their village, a girl he had never met and the idea of whom he was totally resistant to. The friends all attended the rustic wedding in the faraway town. When they returned, something had broken inside Jehan—his eyes showed the wounds of betrayal. Poor Prashant, handling a new relationship and overwhelmed by responsibilities, did the only thing possible to preserve his own sanity and peace of mind. He simply disappeared, ignoring Jehan's frantic and overt attempts to maintain their former closeness. In fairness, Prashant turned his back on all his friends after his marriage, not just Jehan, but Jehan was unable to look at this rationally. To him, it was a cruel stonewalling and so similar to the way Paul had dropped out of his life.

Did Honey see the pattern? Did she get Jehan to confide in her, help him to get over his obsession? Or did she choose to ignore it, hoping it would just go away? Eruch was the typical dad, old fashioned about feelings and emotions. It would never have occurred to him in those early Bay City years that his son desperately needed a person to talk to. Perhaps Fali, Hari or Sid tried to talk Jehan out of the depression. I have no way of knowing for certain. I was still the baby sister, overly protected, not a part of these confusing goings-on. All I could do was watch and observe and unconsciously absorb the emotions swirling around in my family.

That was the year Jehan failed standard ten and slid into a zombie-like existence. Nothing could shake his blues, which took him into a world we had no entrance to. At first, I had tried to tease him out of his megrims. But the glassy look in his eyes frightened me and his prolonged bad mood then became the new normal of my life. Even Tina's unplanned pregnancy, the result of a whirlwind romance with a street Lothario, didn't help. She gave birth on a soft bed under the bathroom sink. As soon as her puppies opened their eyes, she picked up each one and brought them to snuggle in Honey's lap. Jehan ignored her and the pups too.

~

Later that year, we moved out of the apartment complex to a ground floor bungalow set in a dark and unkempt garden. We were growing up—I was twelve, my brothers almost done with their teenage years. This time, the boys promptly snagged two of the three bedrooms for themselves, arguing that giving me my own room had been a failed experiment. Fali reluctantly allowed me to keep my study table in his large room, and to use it while he was away at work. Though I spent all my time in Fali's room (and thought of it as my own), I had to sleep in my parents' bedroom. My trundle bed was set up along the wide window, through which I could see a beautiful guava tree. This house was even closer to school, a couple of avenues down the same road. Tina died soon after we moved, of old age and tick fever. Honey cried as we buried her under the papaya trees overhanging the well. I never saw my mom cry again.

It took the concerted efforts of Hari and Sid, the company of friends and the formation of a fledgling rock and pop band to finally shake off Jehan's depression. Almost immediately, Jehan crushed on Bablu, the hunky and very masculine drummer of the band.

We were once again on the roller coaster of Jehan's relationships. By now, it had begun to dawn on me in a vague sort of way that these were not just friendships for him. As for our parents, I suppose that they hoped it was 'just a phase'. Fali, as always, didn't say much and I wonder now if he too was embarrassed by Jehan's behaviour or just worried for him. None of this deterred Jehan at all. He flung himself headlong into his new friendship, with no checks or balances. He simply gave his all to one person and didn't care who knew it. At the same time, he was very cool, flirting with the girls in his class, gaining the reputation of being the best dancer on the floor at any party and the hippest-dressed dude in our circles.

His current obsession was not going to end well either. Whereas Paul had been a kid and probably just instinctively shied away from the cloying and intense attention that defined friendship to Jehan, and Prashant an androgynous, ineffectual young man with not much self-esteem, Bablu was neither a child nor unclear about his masculinity. Bablu was a stud; we all acknowledged this undeniable fact. His biceps were carefully cultivated and on inviting display, especially on stage when he played the drums with ferocious strength, if not much talent. The girls swooned over him in his tight tee shirts with cut-off sleeves, and so did the frontman of the band, striding the stage as if he owned it. Bablu was all about female attention though. When his status was threatened by the unwelcome attention of this slight boy with an unkempt moustache and the reputation as a baker, candle maker and dancer, Bablu reacted predictably. He publicly informed Jehan that they were no longer friends. He chose an impromptu party at the end of another raucous concert to do this.

I had been finally deemed worthy to attend one of Jehan's shows. I sat in a row of giggling girls, sisters and cousins, a couple of surreptitious girlfriends of the band. My brother strutted about that stage, belting out 'Hotel California' and 'Bohemian Rhapsody', bringing the house down. He interlaced the rock anthems with soulful renderings of 'Feelings' and 'Killing Me Softly'. The joints lit up, and we sniffed appreciatively at the sweet fragrance wafting all around us, getting gigglier. Once the concert was over, a few of us younger girls left for home.

Ziya whispered the details of that evening to me the next day. At the after-party, Jehan had draped his arm around those muscular shoulders, and Bablu had snarled at him to keep his hands to himself. Fali pulled Jehan away but not before Jehan dissolved in tears. The rest of the band, the girlfriends and groupies, were stunned. The band broke up over this incident because Bablu gave up drumming. It was the last concert Jehan ever fronted.

Bablu still treated me kindly enough when I visited Ziya. But some unknown fraternal loyalty kicked in and I gradually lost touch with him. Fali and Bablu stayed friends, bonded as they were by the clear rules of masculinity. Did this incident bring my brothers closer together? I'd like to think so, though Fali's world was clearly black and white, and even I knew that Jehan lived in Technicolor.

If it hadn't been for Fali and three of our more mature friends, Jehan may never have recovered from Bablu's rejection. By now, Hari was doing his post-graduate studies in social work and mental illness. He tried to be there for Jehan, talking him out of this latest slump. Jehan's moods were unpredictable and prone to violent swings. And when they did swing, Jehan was cruel, even sadistic, with a cutting tongue and given to uncontrolled emotional outbursts. Of all his friends, it was Hari who kept calm when dealing with a screaming Jehan, maintaining a low-key front.

'C'mon, Jehan, let's just chat, okay,' he would say. 'Let's go for a ride. Just relax, man.'

Sometimes it worked and Jehan allowed himself to be cajoled out of the depths. But there were many days when he would physically push Hari out, slamming his bedroom door on Hari's genial face. A barrage of screams would ensue, Jehan venting his fury through the closed door.

'Go to hell, Hari! I don't need your lectures!'

'Someone please tell Hari to practise his shrink stuff on someone else!'

'Has that nosy bastard gone yet?'

Jehan strenuously denied every truth that Hari tried to make him come to terms with. He refused to acknowledge his mood swings and the underlying mental health issues to anyone, but more importantly, to himself. Hari would laugh ruefully, faced with this stubborn assertion that all was well, but be back the next day.

'Hari, man, I don't know what happened yesterday...' Jehan would apologize, shed a tear or two. 'Here, I made some pineapple upside down cake. Linu, cut him a slice. We're friends, right, Hari? Here, sit down... I'm sorry, Hari.'

And just as easily, Hari would be forgiven.

I lost touch with Hari for thirty years, but contacted him while writing this book. The voice, the affection in it, nothing had changed. It all came back as if we had met only yesterday.

'Jehan was the sweetest, kindest, the best person I knew, Liana...' he said. 'It was a different time then. We had no language, no words for what he was going through. His being gay made no difference to any of us. We just felt the need to shelter him—he was so vulnerable, more sensitive than any of us rough-and-ready fellows. All we could do was protect him as best as possible.'

Jehan managed to clear his standard twelve Board exams on the second attempt in 1985. He had taken two years to clear standard ten as well. Head Miss was kind but firm with Eruch and Honey. She maintained that her school was meant to help students exactly like Jehan, who struggled academically. There was no shame in failing; she was there to help him and support him until he was ready to face the pressure. Bright students like me would manage just fine; her concern was to get those with failing grades to pass the damned examinations. And so Jehan passed out of Wayland Manor the same year I completed standard eight. At home, Head Miss' attitude was privately scoffed at.

'That Mrs Klugerman, with her highbrow ideas. Ignores my Linu, a topper, and has the nerve to tell me, a college professor, how to educate my sons? *Mrs Chinoy, all I care about are the duffers.*' And here Honey's voice would take on Mrs K's clipped accent.

By the time Jehan passed out of school, he was once again in love. Sid stood by him through this latest upheaval. A quiet, mature young man, Sid didn't claim to understand Jehan but treated him firmly and gently. This time, Jehan was older, more circumspect. Possibly even resigned to the skewed equation of his relationships. Sid might have told him upfront that he wasn't looking for an emotional relationship but they could be close friends. To a boy desperate for affection from other men, this was a new equation. One that was far more dignified. Instead of once again losing a friend, Jehan settled for a one-sided and calmer relationship.

My friend, Amita, recounted to me a conversation she had with Jehan around this time. She must have been hanging out at our house one lazy afternoon and perhaps I wasn't around. She had a crush on Jehan herself, and trying to gauge his feelings for her, asked him as casually as she dared:

'Jehan, is it, you know...is it possible to, like, to love someone who's a good friend?' meaning, of course, herself and Jehan.

Jehan paused in the middle of braiding her hair with ribbons, and replied: 'Yeah, look at me. I love my best friend, you know. I love Sid.'

Years later, Amita remembered the gentle smile on his

face, the calmness with which he told a thirteen-year-old girl about this love, and how special she felt that he had chosen to confide in her.

'I think he knew by then...' she reminisced to me, 'that love for him would always be secret and hidden. He seemed to have come to terms with it.'

She spoke lovingly about how he had smoothly changed the subject and brought the focus back to Amita and her woes.

'You're such a lovely girl, Amita. You'll have boys breaking down your door soon, really you will. Then you'll forget all about me. Now, do you like the red ribbons or the green?'

~

Sid was in love too, just not with Jehan, but with my friend Ziya. The families would have had conniptions if they had been found out. And so Jehan opted to play cupid, in a martyred, perverse way. If he couldn't have Sid's affections for himself, well, then Jehan would win Ziya over for Sid. He would make elaborate plans that only he understood.

'Linu, call Ziya. Tell her you have tickets for *An Officer and a Gentleman*.'

'It's got an A rating, Jehan, mummy will yell if we go for it.'

'Who said you're going for it, stupid? The tickets aren't for you—they're for Sid and Ziya!'

'But then why should I invite her? Tell Sid to invite her, na.'

'Oof, you are so dumb. Call her right now, she'll say yes if you ask, and then when she gets to the theatre, Sid will be waiting. Simple.'

'And then she'll get mad at me—no, Jehan, I'm not calling her.'

'Call. Her. Right. Now.'

The upshot was that I got to see my first Richard Gere movie as a result of Honey stepping in to end the fight.

'I don't care, Jehan. If you managed to buy two tickets, you'll manage two more. Yes, you are taking your sister for this movie... Why? *Why?* Because I said so, Jehan.'

'But, but, mummy, it's an Adults Only movie. And Sid and Ziya, I mean, Sid and me...'

'Look at me, Jehan! Do I look as if I care? Now, if her mother thinks she's old enough to see the movie, that's what you'll tell the theatre people. And Sid and Ziya would love Liana's company. No, no more buts. Take Liana for the movie, Jehan.'

'Mummy, I don't even want to go with them.'

'Stop your whining, Linu. First you want to go, then you don't want to go. I swear, these children!'

'But...but.'

I don't recall anyone asking sixteen-year-old Ziya's opinion. But it was quickly apparent to her that I could very well be the shield she needed from Jehan's machinations. As a result, I got embroiled in this mess as designated chaperone, reluctantly tagging along with the ménage à trois to movies and restaurants. The more Ziya balked, the more effusive

Jehan became, extolling Sid's limited charms to her. Sid himself played the diffident, reticent lover to the hilt. The affair died a natural death when Ziya defiantly began to parade a string of highly unsuitable boyfriends in front of us all. I heaved a sigh of relief. Jehan was left to comfort Sid.

~

Honey couldn't accept that her sons were never going to shine academically, at least not in a scientific discipline. The distance Fali cultivated meant her censure had no effect on him and she gave up. He studied English Literature in college, graduating third in his class and the university. Was Honey impressed? It was a praiseworthy BA, after all. With Honey though, approval and praise came grudgingly and rarely, her own distant achievements always overshadowing and eclipsing most of her children's efforts.

Jehan had no defences like Fali's. Honey and he were at constant loggerheads over his lack of interest in studies. She was convinced that it was a simple matter of trying harder, and he—he was simply miserable. I think now of the stress of maintaining a brave front and a smiling face while juniors came and went, being the butt of not-so-secret jokes—Jehan, the fixture in school, the guy who refused to leave. Paradoxically, his refusal to show his inner hurt each extra year that he stayed on in school also made him very popular. Female teachers adored his charming ways and the slightly flirtatious attitude Jehan could turn on and off like a tap, though he gave them no indication that he heard a word they said in class. His popularity with the girls had never waned—he was the ultimate friend, confidante, mentor and counsellor. Most of the boys too liked him at a certain wary distance. But that dreaded Board exam wasn't going anywhere—it needed to be confronted again and again, bruised and bloodied though it left him. It hurts to remember how I casually laughed at his feeble attempts to study. When he asked me to help write a couple of assignments, I did it readily but gloated about it too. I boasted to common friends how the writing had been a piece of cake but my brother was just too dumb to complete a silly little assignment.

Zarir

IN THE EARLY part of 1985, we befriended a twenty-two-year-old boy who had tragically lost his parents the year before. Zarir was a bit older than Fali, pink cheeked, very straight, very upright and very (to my immature tastes) boring. He was earnest and enthusiastic, possessed of a loving and giving nature, but that was not remotely interesting to a fourteen-year-old girl. He was prosaic even while riding a motorbike, the worst crime in my book.

He was introduced to my brothers at the Parsi Club, at a monthly dinner anyone under the age of thirty dreaded. Living in almost ghetto-like closeness with just around two hundred other community members meant that we were all trooped off on the last Saturday of the month to participate in horrific rituals such as elocution, housie (bingo or tambola), or most dreaded of all, lectures by eminent religious personalities.

A rite of passage at the Parsi Club was the quitting of the first few rows of beribboned, scrubbed and spotless children to join the rabble of teenagers, rebels and assorted misfits at the back of the hall. Of course, at one time or another, we had all been the apple-cheeked darlings who hung on to every word uttered by the guest speaker or by the leaders of the community. But the irony was completely lost on us. We slouched at the back, booing quietly, and lighting up forbidden cigarettes in the ante-room of the hall.

Zarir made his debut at the back of the hall along with me. He was a much protected only child of older parents and had grown up into a very prim and proper young man. Now that his dear parents were gone, he was enticed by us ruffians to break out of his little world. Everyone could see the conflict raging in Zarir's docile heart. But still, he was a good sport and tried his best to keep us wild Chinoy children out of too much trouble. In turn, we very quickly made him a part of our family.

My brothers invited him over for dinner one night, and our parents quickly welcomed Zarir into our home with open arms. Honey and Eruch loved him to bits. Here, finally, was the obedient, respectful, prayerful child they had never managed to bring up. Zarir reciprocated with his big heart, which had been badly bruised by the passing away of his elderly but clearly beloved parents. He continued to live in their big house, crammed with Chinese vases and Wedgewood plates, but it must have been awfully lonely to come home to. He spent more and more time with us. I have to say that our world was strange and alien to him—the shouting matches, the tantrums, the midnight ice-cream runs, and later the drama—and till the last, Zarir was never ever sure whether he approved or not. But we loved him, each in our own fashion, and he loved us back.

Anyway, Zarir was soon eating his dinner with us every night, smiling quietly into his moustache as we teased him mercilessly. Honey would squeeze his shoulder in commiseration, earning her a grateful look. Eruch enjoyed his company. Curiously, Zarir was a mini Eruch. They even looked alike. Fair, round-cheeked, ever smiling. I think I liked Zarir as much as I did in the beginning because he reminded me of my beloved dad and because he was so very different from my morose, often bad tempered brothers. Zarir liked me too. We just hit it off—and in spite of the difference in age, we were soon chattering about music and movies. He introduced me to Al Stewart and Alan Parson's Project, I bullied him into taking a chance with Rainbow and Scorpions. It was like he had always been around, the uncomplicated big brother I'd never had.

Bay City, 1985–1986

FINALLY DONE WITH Wayland Manor, Jehan had enrolled in the same course in the same college as Fali. Jehan was a somewhat senior freshman. In his first week of college, a couple of professors would stalk into the classroom, take one look at him and shout:

'You! You are back? How dare you, Chinoy? Get out, get out of my class.'

Jehan would only too happily leave, but this was a mystery. Why did the professors hold such a grudge against someone they had never seen before? He would narrate the incident at home and we puzzled over it.

Until a couple of weeks went by, and Fali airily admitted to secret knowledge about this daily rustication of Jehan.

'Oh, they probably think it's me. I liked to swing from the rafters in the lecture halls. And oh yeah, I was a bit rude to those two professors. Yup, they probably think I'm back! Relax, mom, I graduated without you knowing all this, right? He he.'

In their early twenties, they even looked alike. The

moustache, trimmed neatly on one face, left shaggy on the other, à la Marlboro Man in the advertisements. The slight physique, neither touching five feet ten inches in their shoes. Only the eyes were different. One pair looked at the world with an arrogant, clear and steady gaze. The other pair were shadowed, framed by long lashes that often swept down to hide the truth, but they were also laughing, merry eyes.

As for me, I was in standard nine; my greatest ambition was to be made captain of my school in the next year. Besides that, there was my little group of girlfriends.

I had known Pia and Nalini for six years now since standard four, when I joined Wayland Manor. Nalini was the first classmate to make friendly overtures—she had been put in charge of the new girl and she went out of her way to make me feel welcome. Still, for the first month, I sat at my desk during lunch break and cried; I missed my Rama Miss and my Backwater Estate friends so much. Nalini would then go and find my brothers, important seniors in standards ten and twelve, to come and comfort me. Each day, one of them would spend his lunch break cheering me up while Nalini hung around, a kind little presence who made motherly clucking sounds, struck dumb in the presence of the big boys. The weeks passed and so did my blues.

Pia, Nalini and I had quite quickly formed our own small group in our class of thirty-five, with only ten girls. In the following year, we were joined by a fourth girl, Amita—the niece of my beloved Rama Miss. Rama Miss had herself recently moved to Bay City and lived with Amita's family.

Amita and I soon became inseparable. She was the exotic one, with a twang in her voice and amazing new ideas about everything. Amita became our gang leader. So our group became two pairs of special friends who hung out together. Pia and Nalini came from far more conservative families. Their parents were strict and kept a close eye on the girls, the friends they made, the clothes they wore. I think their family lives were humdrum and normal. Amita had two brothers and so did I. Our families were pretty normal too, just more relaxed and careless, with a blip every now and then in the Chinoy household. We wore miniskirts, hers recently bought in that Mecca of fashion, the US, mine inherited from my mom's stay there before I was born. This US connection was another common factor: Amita would speak of the US and I could echo her, albeit vicariously, through the stories Honey had brought me up on and that I fervently believed in until I was fifteen years old.

Honey's sojourn in a country far away from home, her temporary freedom and renewed single status, the young friends she mentored and the world she created for herself, far removed from the prosaic existence of her family, all these took on mythical proportions to me. The more she embellished and romanticized the experience, the more I was convinced that my mother was an adventurer and a pioneer in the struggle for women's rights. I was proud of her academic achievements and her willingness to break all conventional shackles and take off for the great unknown. One little part of me still holds on to that romance, though the intervening years have taught me that sometimes abandonment can hide behind independence and cowardice masquerade as rebellion.

My fourteenth year was turning out to be particularly special in a series of wonderful years. Up until then, I had been a quiet, studious girl, one long braid draped over one shoulder, ungainly, with black framed spectacles that made me look like an owl, though I secretly thought these made me look cool. But now things were looking up. I was slated to be captain of my school the following year, surrounded by amazing friends, discovering the heady taste of teenage power—all innocent glances and secret smiles, swinging hair and hips. In spite of this strange new me, I got on with the guys and would always feel more comfortable around them than with my girlfriends. That was the inevitable result of growing up with two brothers, I suppose. But it was also in my nature—I just understood the direct ways of my male friends a lot better than the innuendo-laden doublespeak other girls seemed to comprehend so easily.

One exception to that preference for male company was the new boy in class.

Karthik had joined our school halfway through standard nine. He had arrived from Singapore, a tall, handsome and most unlikely local boy made good. His style, in comparison to the louts in class, was polished. He had beautiful manners and the girls, with one exception, loved him almost from day one. For some reason, he irritated me. The day in our classroom when he sprang up to help me carry a pile of books from the cupboard, bowing slightly as he offered his assistance, sealed his fate. From that day on, we were at war. At least I was. My sarcastic retorts to his friendly overtures scaled ever new heights of unpleasantness but Karthik didn't seem to mind at all. He just smiled and offered his friendship again the next day. Honey and Eruch adored him from the moment he walked into our home one Sunday morning. Too late I remembered that my teacher had asked me to lend him some of my notes, and here he was, politely prompt, to collect them. He was polished, respectful and confident. I soon got used to Eruch's plaintive query:

'Why can't your other friends be more like Karthik?'

He was popular. He was in my beloved Bears house and I had to grit my teeth as he won awards for us on Sports Day. He was a musical prodigy. But the more he tried to be friendly and helpful to me, the ruder and more obnoxious I became. He was just too nice to be true and I was deeply suspicious of his motives.

~

1985 was drawing to a close. The Chinoy household was peaceful for the most part, and we all looked forward to the coming year which promised to be far more exciting. Fali, for one, was planning an October wedding. He had obtained a degree from a city college two years earlier, found a job, and a girlfriend. He was still the quiet rebel, resolutely stubborn and not averse to giving any of us a piece of his mind when provoked. And we provoked him often enough. He chose his friends with care; not many people could claim to be close to Fali. As for us at home, he clearly bewildered Eruch and Honey. He was loving but barely. He tolerated us in the kindest way. A prickly wall surrounded this eldest child, and he assiduously added barriers to it, keeping his defences up. They had left behind a pliant, content child in 1976 and this grown man, critical of their parenting of his younger siblings, determined to make his career and his life on his own terms, came as a shock to them. Parental control is a phenomenon I had heard about but certainly never seen put into actual practice in my home. Eruch and Honey tended to let things slide, preferring to turn a blind eye, whether to Fali's silent rebellions or to Jehan's flamboyant showdowns. I was Miss Goody Two-Shoes, never putting a foot wrong or uttering one word against my adored Eruch and Honey, whom I loved and feared in equal measure.

Only one thing made home life uncomfortable. By late 1985, Zarir, whom I treated pretty much like another brother, was behaving strangely. It seemed as if Zarir had begun to dream of company in that big echoing mausoleum of a house, crammed with rare and antique Chinese vases the height of a man. He could never quite work up the nerve to declare himself—I was only fourteen, though I was a precocious fourteen he couldn't have imagined if he tried. He was almost twenty-four and his morals wouldn't let him even ask me out on a date. To be fair, I never encouraged him at all. But I couldn't help but be myself around him—and the more I treated him as one of my own people, the harder it must have become. A few months later, when I fell madly in love with someone quite different, and in the face of much fraternal opposition, Zarir even became my reluctant confidante.

Though I had no feelings other than the purely platonic towards him, I confess that the feeling of power over this grown-up, very capable young man was heady. I was also beginning to understand that candour and affection, an open face and feelings laid out like a deck of cards could so easily be misconstrued. After a childhood spent agonizing over silly things like whether my panties would show if I swung upside down from the jungle gym, it was a relief to find out that I was never really going to be comfortable hiding what I felt. In those days, it was called being bindaas (carefree or even careless) or a rebel, or some such label. A well-brought-up girl would never dream of telling a boy she liked that she did indeed like him. Instead, one was expected to play fast and loose with his affections, leave him guessing and begging for more. Perhaps that's the kind of girl Zarir thought I was.

The Parsi community of Bay City in the eighties had a clear problem of demand and supply. We were a pretty large group of young singles between the ages of fourteen and twenty-four. Among us were at least five sets of sisters, each prettier than the next. Then there were one or two pairs of personable brothers, mine included, much to my everlasting amusement. (I was oblivious to the so-called charms of my irritating brothers.) The rest of us made up the loose change. The problem was that not everyone hit it off and ended up as convenient pairs, as fondly hoped for by our parents. The sets of sisters positively loathed each other, spreading ridiculous rumours about each other's morals. Frustratingly for them, the boys were proving difficult to pin down. Some, like Fali, had early on declared their intention to never get saddled with a Parsi girl, and were given up as lost causes. And the eligible, willing young men like Zarir tended to fall for the entirely wrong girls. As in, me. I suddenly became the unwitting target of a concerted campaign of vilification. All I had done, inadvertently, was to become Zarir's not-so-secret love interest. The sisters were all united against a common enemy.

Jehan's gossip radar was acute at worst and positively cutting edge at best. He rose up in affronted arms at this deliberate insult to his sister, for whom he suddenly discovered a protective streak. That boy lived for drama and this intrigue was right up his boardwalk. His own network of spies and informants in the enemy camp was formidable. He retaliated by spreading mostly unsubstantiated but hard to refute rumours about the sisters. Attack followed counterattack and the situation spiralled out of control. Teary girls began to confess alleged or imagined misdeeds to shocked parents (unsuitable boyfriends, nights out on the town, and such) until a couple of furious mothers stormed into our house for a showdown.

Honey and Jehan put up a spirited defence of my lily-white and supposedly virginal reputation.

'Linu is so young! Do you think I would encourage her to dangle after an older boy? She is going to study, be a career woman—like me. Boys can wait! Perhaps your girls could also pay more attention to their books.'

'Aunty,' Jehan would interject innocently, as if taking her side, 'you know how it is with these girls—heads full of dreams. The other day, your daughter was telling me how much she adores boys and going on dates. I told her not to think such shameless thoughts but...'

Zarir turned all shades of red and purple when confronted by the aggrieved parties and hastily denied any interest in the female species at all.

'Me? Helaine Aunty, you know I have no such intentions! I swear, on my mother's soul. And Liana! Why, she's like a sister to me,' he would say, and subside into incoherence as Jehan pointedly cleared his throat.

When the furore died down, we were back to square one. Zarir still was a regular fixture at our dining table, and I was still resisting Jehan's efforts to set up Zarir and me happily ever after. Jehan, in fact, had played his cards beautifully. While he secretly encouraged foment and strife among the gaggle of girls, he continued playing mentor and confidante to them as well. Somehow, no matter what he did, these girls simply couldn't stop loving him. My chief tormentor among this group was a flamboyant, oomphy ex-model, used to strewing broken hearts and broken libidos in her wake. She was unable to fathom what anyone, leave alone a lovely young man like Zarir, could possibly see in me, a flat-chested, bad mannered, unattractive kid. And this, when she had gone out of her way to broadly hint that she was very interested in becoming mistress of that big house of his. So, Jehan would spend long hours boosting her confidence and self-esteem on the one hand, and on the other, cry vengeance on her in front of us for bad-mouthing his sister.

'You're *the* one! You can have any guy you want. Forget Liana, she's just a kid. You should wear that sexy red top to the club next week. You look amazing in it!'

I flatly told him on a number of occasions that I did not need his help with my budding love life, and that I had little interest in Zarir. I was beating my head against an obdurate wall. Zarir and I were made for each other, decreed Jehan, and if it was the last thing he did, he was going to make me see that.

Zarir was Clark Kent. One day, he would turn into Superman, but I would never be his Lois Lane.

I was beginning to find out two things about my future self: I had a sense of intuition beyond my age honed by the drama at home. And I refused to play the charades other girls my age did.

Paribesa

AMITA, SHE OF the US antecedents and miniskirts, my almost best friend and not quite soul sister, had an older brother, Sunny, who treated me mostly like a kid sister, but sometimes flirted with me in a teasing way, as if to practise his skills. I liked it. No one had ever flirted with me before and it made me feel a little bit reckless and dangerous. We were growing up, and change was just round the corner for all of us.

The thing that altered our group dynamics in the latter half of 1985 was Paribesa Nature Club. Paribesa was the money-making brainchild of a pseudo-intellectual—pseudo-everything really—guy called Subrato Banerjee. Anyway, he had roped in a group of environmentally concerned teenagers to form a nature club and they came to our school that year to look for new members.

Amita and I were immediately enamoured of the idea, being proud owners of personal menageries at each of our homes. I'd provided foster care for baby squirrels who fell out of nests perched in coconut trees (one, Nutty Fruitcake, survived my attentions and grew to adulthood, becoming a semi-house pet before heading off to claim the garden as his territory); a kite—or was it a quail?—with a broken wing; a baby bat I found behind our Biology lab in school. That little thing, the size of the nail of my little finger when I found it, actually survived three weeks, though I'm convinced his/her death was finally brought about by my grandmother who stood muttering evil incantations over its little shoe box kept on top of the fridge, snapping her fingers and saying things like: '*Ja, ja, shaitaan* (Go away, devil).' No bat stood a chance against powerful voodoo like that, poor thing. In any case, I felt confident of my position as the family naturalist (helped along, no doubt, by the slavish reading of Gerald Durrell) and convinced my parents to allow me to join Paribesa.

The Club was, in hindsight, perhaps an unconscious ruse by those founder members to meet some chicks, as they all seemed to come from boys' schools. Oh well, it only took twenty years for that to register!

Three guys came to our school that morning—one was an absolute dish called Abraham, Baro for short, older, with soft brown eyes, a dimple in the chin and a velvety drawl. We all fell hard for Baro. The nice thing about the guy was that though he had a string of besotted girlfriends, he never tried to patao (flirt with) Amita or me. We were much younger and hero worshipped this gorgeous hunk of a Zoology graduate student from a safe distance. Subrato was sleazy and we didn't pay him much mind. It was the third nerd who stuck around and remains a good friend to this day.

This was Pradeep Pillai, nicknamed Paddy for his tendency to pad through the undergrowth in search of snakes. Earnest, awkward, with a huge handlebar moustache and the kindest eyes, he was nonetheless the real whiz with animals, reptiles in particular. His other nickname was Snakeman. He volunteered at the famous Snake Park, and often brought sick snakes home to tend to. Roshan Kaki was visiting us one summer when Paddy made an afternoon appearance at our house with a Bata shoe box tucked under one arm.

'What is in that box, *beta*?' my aunt asked him, attempting to make friendly small talk.

'Aunty, this poor guy's not feeling too well. I'm taking him home to look after him.'

And he opened the box to show this sympathizer the drowsy rat snake curled up inside. The hysterics the woman exhibited that afternoon were epic. Needless to say, Paddy was banned from bringing sick patients around to our home for a while. But he became a good pal, and my parents liked him, so he also became my de facto escort around town. Amita and I enthusiastically began attending the fortnightly meetings.

Each meeting, for me, was an adventure. I met new people, learnt to handle strange animals, went bird-watching and on nature trails. Paddy and Baro were the storytellers—they spun yarns of the snakes they had caught; the birds they had identified.

Every so often, they would refer to a couple of friends of theirs. They never came to the meetings but seemed like fun guys. These absent friends owned bikes, their family owned shops. They seemed very exotic to me. Amita knew them already—they were schoolmates of her elder brother Sunny at Boys' Academy. Eager to see them, I would sometimes scoff at the stories or proclaim these guys to be figments of everyone's imagination. To which Paddy would laugh and say, 'Wait, you'll meet them and see for yourself.'

Amita, Ziya and I were the only girls at the Paribesa meeting one December morning of 1985. Ziya was my old friend, the girl Jehan had decided was the one for his Sid. We had drifted in and out of friendship, sometimes losing touch. Right now, she was trying to get Jehan and Sid to leave her alone. She had declared recently that she needed a new group of friends, and so there we were, gathered in the Reptile Room of the beautiful red stone City Museum, standing under a display of one of the longest cobra skins ever found. Paddy was bustling around, getting us to stand still so that Subrato could pontificate on whatever.

Then, suddenly, there were these two guys, standing quietly with us. One shorter, older, with a trim moustache. The other, taller, with glasses and a bit of a strut. This one had sleeves rolled up to show off non-existent biceps, a wooden tribal chain tight around the throat. And a smile that did crazy things to my insides. These were the guys Paddy and Baro had spoken about. Two brothers, Joseph and Lucas, aka Joe and Luke. Many years later, Luke told me that the one he noticed first was Ziya—she looked like a doll. Ziya wasn't really into creepy crawlies and never came to any meetings again so that came to naught. But I was and I did. And Luke was there too. There was attraction right away. Maybe it was only that we were so unalike in every way. Him, cool, cocky yet peaceable, with skin so dark I was enchanted. Me, shy, argumentative, quick to take offence. Anyway, I was determined to nip any budding feelings I might have had. There were other currents in my life that year and I pushed any ideas of romance to the back of my head.

~

The first turtle walk early next month almost didn't happen. Turtle walks were a rite of passage for young people in the Bay City of the eighties. It was a cool way to declare one's independence—spending the entire night out on the beach with friends and strangers. It was a good measure of whether you were cut out to be an environmentalist, a slightly disreputable occupation in the local conservative society. Starting late at night at the beach, we would walk the dark stretches of sand searching for nesting sites of the endangered Olive Ridley turtles. If we were successful, we would then reach the eggs safely to the turtle hatchery further down the coast. This was my first night spent away from home and/or at least one member of my family. My childhood fears meant that sleepovers were the stuff of nightmares. I had never been a carefree child, the monsters created by my imagination had seen to that. I'd spend a few hours happily enough with friends but I was petrified of using a strange bathroom or even waking up in a strange bed. So this was huge. I couldn't believe I was actually looking forward to meeting strangers and spending the night on a lonely beach. Paddy was instrumental in persuading me. He had scoffed at my fears and cajoled Eruch into approving. That was probably the first and last time I waited for Eruch's permission to spend time away from home. Eruch liked Paddy, his straight back from years of NCC training and his clear-eyed gaze—nothing shifty there. And so the stage was set. Perhaps if Jehan hadn't been so obsessive about pushing Zarir at me and making his dislike of my new friends at Paribesa apparent from the very first, I wouldn't have been spurred to make this break from the friends and life my family planned for me to have. Turtle walks came to represent freedom, breaking away from filial control, and from the malaise that had blanketed my home.

~

That was the year that Jehan tried to kill himself.

That first attempt, at least in Bay City and in my certain memory, was such a surreal experience that unlike the episodes that followed, my mind has blanked out most of the details. It must have been a Saturday in early January 1986. I was looking forward to my first turtle walk that night. Jehan was sleeping in. He didn't emerge from his room for lunch, which wasn't unusual. These days, Jehan had his own schedule, eating at odd hours and sometimes missing meals with the family altogether. We had never been conventional about meal times: 'the family that eats together stays together' was loosely interpreted in the Chinoy household to mean 'the family that has its heads stuck in novels doesn't really notice when one of its members stops eating his meals with the rest'. The new routine had become normal quickly and without question—Jehan ate on his own, in his room or late at night. No one noticed, no one commented. Hari ambled in at around three that afternoon. I barely took note of his arrival. Hari and Sid, our friends from the apartment block we'd lived in earlier, were daily visitors in our home.

Jehan slept on. Hari took out a book, sat down in Jehan's room and waited—for two hours. Jehan refused to wake up, even after repeated attempts by Hari, now bored of waiting. It was then that Hari came out, alarmed, asking if Jehan had been sleeping that soundly all day. I overheard raised voices, but still lost in my own dreams, failed to register fully the tone of the conversation.

'What did you take, Jehan?'

'Jehan, wake up, you need to wake up!'

And a slurred voice, not my brother's at all, crying:

'Leave me alone, I want to die.'

Honey's voice, just a bit shaky:

'Fali, should we call a doctor?'

As the house swirled with friends making strong coffee, Honey and Eruch trying to keep Jehan awake and Fali calling the doctor, all I could think of resentfully was: 'Typical Jehan, hogging all the attention. There goes my turtle walk.'

Jehan had attempted to overdose on sleeping pills on Friday night. They had been prescribed for Eruch—to use during emergencies—and Jehan had been stealing them. By then, Eruch was a 'heart patient'. He had survived three heart attacks between the ages of forty and forty-eight, the combined result of a desk job, zero exercise and soaring cholesterol levels from a supremely careless attitude to his diet. Suffering from indigestion, he often found it difficult to fall asleep. I suppose the wisdom in the 1980s dictated that heart patients needed a full night's rest more than anything else, and so the doctor prescribed a mild dose of sleeping pills to keep as standby for sleepless nights. Eruch's picky ways meant that as soon as the stock ran low, he would order a fresh lot without stopping to check if he needed to. This suited Jehan very well. He had been squirrelling them away to his bedroom. It became apparent only later that he hadn't swallowed the whole lot, just enough to make him extremely sleepy.

I was quiet, unable to bring up my own silly plans for the evening. Hari sat with me and tried to distract me with joking offers of coffee and cigarettes.

It was late evening before things calmed down. Friends began to make goodbye noises. When Zarir came by as usual, we all looked a bit guilty that we'd forgot to call him. Though what it was we'd have told him over the phone is anyone's guess. Anyway, Fali didn't seem in the mood to chat, and so it fell to me to tell Zarir the day's events. He was almost family. He gawped at me, a goldfish dumped out of its safe little bowl.

He made up excuses for Jehan:

'He must have found it difficult to sleep. He just took too many...entirely by mistake. Could happen to anyone...'

I gritted my teeth.

By then, I was caught in a state between extreme hysteria that is common to teenagers denied their current life's wish and total numbness over the events of the day. Finally, Honey stopped looking preoccupied for a moment and said in a vague sort of way, 'Don't you have to go for a turtle walk tonight?'

'Yes, I do. Can I go?'

She looked surprised that I was even asking. Honey's ability to act normal under moments of high drama was beginning to impact my life.

'Of course you can go. Why ever not?'

I ran to phone Paddy to beg him: please pick me up right away.

~

Later that night, we sat on Subrato's terrace, waiting for everyone to arrive. Baro, the lofty senior member of the club, who knew everything there was to know about turtles and other exotica, sat down next to me in companionable silence. That's when the shock hit me—I was floundering, here with these friends who seemed too grown up and in a setting where I was out of my depth, while my brother slept off an overdose of sleeping pills at home. I couldn't think straight, much less speak, my mind numb with the events of the day and a feeling of being overwhelmed.

The night was magical though—the low murmur of voices, the breeze blowing off the ocean, faces in shadow, lit by the glowing ends of cigarettes. It was all very peaceful.

Baro sat quietly, not much of a talker, as we watched some guy, high on grass, trying to demonstrate Transcendental Meditation.

I turned to Baro and found myself saying, almost reluctantly: 'My brother tried to kill himself today.'

He sat in silence, listening as I stumbled through the day's events, trying to make some sense of it all. We talked all night long, walking down that long stretch of beach. We spoke about relationships that didn't quite conform to the straight and narrow, and how to deal with this new aspect of death as a constant family member. About families that hid their dysfunctionality behind a façade and how surprisingly common these families are.

'Good you came tonight though. No point hiding in your house,' he said.

His quiet voice, unemotional in the face of my turmoil, but comforting in its calm matter-of-fact explanation, has stayed with me through the years.

'You'll learn not to drown in it. None of this is your fault, Liana. Just concentrate on living your life the best you can. His demons are his own, not yours.'

I think of that night and subsequent turtle walks often. It calms me down when things start to go awry. Though we've lost touch over the years, Baro was a good friend in the following months of continued crisis. It was a time of such exquisite pain and pleasure, and yet, it was the calm before the storm.

~

Jehan tried to kill himself again a couple of months later. It might have been earlier, Valentine's Day perhaps. Maybe he'd had a fight with Sid. This time, the pills he took were stronger. The young doctor who lived down our street had to be called home, his stomach had to be pumped clean and he slept off the remainder of the dose over the next few days.

Honey sent me off to school without a packed lunch, and by the time I returned home, there was only a vague sense of unease in the air. Fali disappeared after the furore subsided and avoided coming home for dinner. I had to tell Zarir not to come home that night. I didn't have to explain, Zarir was far more sensitive to the undercurrents swirling around us than he let on. So it was only Honey, Eruch and I who sat down to dinner. I didn't quite know the details, but some part of my brain knew exactly what had happened that morning. This time, there was no shock, no blanking out. The parents spoke to each other in coded undertones and Jehan snored in his bedroom, the door carefully left ajar. Did someone keep vigil over him that night? I'd like to think so, but it seems unlikely. That week I learnt that hoping for the worst to be over was far more painful than the actual event. There were maybe two or three days of tiptoeing around, whispered consultations and shuttered eyes and then life slid back to normal.

There was also, after a gap of another couple of months, (what, until recently, I remembered as) a slashing of the wrists. He came out of his room, crying with the pain. He had only managed a skin-deep cut on each wrist and the result was a lot of superficial mess, awful pain, but not much else. His wrists were bandaged, the white startling against his brown skin. He would pull the sleeves of his shirts down to hide them.

While writing this book, thirty-four years later, I happened to speak with an old childhood friend of Jehan. She still lived in our hometown then and used to correspond regularly with him. She revealed that he had written to her not about slashing his wrists but spilling hot wax on them. She couldn't say whether it was by accident or on purpose. It made me realize just how much of those months I have had to imagine in my head, to fit into a narrative, because there was no one who could or would set the record straight for me.

As I write this, I am overwhelmed. Hot wax on his wrists? He made the most beautiful frosted candles, whipping up melted and coloured wax into a foam which he then used to decorate a plain candle. These frosted beauties were much in demand among all the neighbourhood aunties, and he had a flourishing little business supplying custom-made candles. It is entirely possible that he spilt some of that boiling wax on himself. And equally possible that he was self-harming. Still, it could only have been a cry for help. Even Jehan, swamped in misery, must have known that hot wax, unless it covered larger surfaces of one's body, couldn't possibly kill.

After this incident, an impromptu intervention was held in our living room. The family was there, Sid, Hari and some of Fali's friends, even Zarir, looking pained and uncomfortable. It was an amateurish attempt and possibly did more harm than good to Jehan's fragile psyche.

Eruch, well-meaning but clearly out of his depth, confronted him, 'Why are you doing this, Jehan? Don't you have all that you need? Your family, your friends, have we ever stopped you from doing what you want? Tell me...'

Fali and Honey were silent.

Eruch tried again, 'Are you homosexual, Jehan? You can tell me if you are, beta.'

In the pin-drop silence that followed, Jehan's groan of despair was like a wail. Which twenty-one-year-old has the capacity to confront his innermost demons, laid bare in front of the very people from whom he has desperately hidden them? Reeling under the shock of what he had done, face as white as the bandages around his thin wrists, confronted by a well-meaning but belligerent dad, he collapsed. Fali or Sid half-dragged, half-carried him into his room, and together with Hari, they calmed Jehan down.

'What did I say wrong?' Eruch said helplessly. 'I was only trying to help him.'

Fali wouldn't meet anyone's eyes and Honey just sat there, small and deflated, all life seemingly sucked out of her. I gritted my teeth some more—it was becoming a habit, one that would last a lifetime. Zarir took me out for a drive and thus ended the first and only intervention that I can recall being staged for my brother in my presence. It must be said that not one of us dared to drag it out into the open, nor did we seem to have the collective emotional resources to confront the demons that haunted Jehan. I never knew if he ever did get the professional emotional and medical help he so urgently needed. It felt as if the family was paralysed by social strictures, by the fear of what people would say. Perhaps each of us tried in individual ways, to talk to Jehan, to bring him back to us. I see now that what he needed was urgent and professional intervention, not our well-meaning but ultimately futile amateur efforts.

Many years later, it came as not much of a surprise to read about cases like his, diagnosed as bipolar disorder or borderline schizophrenia or manic depression. It doesn't seem possible that no treatment existed for any of these disorders. Diagnosis and medical help were not out of our reach. Hari had pushed as diplomatically as he could to get Jehan to a therapist or a psychiatrist. That would have been the first step to helping him cope with whatever was going on in his life—his homosexuality, his manic episodes, the obsessive relationships and the depression that came like a wave when these relationships collapsed. But Hari, sensitive and articulate as he was, was an outsider and consequently no match for my family. And the basic fact was, no one could force a twenty-one-year-old to go to a psychiatrist if he wasn't willing to cooperate.

What will people say? No one is to talk about Jehan's problems to the outside world, they appear to have decided. We ought to be enough to sort out this mess—father, mother, brother. (I was inconsequential and therefore ignored.) He's homosexual/depressed/disturbed and it upsets/embarrasses us!

Were these the unspoken truths in our world? Jehan himself was in complete denial, refusing to go to a doctor even to treat the eczema on his foot because he was terrified that he would be tricked into meeting a psychiatrist instead, or, in his frantic imagination, that he would be institutionalized in some ghastly psychiatric ward. I don't know who had left him with this lasting impression, but Jehan fought with all his might to stay away from a hospital. He just kept saying there was nothing wrong until the family began to believe him, if only to preserve their sanity. Because the stark truth was that we all—Honey, Eruch, Fali and Jehan himself—were paralysed with fear.

It seemed that the intervention had worked—at least, enough to frighten Jehan with the threat of hospitalization. Summer was upon us, and thankfully, he showed no signs of another attempt. In fact, he was calm, and life was as normal as it had been in the last six or seven months.

Luke, Summer of 1986

THEN THERE WAS Luke. And bus route 47A. Luke and I both lived at various points along its route during our friendship and later romance. At first, when we lived down adjacent avenues in the same colony, both of us caught the bus at the same stop, then further apart down the route, as his family, then mine, moved away. We met usually on the beach. This was before the shops and crowds and floodlights took over the empty spaces, when the stretches of sand and ocean waited quietly for secrets to be shared and memories to be made. The particular stretch of the beach I'm thinking of was bracketed by a broken bridge and the locally revered church. Beyond the church lay the route to the turtle walks and the hatchery further out along the hazy coast.

The second time I went on a turtle walk, it was early May. There had been no drama for some time at home. No one threatened my plans. In fact, Jehan and Fali were not even home that night. I finished dinner, said goodbye to the parents and a forlorn Zarir. Luke and I waited at the bus stop until a 47A, Paddy on board, pulled up. We headed to the beach, picking up Amita and others along the way. It was a merry group that clattered off the bus at the depot. By now I had been nursing a crush on Luke for a few months already. I had characteristically kept silent about these feelings to Amita, my friend, my co-author and conspirator in all manners of mischief. Flamboyant, extroverted, talented, the one thing she couldn't match me at was keeping secrets.

That moonless night, the turtles cried black tears as they laid their eggs. The coastline curved around so that the distant lighthouse sent a faint light arcing over the mothers as they ponderously made their way back to the water's edge. No other light disturbed that lonely beach. Halfway to the hatchery, I found myself walking next to Luke.

'We need to talk,' he said quietly.

We stopped near a beached fishing boat.

Then, even more quietly: 'I like you.'

Nothing more was said. Everything was understood. The group stayed up all night, collecting turtle eggs, and depositing them in the turtle hatchery. Then we sat on the beach, watching the sun come up in a hazy sky. Later, we wandered over to the National Park for breakfast. Here, we lingered, reluctant to end the mood. Amita was quiet, watchful. As I sat, back propped against a tree, there he was, cheeky grin asking permission as he dropped down, laid his head in my lap and stretched out. I froze. The thought popped into my head that the heat generated right there and then would implode everyone around us. No one said a word. I couldn't look at Luke or anyone else, and I could feel my face burning scarlet. It was his way of saying without words that we were together. Amita's eyes widened in amazement. And everyone understood.

We all rode 47A in silence back home. Amita got off first, after trying in vain to catch my eye. Luke and I rode the bus till our stop, and separated at adjacent avenues to go home and relive the memories, to wonder and worry over the interlude in private.

By now, Zarir too had reached some kind of internal tipping point, as far as I was concerned. There were times when he seemed ready to blurt out his thoughts to me, usually when we were out driving in his little car. Zarir was given carte blanche partly because my parents knew that there was no way he would ever take advantage of their trust, partly because they saw, to their secret dismay, that I wanted nothing to do with him except on a purely platonic level. But I think they hoped that I would see the virtues in this fine, upstanding Parsi boy and forget about the strange, awkward boy who was still only 'my friend'.

So there we would sit, parked at an ice-cream parlour or in the drive-in restaurant, and it would start.

'Linu...'

And just the sound of my nickname, uttered softly, hesitantly, would set me off.

'Now what?' I'd snarl.

'Uh, no, no, nothing...just that Jehan said that the new movie is good...'

'Then take Jehan for the movie.'

'He he, no, I thought we could...'

'Nope, no way.'

I would cut him off before he started with his criticism of my unworthy friends, whom no one liked—not my brothers, not my parents, certainly not Zarir. I wondered how he never got it.

'Are you still seeing that Luke? You know your parents don't like him.'

'He's a friend. And Zarir, you're not my dad, so, you know, screw you.'

'I'm just saying it for your own good...'

'Maybe I don't want to be good, Zarir. Maybe I want to be bad, bad, bad. Got it?'

'Liana, if you'd just let me...'

'No, Zarir! Get me another ice cream, na!'

That was the best reason for the new friends I'd made—they had helped me break out, think for myself and explore the kind of people I liked. These were not friends chosen for me by my family and that suited me just fine. The conversation would quickly disintegrate into a sullen silence on my part or a screaming match, with Zarir very quickly capitulating and restoring the peace.

I walked a finely splintered line that summer. Luke and I were meeting secretly, some deep-rooted instinct telling me that the family would not approve—I was too young for a boyfriend, he was too dark, too rough at the edges for the protected youngest child. Though he lived in the next avenue from ours, and even came home a couple of times, chaperoned by Baro or Paddy, we were just friends. Honey's eyebrows disappeared into her hairline the afternoon Luke came over alone, carrying a bunch of red roses, thorns and all. Those roses were still there at home, dried and fragile, four months later. That hot May afternoon, I accepted them with as much insouciance that I could muster, while Fali and his fiancée Preeti peeked out at this unlikely intruder, Cherie, our dachshund, barked at his unfamiliar smell and Jehan refused to leave us alone, instead making small talk which left Luke speechless and me furious.

'So *you*'re Lucas. Hmm. From Paribesa—what kind of a name is that anyway?'

'It means one's surroundings in Bengali, I think.'

'Ooh, you speak Bangla too?'

'No.'

'You stay just next door, in 17th Avenue, right?'

'Yeah.'

'Roses? How interesting, the thorns are still there—ouch! Linu, I say, careful of those thorns—wicked sharp, they are.'

'Jehan, shut up,' me, trying to get a word in edgewise.

'Just getting to know...Lucius, was it?'

I couldn't speak to Amita about Luke. It was hard enough to accept these startling events myself—I liked a boy, and he actually liked me back. It went against the very nature of things in my straitlaced world. She prodded and teased me gently but it ended there. This thing with Luke, whatever it was, was a secret I kept to myself.

Even so, we were aided and abetted by Sunny and Amita,

agog over this most unexpected mismatch, as we continued to meet all through the summer holidays. They had figured out that neither of us would talk about it, but that we still needed their help to keep our rendezvous. Amita provided me with alibis for long afternoons, and Sunny would drive me to our usual meeting spot, a shop owned by Luke's father, which he minded in the afternoon. I'd duck under the half-open shutter, he would bring it down fully, and we would sit carefully separated by the cash counter, getting to know each other and staring at each other's faces when we ran out of words. Our personalities were different, we had very little in common and the affair should have fizzled out in a few months. But it didn't, mainly because of events he had not imagined in his wildest dreams. Events that loomed over my life so that I lived alternately between dream-like days that summer and nights filled with terror. And then there was the small matter of the attraction between us. Unrecognized for now and unacknowledged, it was there, flickering and growing. Still, it was the most non-physical romantic relationship in those early days, even by Bay City standards.

Joe wasn't sure what to make of us kids. Their dad was an autocratic man, their mom kind but cowed by her limited education. They would have approved of a teenage romance even less enthusiastically than my parents. So there were secrets all around.

He once said something I'll always remember with a smile. He was giving me a ride over from Amita's place when, as we rode past the road down which we both lived, he said:

'Hey, Liana, close your eyes—that way, no one will see you.'

I did confide in two friends about this new and very secret relationship. They were very far removed from my gang of friends, and I judged it safe. Both girls came from stricter homes than mine. One was the younger of two sisters who lived down my road. They were fun-loving, jolly girls. The older one had a mild crush on Fali for a while, but they sorted that out between themselves. They both adored Jehan, their fashion mentor and go-to advisor in all things culinary and creative. Their parents were close friends of my folks, though later Honey was to develop a hearty dislike for them that she kept well hidden.

It was only on her deathbed, when her mind was rambling, that she once again remembered why her feelings had soured. It had something to do with a motorbike that Fali wanted to buy, for which Eruch, living a salaried life, could not shell out the money immediately. Honey convinced him, against his better judgement, to request these close friends for a loan of ten thousand rupees, no small sum. What Honey hadn't bargained for was the very business-like attitude their friends took towards that loan, and repeated reminders of their munificence as well as periodic hints to pay up, did not sit well with her idea of friendship. The loan was repaid in full but Honey never tired of brooding over her grievance. As she lay dying in hospital at the end of her long life, the couple came visiting and Honey, blithely ignoring them, loudly warned me:

'Don't mention that loan, Liana, they are shameless. They'll ask for the money even here in hospital. With friends like these, who needs enemies?'

Hushing her was useless, so I had to hustle the friends out of the room as quickly as I could. The thirty years that had passed had been erased by the growing tumour in Honey's formidable brain and she felt the hurt and insult as keenly as if it had been only yesterday. I think the hardest thing for her to forgive was her own misjudgement, her false reading of character, something she had always prided herself on having honed to a fine art. And the galling thing was that Eruch had been right for once, refusing to ask for the money until goaded beyond his limits by Honey's nagging. Honey never forgot and rarely forgave slights to her beloved Eruch. Only she was allowed to dole out veiled insults and accusations to him.

My other friend was an even jollier girl with a pesky younger brother; and her mom was quite one of my favourite aunties, a stern but fair-minded Physical Education teacher at one of our leading convent schools. The three of us had an unequal but happy enough friendship. The two of them would often moan about how their parents had warned them of disownment and perpetual disgrace if they ever brought an unsuitable son-in-law into their homes.

Their conversation usually went along these lines, while I sat, laughing quietly.

'Dai, tell me this, where are we going to find boys, ya?'

'Not just boys, good boys, good little mamma's boys...'

'Where? In this lot of duffers? Tch, don't hold your breath.'

'And Liana, you just shut up, di! Stop laughing, you stupid girl, this is serious!'

'She's clueless: she'll waltz off with that chocolate boy of hers and her folks won't say a word to their darling Linu!'

This was true. My parents had no expectations of a Parsi son-in-law: two of my beloved aunts were not Parsi, and Fali would also marry outside the community. Honey and Eruch were rather proud of their magnanimous acceptance of their cosmopolitan relations by marriage. In fact, Eruch and Honey had recently helped my friend's elder sister, she of the mild crush on Fali, to marry her unsuitable boyfriend and later convinced their friends, the same couple that Honey would never forgive, to welcome the happy couple back into the fold. Of course, the liberal attitude they were so fond of displaying fell a little short when it came to their daughter. When Honey realized belatedly that Luke meant something more to me than just a friend, it wasn't just his complexion or his ethnicity that she objected to, it was also the social distance she perceived between his family and ours.

Luke and a few other friends had got admission in the same college as Jehan. Luke and I anticipated some fireworks once college reopened because Jehan's radar for romance was uncannily sharp and he had already made his displeasure known to me in no uncertain terms.

'I'm putting in all this effort for *you*, Linu! Finding you nice boys, people like us. What about Zarir? He likes you. I honestly don't understand why he does but still...'

'Why don't *you* date these paragons, then, Jehan?'

'You're such a cat, Linu. I'm telling mummy all about that dork friend of yours!'

'Jehan!'

And, again, 'I've never seen such an ungrateful girl! Still mooning over that Lucy fellow? He barely speaks, he wears specs, and oh my God, he's always falling over his own feet. What a clown!'

He wasn't wrong. Luke had no social graces and was inarticulate to boot; two solecisms Jehan could not overlook. And, as we found out, he couldn't even dance!

I had only ever been to one dance party, one hosted by Nalini earlier that year. Jehan and Honey had probably been more excited than me on that momentous occasion. Sure, I had overcome my awkwardness in the past few months but I came from the same genetic material as the smoothest mover on the dance floor. And he had a *rep* to protect.

The lessons happened over a series of excruciating afternoons in our garage while my neighbourhood friends gawked, giggled and secretly took notes. There were lessons in jiving, appropriate slow dancing and party etiquette by Jehan. I paid the closest attention to the lectures on party etiquette. You wanted to be grown up and look blasé when a guy (nervous as all hell and sweaty too) asked you to dance to a slow song, but you also had to know the tricks. How to keep his hands from wandering, how to maintain that crucial distance? My brother glowered at me and quickly dispelled any illusions I might have had about these mysterious rules.

'Arm's length at all times. Hands at waist or nothing. Don't even think of trying anything—I'll come to know. You know I will.'

It was all very disillusioning and comforting at the same time. Jehan had always been clinical in his supervision of my wardrobe, collaborating with Honey to get me out of old jeans and kurtas and into dresses and skirts. He was categorical about my shortcomings in the fashion department, frequently reducing me to tears with his sarcastic and accurate assessments of my self-styled looks.

'No sister of mine goes out dressed like a frump!' was his battle cry.

He supported my dad in his old-fashioned and wildly patriarchal preference for my waist-long hair, directing Honey when she tried out different hairdos, the stylist to her hairdresser. On this occasion, a new pale pink dress with a dropped waist (virginal and just slightly seductive) was produced, my long, straight hair, possibly my best feature, left hanging down my back, and my spectacles were confiscated. Jehan declared himself satisfied with the result and off I went to the party.

It turned out to be a nerve-racking but memorable evening, even if the dance floor was just an open space created by pushing Nalini's bedroom furniture aside. I had my first slow dance to 'Self-Control' by Sheena Easton, partnered by the most popular boy in school, Callum. I came home starry-eyed and full of praise for this brave attempt at cutting the nursery strings. Nalini had pulled off something none of us had dared to—a proper evening dance party. With boys!

Jehan of course scoffed at my breathless description and decided to launch an all-out and immediate offensive. Just before school (and college) reopened, he decided that I wanted nothing more than to throw a huge party. He planned our debut meticulously, roping in the entire family. Eruch took charge of the soft drinks and agreed to serve wine to the older guests, flatly refusing to open his bar to underage drinkers. Jehan begged and threw a tantrum but Eruch stood firm. Honey promised to send out delicious snacks from the kitchen, and turned her bedroom into a powder room for any hysterical girl to retreat to, if needed. Fali strung up the mood lighting and was assigned bouncer duty if any kid got too excited. And Zarir?

'Please, please, Zarir, try not to be such a good boy! Cut loose!' cried the Master of Ceremonies, when he thought I was out of earshot. 'You have to *slay* the competition.'

Zarir wilted at the prospect of slaying anything, and Jehan hustled him away to give him last-minute secret tips on how to win over his reluctant sister, I presume.

Everyone I knew was invited. Waylanders of course, including the cool kids who came because Jehan told them to. He was the acknowledged coolest of the cool: what Jehan wore today, the dance steps he taught us all, that set the fashion. There was no doubt about his sense of style. The Sri Lankan kids knew the latest dance moves and had access to American jeans but even they bowed to Jehan's natural flamboyance. The Paribesa kids came too, far more awkward than the Wayland crowd but game for a good time.

Jehan wore his brand new baggy red pants, straight out of a Michael Jackson video, and I was extremely uncomfortable in a sexy little velvet number. My mom had gone a bit crazy at the last YWCA jumble sale, bringing home the dark blue velvet dress held up by two little buckles through which the shoulder straps were casually looped. It was far too sophisticated for a fourteen-year-old with a flat bosom and very little self-confidence.

What a party though! Two boys almost came to blows over a girl, the long-standing girlfriend of the dorkier one, who was being hit upon by the school stud. The dorky boyfriend stormed off in a huff, while the girlfriend spent the rest of the evening wrapped dreamily in the stud's arms. One of my shoulder straps came undone and I almost had a wardrobe malfunction in the middle of the dance floor. My partner was gallant enough to simultaneously point it out and look away and disaster was averted. Luke did not dance. He hung out with the other non-dancers, all Paribesa guys of course. Waylanders will never, never be wallflowers. Jehan was everywhere all at once, pulling this girl out for a fast jive, serving drinks, introducing shy boys to shy girls, keeping one eye always on Sid and Ziya, or on Zarir and me. I danced all night, managing to avoid Zarir until the very end, when I ended up in his nervous clasp.

I watched Luke out of the corner of my eye. Zarir was the one, Luke knew. The kind of boy my family approved of. But even then, he couldn't make himself cut in and dance with me himself. Convinced that he had two left feet coupled with facing down two very intimidating brothers (Jehan having pointed him out to Fali), he decided to leave things well alone. I escaped from Zarir as quickly as I could but the evening was winding down, people started leaving, and suddenly, the party was over.

~

It had been an amazing time—falling in love, parties, friends... and my brother hadn't tried to kill himself even once all summer. Standard ten loomed. College for some of my friends. The thing uppermost in my head was: Would I be made captain of my school? That really was the extent of my ambition. To lead my beloved Wayland Manor, to carry the school flag in the annual Sports Day march past, never mind if I couldn't really march. To have the little ones look up to me. It never occurred to me that I wasn't half as popular as I imagined. That my up-tightness and stick-in-the-mud image (in spite of the boyfriend, an anomaly no one in school could quite accept) had made me the object of ridicule behind my back, and that my closest friends were party to the mockery.

Amita and I had grown distant that summer. She was no longer my go-to person, because suddenly, there was Luke in my life, and I couldn't talk about Luke to her. But would I have talked to anyone about him? It had had to be such a secretive thing from the beginning, knowing my family would strongly disapprove. Not because I had a *boyfriend*—that would have been okay. After all, Honey and Eruch had got together at around the same age. No, what they all disapproved of or would disapprove of were other uglier factors—the things that no one spoke about and yet were quietly acknowledged.

Amita, for all the unobtrusive help she and Sunny gave me, must have felt hurt for being kept out of the loop. Pia and she were also the most mature among our group of four so it was only natural that they grew closer as standard ten began.

Jehan had spent the summer vacation in agony over his eczema. It was a family trait. Eruch had a patch on the crook between his thumb and forefinger, which he rubbed at incessantly. Honey had the worse habit of digging around in her ears with the blunt end of a bobby pin, instead of visiting a doctor. Her ears probably had a fungal infection which had never been treated, and she made things worse by sticking unhygienic pieces of metal inside. For the well-educated woman that she was, she had a singularly superstitious nature and a philosophy of 'leave well alone'. She was convinced to the end of her days that visiting a doctor was the invitation to mostly unnecessary diagnoses and that there would be no end to the bloodsucking and prescribed treatments. Come to think of it, for the daughter of a dentist, she had the most awful set of teeth I have ever seen. Discoloured and crooked, she always hid her mouth behind her palm when she smiled or laughed.

Jehan's eczema was on the soles of his feet. The sensitive skin bled and wept, flaked away and itched until he cried. He wore thick, soft socks to keep himself from scratching the skin raw. No ointment or oil seemed to help. Only one thing provided relief, temporary at that. Dipping his feet in the ocean cleared the skin up miraculously for a few days. Salt water baths at home had no effect at all. That summer was particularly bad, to the point that he even agreed to visit a skin specialist who prescribed more creams and unguents. The results were unpromising. Zarir and Hari spent many evenings just distracting him from the severe urge to scratch. When my younger son was five years old, he had a flare-up of atopic stress-related eczema. The first time a doctor asked us about a family history of skin ailments, I almost neglected to mention Jehan's feet. I reluctantly disclosed it as if it were a guilty secret. As with most things related to my brother, this too was filed away in my brain under the no-need-to-let-anyone-know compartment.

~

Then the vacations were over and the academic year of 1986 began—my big year, standard ten. Jehan was in his second year at college. He left for college the first day wearing the red pants he was so proud of. He came home subdued, saying only that some boys had teased him. He wore them again a few days later and returned clearly scared. Zarir, Fali and he went into a huddle from which I was pointedly excluded. I think Luke may have mentioned that they bumped into each other in college but Luke was a freshman, Jehan a second year senior; it was unlikely that they would have much in common.

By then, Jehan seemed to have settled into his life. The three attempts to kill himself were distant nightmares and we seemed to be past all that. Life was looking up for our family. He now held down a night shift in a five-star hotel bar, where he was a very popular waiter and enjoyed learning to mix cocktails.

'This one client of ours—he tips really well. And he only drinks Campari—it's like blood, Linu, or like mummy's rubies.'

Jehan's fascination with blood and jewels was always a little unsettling. It was like living with a hedonistic vampire and I told him so.

'Pooh, don't be squeamish. Listen, na. After he left last night, I took a teeny-tiny sip of Campari from the bottle—it was *foul*! Like bad cough syrup. Can't believe this guy pays so much for a glass. Maybe I should give him some Benadryl next time—it tastes a lot better!'

Zarir and I collapsed laughing as he made horrible faces to explain exactly how foul it had tasted.

He had even started talking about applying to catering college and planning the parties for Fali's wedding. Yes, things were as normal as they had ever been.

Except Sid didn't come around much any more and Jehan hardly mentioned him at all. Jehan was writing poetry now; he never showed it to me of course. I once opened his cupboard hunting for a tee shirt, and found a love poem drenched in tears scribbled inside the door in his signature green sketch pen. I read it, and it disappeared quietly into my subconscious as so many other signs did in those strange times. The feeling, however, burnt itself into my brain even though I couldn't remember a single word of it in a few days, as if my gaze had skittered over that poem, and I hadn't actually read it. All I remember is the clarity of vision it gave me and the knowledge that it was there, waiting, for someone to open the door and read.

And each time there was a fight at home, the screaming matches between Honey and Jehan or his meltdowns following squabbles with one of us siblings, I went to bed with a single thought in my head:

He's going to try again tomorrow. Please, let him just do it and get it over with.

But he didn't. It was as if he was on mute—the scream that I anticipated on those nights never came. And Head Miss was delaying the announcement of school captains—it was I, it seemed to me, who would scream with frustration the next time the morning assembly ended without her letting us know who'd been chosen. The nights and the mornings kept coming and going though, without the frantic rush of friends and doctors and drama, or the euphoria of having been selected captain of school.

~

Luke and I had decided to go steady. Well, I had decided and bulldozed him into agreeing. At that point, I was in love with the idea of being in love. He confessed later that he just couldn't get over how such a cute girl could see something to like in him. But the cute girl saw a lot in him to like. The later insecurities and intense obsession hadn't set in yet. His family business was still up and running, the boys had two-wheelers and money in their pockets. He was quietly cocky, properly deferential to my superior academic track record, and flatteringly attentive. There was a crazy amount of physical attraction as well.

Every evening, at 7 pm the phone would ring. It'd be Luke, calling from the shop. I would pull up a dining room chair to the alcove by the window overlooking the garden, and we would talk some, but mostly just listen to each other breathing. I pictured him lolling in the swivel chair behind his father's desk, lazily smiling or eyes crackling with some exciting adventure of the day. After a while, Honey would clear her throat and noisily begin to set the table for dinner. I would hang up and she and I would lay the table without quite meeting each other's eyes.

The morning that Head Miss finally announced the names of the two chosen ones to be captains of Wayland Manor was fairly ordinary. By then, I was past the stage of breathless excitement each morning and I barely noticed when she called Venkatesh and me up to the front of the hall and the school began to clap. I was so taken aback that I failed to register what she said to us as she hung a medal around each of our necks. It was probably one of her rousing pep talks: Play the Game! One for all and all for one! I walked home on air that evening.

I waited until dinnertime to make my big announcement.

I'd whispered it to Luke already. He laughed hearing the pleasure in my voice. It wasn't his kind of news. He went to a huge, impersonal boys' school, where personal achievements were often passed over, or, for most of the boys, just out of reach. So when I did show my medal and give my news to the family, I was already a little deflated. Perhaps this meant something disproportionately important to me and the rest of the world simply didn't understand its significance. For me to speak up at the dining table had become increasingly rare. I used to jabber away as a child, showing off for my doting Eruch, and give the boys a chance to grab choice pieces of mutton from my plate or the five shrimp that were my share. Lately though, especially after Luke and I had met, I had become far more reticent at family conversations. My announcement therefore was met with a whoop from my mom, a beaming smile from dad, and not much reaction from the brothers. Zarir was the most vocal in his praises, but Fali was far too lofty a personage to react with enthusiasm to such local news. And Jehan had been oddly distracted for weeks now, so I didn't pay him much mind. Still, I missed being in the limelight on this most significant day of my school life.

Becoming captain of school brought out my worst traits—I became a stickler for the letter of the law, I pontificated and preached to anyone unlucky enough to be caught in a minor transgression and I became even more of a stick-in-the-mud than before. In short, I made myself quite unpopular within the first couple of months. I was too busy basking in my newfound self-importance to notice a distinct lack of enthusiasm from my closest friends.

One day, I heard some giggling as I was walking past the empty standard eleven classroom. I kept going, my head well below the level of the window, when I heard one of the older girls, a brash, hearty girl very popular with the boys.

'Oh, that Liana, she's so preachy...such a bitch! So what if Head Miss made her captain, I'm just going to ignore her.'

I stopped, not because of what she said, but what came after.

'Yeah, she's such a teacher's pet...' Pia's voice was unmistakable, and Amita's half-hearted murmurs too. They had begun to hang out with girls from the higher classes.

I hurried away, close to tears. Why did I feel so betrayed? They hadn't said anything wrong! I never mentioned it to anyone, not even Luke. It must have cut very close to the bone, injured my pride, if I can remember it as clearly as if it were this morning. At the time though, I chose to ignore it, like it never happened. I didn't breathe a word of the hurt to Amita or Pia, surprising even myself with my acting.

Nalini, kind-hearted and agenda-free, continued to stand up for me in her own quiet way. Surprisingly, I also had a quiet champion in Karthik. No longer the new boy in class, and much adored by all, he remained unfazed by my rude rejection of his friendship.

In any case, that incident aside, the first term of standard ten was fun.

Mrs Klugerman had selected the cast for the December school concert. This was an annual extravaganza, featuring song and dance routines, excerpts from Shakespearean dramas and the Nativity play. With a sublime disregard for the syllabus and the teachers' burdens, she proceeded to give most of the starring roles to us students of Standard Ten. I was Portia in *The Merchant of Venice* to (the other school captain) Venkatesh's Shylock. Karthik was a very bashful Joseph to our school beauty Arwa's Mother Mary and Amita's Angel Gabriel.

At home, too, the excitement over Fali's forthcoming wedding was building. As he had promised my aunt all those years ago, he had met and fallen in love with Preeti. Eruch, funnily enough, came over all Parsi, arguing, 'But how will she fit in?' It took a stern talking-to from Jehan to make him pipe down. This is the one story Eruch willingly shares about Jehan even today:

'I was in two minds about Preeti. Then my Jehan said to me: Dad, do you want to lose your son? If you object to Preeti simply because she's not Parsi, Fali will leave us for her. Just accept it with a good grace. *Samajyuné?* (You understand?) And I listened to my wise son and welcomed Preeti with open arms.'

Finally, the parents met and liked each other very much. And we had a wedding to plan! Zarir and Jehan became de facto groomsmen, though Jehan's contributions to the wedding planning were usually far too flamboyant for a quiet Bay City affair, and more suited to the kind of tabloid weddings he enjoyed reading about.

The wedding was planned for October. The talk turned to the plans for it one hot August evening as we sat around on the front porch chatting of this and that. Dinner was done, Honey and Eruch had retired to their bedroom and the rest of us lolled in the humid air with the lights switched off to prevent an onslaught of mosquitoes.

Fali had become a softer, kinder brother. Jehan and Preeti had got on famously ever since we'd met her. They were conspirators, ganging up on a hapless Fali in all sorts of escapades. It was nice to see an indulgent, loved-up Fali—a very different and very likeable person. We had Preeti to thank for that transformation. Fali and Jehan actually spoke civilly to each other these days, at least when Preeti was around. Zarir and I had learnt to slowly relax, the stress of constantly jumping between the two sparring brothers having vanished. Today, Fali and Zarir loudly vetoed the idea of a huge engagement party being planned by Jehan and the bride.

'And Preeti,' said Jehan excitedly, 'I'll organize a DJ, and a champagne fountain! Zarir, you must be having champagne flutes somewhere in that mansion of yours?'

Fali groaned. 'Zarir, my man, hide all the glasses you own. These two will bankrupt me!'

'Nonsense, Zarir will pay for the champagne as part of his wedding gift. Right, Zarir?'

'Umm, yeah, sure, why not?' from a flustered Zarir.

I sat quietly, listening in amusement as Fali shot down one after another of Jehan's increasingly grandiose and airy schemes. A three-tiered cake was the next item on the agenda.

We all laughed at the idea. No baker existed in our city with the skills to create the confection Jehan was describing to us.

'Butter cream, scalloped around the edges, and where can we find a sword, like Charlie's?'

He had pored over the double-page spreads of Princess Diana's wedding a few years ago, when Honey brought home *Woman & Home* magazines. Now it was apparent that he was aiming to recreate, if not the meringue dress, then at least the cake.

'You'd better start baking now, Jehan, if you want all those layers ready by October,' Zarir teased him.

And then, suddenly, in one of his quicksilver mood changes, Jehan said, very quietly, almost to himself:

'But I won't be there for the wedding.'

I heard the note in his voice, I know Zarir heard it too. We both glanced at him, then at each other. My heartbeat hitched, the breath caught in my throat. It was a feeling that would become increasingly familiar in the days and months to come. Zarir looked away. The happy couple laughed it off.

'Where do you think you'll be, Mister Jehan?' demanded an imperious Preeti. 'You're going to be run off of your feet—my Master of Ceremonies. And oh, first you'll be decorating the house... I want lots of your frosted candles everywhere, and you'd better take charge of the flowers as well.'

The conversation passed on to other topics. I had heard it though. The pain, the wistfulness in his voice. It has haunted my nightmares ever since. Why did I not say or do something, anything? For years afterwards, I was told by well-meaning people trying to comfort me that it wasn't my fault, that I was only a child, and that there was nothing I could have done. Tell me, reader, having read my story thus far, was I really a child? I try and reconcile myself to one of two truths, both equally ugly: That I was either so caught up in myself, that even my brother's three attempts at killing himself hadn't shaken me out of my self-absorption. Or—and this is the one that cuts deep—that those three cries for help, loud and clear, had deafened me to the point where I just wanted it to be over. The drama, the tension, the emotion, I wanted an end to it all. Did I, then, deliberately ignore all the warning signs? If no one else heard it, and I did, why didn't I run to someone? Teachers in school, and there were a couple who would have listened. Teachers who might have had some inkling, as my writing got darker and far too morbid for a fourteen-year-old amateur writer. Visiting relatives. A young aunt who hung out with us, smoking Virginia Slims and as crazy about comics as us. Or an uncle, wise and trained as a counsellor, but far away in our hometown. That begs the question of questions: Why didn't I tell Honey or Eruch? Fali? About the poem written in green sketch pen on the inside of Jehan's cupboard door. About his latest hint over the wedding cake. A dozen other signs, flashing their warnings at me. I saw, and chose to do nothing at all.

Then too I wonder at the paralysis of the entire family. Is it optimism or foolhardiness to believe that your son, your suicidal brother will turn the corner with only amateur intervention and no medical treatment or emotional help?

Or is it a fear so debilitating that your only hope lies in ignoring it, pushing the looming threat aside, pretending that it is, after all, a most ordinary life we lead? Did Honey and Eruch speak of it behind closed doors? Did Fali and his bride-to-be? Did we all speak of it together? This is something that I simply don't have a memory of. Have I blanked it out along with so much else?

A cascade of questions.

No answers.

September 1986

IT HAD BEEN a lovely start to a long weekend. Head Miss had given the whole school, including us tenth graders Thursday and Friday off so that all the cricket-crazy kids—and she was just as fanatical as us—could watch the Australia–India test match at the downtown cricket stadium. Though she was Australian by birth, our principal always played fair. This chance of watching her two favourite teams play in her own city was too good to resist. Much to the despair of the faculty, racing against the clock to finish the syllabus, she declared a holiday. We were the secret envy of everyone else, though out of long-standing habit and wounded pride, the other schools continued to jeer at us: we were the losers who watched cricket instead of working hard and bringing home the all-India ranks in the Board exams. Now I look back and wonder who the real losers were.

I had spent the day hanging out with my girlfriends, none of whom had any interest in cricket. Our small animosities and differences laid aside, we'd left home, prepared to cruise the city. Amita had on a new straw hat.

'Dahlings,' she proclaimed, as we walked along, 'my straw hat vill protect my alabaster skin from big, big bimbles.'

We collapsed with laughter at her Greta Garbo act.

I remember a vivid blue sky, the kind of blue only a Bay City sky can be. We preened and twirled our way down the sidewalks, acting silly the way teenaged girls do. We window shopped and ate lunch at Fiesta, the cool restaurant at the best department store in town. Then we headed to a movie theatre to watch *Curse of the Pink Panther*, starring Peter Sellers. At the end of the day, exhausted and happy, we made plans to meet again while school was out and then headed home. Nalini dropped me off on the way and I walked home dreamily, no thought in my head at all. As soon as I got home, I switched on our new stereo system. I slammed *Genesis* by Genesis into the tape deck, turning up the volume so that Honey knew I was home. Almost immediately, the phone rang. It was Luke, calling earlier than usual from the shop, asking how my day had been.

~

My brother Jehan killed himself on that warm September evening, the year I was fourteen and in love for the first time. It's selfish, I know, but I'm trying to give the reader a feeling for my self-absorption. He died somewhere between the time that 'Mama' by Genesis was blasting out of the speakers and I was chattering away with my clandestine boyfriend on the phone. Perhaps if the music hadn't been playing at that volume, I might have heard the bathroom stool being kicked away beneath his feet, heard his breath leave his body, our home, our lives. He had locked his bedroom door, and hung himself from the shower pipe in the bathroom using my nylon skipping rope. I have never skipped since.

The rest of that evening was commonplace: Zarir, who ate dinner most nights with us, came by as usual around 6.30. Eruch returned home from the office at 7 pm, and headed to the master bedroom to freshen up. The cook and Honey were making chapattis for dinner. Fali was at his fiancée's house, having ridden off on his black Yezdi as soon as he returned home from work. October and the wedding were just over a month away. It was just another evening in the Chinoy home, when Jehan chose to go away.

Zarir walked in and went to deposit his tiffin carrier in the kitchen. Mom and he made small talk, then he wandered out in search of the rest of us. I was on the phone. He waved his hand and I covered the receiver and cocked an eyebrow at him.

'Where are the boys?' he asked.

'I don't know,' I said and he looked wounded. 'Oh come on, Zarir, Fali's gone to Preeti's.'

'And Jehan?'

'In his room. He's been holed up all day.'

Jehan had come home on Tuesday complaining of a bad stomach ache and had stayed home for two days after that. He had sounded so low and dispirited that afternoon that when he asked me for a glass of lime juice, I actually went and made it for him. I handed him that bottle-green glass brimming with the drink. His brown hand, the thin wrist festooned with his thick silver link bracelet (I think he and Prashant had given each other similar ones), reached for the glass. Did our hands touch? I don't remember. He thanked me, and retreated into his bedroom. As far as my memory takes me that was the last time I saw my brother alive.

Now that Zarir had been answered, I got back to Luke. I half-noticed that Zarir's face became glum as he heard me whispering on the phone. He knew he wouldn't be getting any attention from me. I turned my back on his hovering form. Finally tired of waiting for me to get off the phone, he wandered away in search of Jehan. The bedroom door was locked, I could hear him shouting Jehan's name over the music but there was no answer. From my perch near the dining room windows, I could look across at Jehan's bedroom windows. The curtains were drawn as always. My brother was rather paranoid about his privacy. I turned back to my phone call and lost interest in Zarir.

Now my narrative becomes hearsay.

Bored, Zarir wandered out into the garden and saw the bathroom light on. Worried that Jehan, who hadn't left his room claiming illness for a couple of days, might've fainted, he hiked himself up on the pipes running along the outer wall to look in through the bathroom ventilator. In the next minute, he came running in, and snapped at me to fetch a knife. When I airily waved him away, he shouted, '*Get a knife!*'

My parents were in their room, and he probably wanted to bring the body down before they or I could see it.

I knew then that it had finally happened.

'Oh God, he's done it again,' I said to Luke and slammed the phone down.

Zarir's face was mottled and sweating with emotion or exertion and I fled to the kitchen for a knife. This young, short, slightly podgy man, my reliable and boring Clark Kent then became Superman. Driven by a rush of adrenaline, he found the strength to break the locked door open.

'*Don't* come in,' he panted. 'Get your mom and dad!'

He ran into the silent room. By the time my parents realized something was wrong, our friend had carried Jehan to the bed and laid him down. He was the only one who saw my brother's hanging body. I can't even imagine the quality of his nightmares. I hope that his deep spirituality got him through the worst of the memories.

My mind wasn't working but I knew that I had to call Fali. His fiancée's sister picked up the phone and settled down for a nice chat.

'Hi there, how's the wedding shopping going? Have you chosen a sari yet?'

'Hey, I need to speak to Fali please.'

'*Arre*, you can speak to him later. Just now tell me, did you see Preeti's reception sari? So heavy, na? I told her she'll collapse by the end of the eveni...'

I spent what seemed like a lifetime convincing her that I really needed to speak to my brother. When he finally came on the line, his voice sounded annoyed at being disturbed.

All I could blurt out was, 'It's Jehan, he's killed himself.'

It's hard to imagine how Fali and my future sister-in-law made that fifteen-minute motorcycle ride from her place to ours in one piece.

At home, my mom and dad held each other and pleaded with Jehan to wake up.

'Jehan, babba, Jehan.'

I comfort myself for my tactlessness by telling myself I must have been in shock because I kept repeating to them, 'He's dead, can't you see? He's dead.'

I don't think any of us heard each other. Now, in hindsight, as I write this, my heart is pounding double time. Back then, it felt like time was standing still. One moment, life was normal—well, at least as normal as it had ever been in the last year—and the next, life, as we knew it, simply disappeared. More specifically, it felt as if all the air had been sucked out of the world. I continued to breathe but it didn't bring relief from the gasping sensation in my lungs or the light-headedness. There was an immediate hollow feeling in my stomach as I stood there over my brother's body, a feeling that has never really gone away. It abates, sometimes for days, weeks, months, but I am never free of it. It always comes back. It seems surprising that I wasn't quite ready for this complete sense of numbness, the lack of emotion, because I had been bracing for this eventuality for the preceding year—he'd given us ample warning, hadn't he? The only surprise should have been that he had finally done it.

Zarir stood at the foot of the bed. He murmured to me, 'We should straighten his feet.'

I looked and his feet were askew, twisted, at odds with the rest of his body. I bent down and straightened them. Zarir then bent and paid his respects with folded hands. Jehan's face was very peaceful. It wasn't mottled, nor were there strangulation marks on his throat. He was dressed in his light baggy cotton pants and a tee shirt with cutaway sleeves. He lay there, eyes closed; he might have been sleeping. But there was no way my brother would have left his body that vulnerable even in sleep. He slept in a ball, huddled around himself. I too sleep in the same position now.

I wandered out, registering everything and nothing as the young doctor, for the third time that year, came running in, alerted by our cook. I switched off the music. I looked at the clock. It said eight o' clock. When I went back inside, standing in a corner to give the doctor room as he tried to revive Jehan, my eyes fell on little yellow notes stuck to every single thing in the room. His records, the little lantern, his knick-knacks, everything had a label on it. Zarir, Fali and I looked at each note afterwards. He had left all his things, pieces of his life, for his friends, nothing for the family. Bablu, Prashant, Sid, Ziya and others. I don't know if his last wishes were honoured. My guess is that they were ignored. I have his thick silver bracelet, the one he left for Prashant. My mother gave it to me when I found it many years later in her cupboard. Hari told me when we spoke after a gap of thirty-odd years that Prashant died a few years ago. I don't yet know what to feel. I wouldn't have known how to find Prashant even if I wanted to do the right thing and give him the bracelet. But I didn't want to do the right thing. That bracelet is my only physical memory of my brother. I don't look at it very often, but like my teddy bear, sitting blind-eyed in a corner of my cupboard, I know it's there, and that comforts me.

Fali and Preeti came running in. I had to leave the room to make space for them. Zarir too came out to give the family some privacy. It was amazing how quickly the word spread. As the cook ran to get the doctor who lived down the lane, she had also managed to alert the entire neighbourhood. It was around 9 pm. Neighbours began to gather at our house gate, keeping a silent vigil, which irritated me no end. Zarir and I sat on the porch, and I became increasingly agitated.

'Zarir,' I said again and again, 'tell them to go away. Please, just make them go away.'

Fali found a long suicide note, incoherently written in green sketch pen, detailing various plots and dramas, leaving behind various personal articles for all his friends and a nightmare for his family. In it, he hinted darkly at my unsuitable gang of friends and that he hoped I would be careful of them. He rambled on about conspiracies, warning me that these friends were no good for me. I read it just that once, sitting out on our porch, and I often wish I had the guts to ask my dad or Fali for it. I'd like to read it again with some detachment.

Some friends who lived down the road came rushing over. Fali must have called them. One gentleman, a prominent businessman and father of my classmate, accompanied my dad to the local police station to deal with the formalities. Now Fali and Zarir had a muted conversation and then came to me. If I don't remember any other detail of that evening, this conversation is the one thing I will never forget.

'Liana, listen to me,' Fali said. 'These new friends of yours. They picked on Jehan in college, just last week. They teased him about his red pants. You know Jehan—how soft he is. Was. Read his letter, Linu. He's told you they're no good for you. He didn't like these guys. You have to stop meeting them at once. You are not to meet them again; do you hear me, Liana?'

My sanity, the last vestiges of it I had been clinging to all evening, left me in that moment. I watched them, leaning forward, elbows on knees, as they explained away my life as I had known it. Almost immediately, the thought came to my head: Did Amita know? Sunny and she were exceptionally close siblings. Had she known that they were teasing Jehan in college? Teasing him about his clothes and maybe his effeminate manner. The things he was most sensitive about. Their words and the words written on those sheets in vitriolic green, seared themselves in my brain. The anger and hurt I felt in those first few moments were overwhelming. Then, mercifully, my mind switched off and all I could do was nod my head.

A hearse arrived and Fali accompanied the body for a post-mortem. The neighbours drifted away. Honey and Eruch locked themselves up in their bedroom.

That night, I was sent to sleep at a neighbour's house. The

little family of three had moved into the apartment building next door just that last year. Having lived in our hometown until their recent move to Bay City, we naturally bonded over this connection. The daughter, Divya, tall, statuesque and comely, had even studied in the same department as my mom. She had found a friend and confidante in Jehan, who counselled and comforted her through her turbulent relationships and growing pains. They had sat huddled on our terrace on many evenings, and giggled over boyfriends and fashion. Just a couple of nights before, we had sat on the bonnet of Zarir's car, parked in our garden, and whiled away the evening in meaningless conversation. Now, Divya, her beautiful dark eyes reddened with tears, took me home, where I scandalized her mother by telling her, 'Well, at least we'll rest in peace now.'

The kind old lady, shocked and sorrowing, could only pat my head with a gentle hand. Uncle, usually bluff and jocular, held my shoulders and shook me gently. His face was like a clown's, the one with the smile turned downwards. I turned away and Divya led me into her room and silently handed me half a sleeping pill. I swallowed it, told her not to cry any more and went to sleep.

~

The next three days went by in a haze. I woke up and went back into a home filled with friends. Now here's the strange thing. I can't remember whether Amita was already there. I think she was. Who told her? How did she know? I never did find out. We retreated into my room and sobbed together, until Preeti came in and briskly told us to get our act together. I was wanted outside. My school principal and teachers were waiting for me. I came out, not wanting to look anyone in the eye. Head Miss took my chin in a big, bony hand and forced my gaze to meet her steady eyes.

She said firmly, with a conviction I did not feel: 'You are strong, my girl, you will get through this.'

I was never as unsure of my strength as I was that morning, and maybe she knew that. My teachers hugged me, most of them had taught Jehan as well. As they left, disconsolate and tearful, I turned to go back to my bedroom.

But first there was Feroza Aunty, one of my favourite aunties, the convent school PE teacher, family friend and the mother of one of the only two Parsi girls I was friends with. She hugged me to her and whispered:

'Just say Ashem Vohu'—the simplest and most powerful prayer in the Zoroastrian religion, the first one every child learns—'and everything will be all right, you'll see.'

I lost my faith that year and never regained it. But still, when things overwhelm me, or when life feels unliveable, I still say an Ashem Vohu in my head, in memory of Feroza Aunty's simple advice. No other visitor could bring themselves to comfort me, perhaps because I was already exuding the thorny, don't-touch-me vibe that was to become my best and only defence and barrier in the coming months. The morning passed. Now it gets confusing again. I can't tell if whatever happened after that happened that day, Friday, or the next. I think the funeral was held on Saturday, as we waited for family and friends to arrive from out of town. It probably doesn't matter.

By the time the following afternoon came around, I longed to be with Amita again, and her aunt, my beloved Rama Miss. I was desperate for the comfort of their presence and equally desperate to understand this rage roaring in my heart. I begged another neighbour, Sanjay, to take me to Amita's house on his motorbike. I climbed the stairs to their first-floor apartment, an old-fashioned South Indian residence with deep windows, cool floors and quaint bedrooms set off from the main rooms by a step leading downwards. The entire family, except for Sunny, was there.

I entered their quiet home, everyone hugged me, Rama Miss crying with anger that she hadn't seen this coming. She loved Jehan and Jehan had loved her. They shared a special bond over their singing and performing. As Jehan grew older, the relationship easily slipped from that between a teacher and student to friendship. They cracked risqué jokes and cackled like two witches whenever they met. In the last year, Rama Miss had often complained that she didn't get to see Jehan as often as before. And now this.

'Why didn't he come to me? Silly fellow...why didn't he talk to me?'

The phone rang, it was Luke.

'I'm sorry, Dumbo.' (I never really gave it much thought, why we called each other Dumbo. It was just our name for each other.)

There was a long silence. I listened to him breathe. 'That's okay,' I mumbled.

He sounded helpless. 'It's not okay.'

This became the refrain of our conversations, real or imaginary, mostly the latter, for the following months. I'm sorry. It's okay. I was never quite sure whether he was apologizing to me or commiserating my loss. I didn't want to think about Fali's accusations. We didn't talk much. Maybe I gave him some incoherent explanation for what I was about to do. As I stood there, my back turned on Amita's anxious face, I began to see with some warped clarity what lay ahead. I was in shock and pain. My body and mind were shutting down. I did not have the resources to confront my friends, nor did I feel able to ignore Fali's words. I would never find the strength to ask these friends if and why they had teased my brother. Certainly not right then, and never afterwards. The only person who could confirm or deny the events was gone. As I withdrew into myself, the plan hardened in my mind. I could no longer bear to be near Luke and Amita, or Sunny, not now. I left Amita's house soon after and I next entered it only after six years had passed.

When I got home, I went to my bedroom, the one I still shared with Fali. I sat down at my study table with the dried-up bunch of red roses from the summer. I cried, I think, as I crushed them and let the dust fall into the dustbin. Then I wandered over to the window and stared out at what I supposed was Luke's bedroom window. I cried my tears until my throat was sore and my stomach ached. In reality,

I didn't know quite where his house was exactly. I just knew it was in the avenue next to mine. We had laughed about it. I had told him I could see his bedroom from mine, and he had insisted that I was looking at the wrong window. That night, nothing could have convinced me that the solitary light in that dark building I could see from my window wasn't his bedroom.

That light in the window sustained me for the next nine months. It was years later that I realized that they had moved out of the neighbourhood soon after and what I'd been staring at was a light in a stranger's house. No matter, it was my lighthouse. Every night, when I was supposed to be studying, I would switch off the lights to my bedroom and speak to Luke from my window. I raged at him, I cried, I said and did all the silly dramatic things teenage girls in love do. It was all in my head and I started to build up this rich imaginary world that lasted well into my early twenties, a world in which we had long conversations, even though in reality we had been in and out of touch for long periods in the intervening years. I became obsessive about those conversations in my head as the years passed.

~

Saturday. Fali and Zarir were leaving for the prayer hall, to receive Jehan's body once it was released from the police morgue where it had been taken for the post-mortem. Fali came to ask if I wanted to accompany them. I couldn't face the thought of being alone at home with my parents so I jumped at the offer. The quiet prayer hall was situated in a small green park next to the Parsi cemetery. Jehan lay there on a marble slab, covered in a sheet of cloth. Zarir and Fali washed the body according to Parsi funeral requirements. When they allowed me inside that empty, airy room, he had been bathed and dressed in clean white pants and a sadra (the sacred muslin vest worn by Zoroastrians). Zarir again bent and paid his respects at his feet but wouldn't touch the body now that it had been bathed. Orthodox Parsis observe these restrictions, but I wasn't orthodox. I bent and kissed his forehead. As I smoothed back his hair, I noticed with a certain clinical detachment that a gash on his skull had been stitched with thick red waxy twine. Three or four big stitches, visible through the thin shirt, ran across his chest and abdomen as well. My brother's brain and heart were gone. This was, after all, only the husk left for us to mourn over. We returned home after making the arrangements with the priest for the funeral.

The family had arrived, the largest contingent from our hometown. I don't know where they stayed, who cooked for them, nothing. I couldn't tell you anything that didn't directly concern me, that is how wrapped up I was in my own grief. For example, I can tell you how I struggled to comb my hair neatly that afternoon. I had very long hair, straight and silky. Only Honey could wrestle it into neat plaits; I had never bothered to learn to do my hair myself. I couldn't ask her, not today. I tied it up as best as I could and emerged from my room, dressed for the funeral in a long white skirt, a black wraparound top and a parrot green scarf. Honey and Eruch, not being religious, had never insisted that the three of us go regularly, or at all, to agiary (Parsi temple). In fact, soon after my Navjote (initiation ceremony), I had quietly taken off the sadra and kasti (the sacred vest and thread), and I just about had one sadra that was kept for funerals. I certainly did not own a white scarf.

When I asked an aunt what to do, she said distractedly, 'Just manage, Linu.'

So I did.

The park outside the prayer hall was packed with people. We were a small and close-knit community, though that didn't stop the gossips from having a field day at our family's expense for the next several years. Still, they were all there to support my parents. Jehan was much loved by the aunties, for his cakes and candles as well as for his charm. He carefully kept the sarcasm and biting remarks to a minimum in their company. To say that the community was shocked would be an understatement. All the young girls of the community had crushed on Jehan at one point or another, so there were many red-eyed young ladies there as well.

Inside the prayer hall, I was sternly admonished when the tears welled up. The soul would not find peace if it saw those it had loved grieving for it. Apparently, the soul hovered close to the body so tears were expressly forbidden. I can't think of a more asinine thing, given the circumstances. The boy had taken his own life. I'm pretty sure he didn't give a damn if I cried or not. The priest droned on interminably, it seemed. Honey and the ladies of the house sat on the floor of the prayer hall, an old-fashioned gesture that raised many eyebrows. Coming as our family did from a mofussil town, we followed many more local customs than the Bay City community, many of whom were more Westernized and modern Parsis. Anyway, I was hustled out and I sat, with Divya and Zarir, on the steps of the adjoining building, crying quietly. Or howling. I couldn't say with certainty.

The silence in that park, muted except for the sound of the priest's voice and my crying, was broken by the sound of motorbike engines, abruptly cutting out at the gate. Luke and Joseph, Sunny and a few others had come to attend my brother's funeral. They hovered at the back of the crowd, unsure about the formalities. I caught their eye and looked away, horribly embarrassed as only teenage girls can be in such situations, acutely aware of my red eyes and untidy hair and green scarf.

Then the prayers were over. Fali and Zarir, Eruch and his brother lifted Jehan's body and carried it through a parting wave of white to the graveyard. The ladies followed. I trailed behind, forgotten in the grim solemnity of the occasion. A little door separated the graveyard from the park. Luke caught up with me there.

He said, again, 'I'm sorry, Dumbo.'

And I said, again, 'It's okay.'

He didn't touch me. I couldn't meet his eyes. I could feel Zarir's eyes boring into my back.

And Fali was there, ordering abruptly: 'Let's go, Liana.'

I turned away obediently, and soon after, I heard the bikes roar away. Maybe I would have said more if I could have seen the immediate future, but as it is, I said nothing at all.

I watched the funeral from a great distance. As I stood with my parents and Zarir, I was already very far away. Fali helped the grave diggers lower the body into the flimsy raw wood coffin and then into the freshly-dug grave. Honey murmured his name a couple of times, and then turned away. The rain should have been falling, a wind should have been moaning. It felt wrong that the sun was shining in a blue sky, and a gentle breeze played around our heads. People slowly began to drift away, and finally only Fali, Zarir and I were left. Fali sat down on the ground, knees pulled up and head hanging. Zarir tugged at my hand and I let him lead me away.

~

It was evening by the time we returned home. Again, Honey retreated into the bedroom, Eruch trailing after her. The family sat in the living room, talking quietly about silly details. Zarir and I sat on the porch, staring out at the garden and at Cherie, running around after being locked up in the house all day. Vagabond, our cat, had disappeared in that eerie way cats have of sensing great emotion and preferring to distance themselves from it.

Inside, the voices slowly grew in volume and one bitter voice said viciously:

'See, this is the result of her leaving them to go to America.'

I reacted as if I had been hit by lightning, storming in and crying, 'How dare you say that about my mother? She's sitting inside, and you are in her home! How dare you?'

The old lady, the aunts and uncles were aghast. I had never ever raised my voice to them before. I was their little darling, their Linu. But in that moment, I chose sides. I would always and forever after be my mother's defender. Wrong or right, her refusal to defend herself against this and many other charges laid at her door aroused in me a sense of justice denied. She never asked me to fight her battles for her, nor did she ever acknowledge that I did so for as long as she lived. We were ourselves adversaries in the great mother–daughter conflict.

~

The next morning, oddly enough, is clearly etched in my memory. It was the third night, when the early morning prayer ceremony is held after a death. We stumbled out of bed around three in the morning, silently avoiding each other as we dressed. This silent avoidance had become the new normal in my home already. It would last for a very long time. Fali had spent the last three nights brushing up his driving skills. Every night, Zarir and he would drive up and down our deserted road in Zarir's Maruti. It was Fali who drove us that morning all the way to the agiary, located next to the graveyard and Parsi club. It was a measure of Eruch's grief that he did not utter a single word of criticism or correct Fali's nervous handling of his precious car. Zarir followed as escort in his car, bringing the relations. At the agiary, the priest greeted us and led us into the anteroom where the ceremonial fire and platter with various offerings were laid out. I began to nod off on the hard stone bench as he intoned the sonorous prayers. Honey caught my eye and glared at me but the yawns kept coming and soon I had infected everyone. The smoke from the fire began to burn our sleepy eyes, and the tears ran acrid down our faces.

After an unbearable half hour, I made my escape to the front porch of the temple. I sat there, gulping in the cool morning air, breathing the smell of night jasmine and the dew wet mud of the compound. When I think back, I think that was the morning I lost faith. Sitting in God's house, I could see no further use for a deity in my life. The cruelty, the ruthlessness, the futility of all that had gone before, the past year of high tension, the days of stress and the nights of uncertainty, all of these could only be the petty play of some vengeful God. There was no kindness or love that I could fathom in his actions at all. The vague realization that one more anchor was lost, and I was drifting away, brought tears to my eyes and hysterical laughter. I smothered it with one hand and Zarir, coming out to check on me, was once again left distraught and scandalized by my callous behaviour.

Sunday dawned and my four-day holiday was soon over. I don't believe it crossed anyone's mind that I might not want to go back to school. Certainly it never occurred to me. Tomorrow was Monday, and I would have the strange new experience of being the girl whose brother had killed himself. I gritted my teeth and pulled all the defences I could muster around myself. I wasn't giving anyone the chance to be kind and sympathetic. I had had three days to plan for the time ahead. Of course, I wasn't thinking rationally. I had convinced myself that Amita must have known all along of the teasing Jehan had endured in college. Even worse, I added Pia and Nalini to this list of the guilty, for no good reason except that the four of us were so close. It seemed to me that Luke had picked on Jehan to exact petty revenge for Jehan's blatant disapproval of our fledgling relationship. His friends, who I'd thought were my friends too, had egged him on. The trauma of the last few days meant that my brain refused to consider the alternative: that Luke and Jehan may indeed have had a run-in at college, words might even have been exchanged, but it had likely ended there. And that Amita and the other two girls had no inkling of what had happened. Most importantly, that Jehan had been troubled by his demons for so long now, the altercation with my friends could hardly be the reason for his death. The last nine months had been one long cry of despair before the voice fell silent.

In retrospect, I think that I was already punishing myself for Jehan's death. This was the worst punishment I could inflict on myself—cutting ties with my best friends, my boyfriend, ironically almost everyone who had made the last year bearable, even enjoyable. And yet, some deep-rooted sense of self-preservation meant that I would hold on to some friends. These were friends whom I hadn't valued before, but who became my safe harbour now. And I found out that even in the hardest moments of grief, a new friendship, tentatively offered for the nth time, can become one's lifeline.

~

I got to school early, as usual, and sat down in my usual place, leaning against the wall separating the basketball court from the football field slash tennis court. Pia and Amita walked up; I didn't say a word to them. They were awkward and unsure of what to say. Then Nalini arrived. The three of them sat with me, making small talk.

Another classmate, Lissy, sweet, bubbly, loyal Lissy came up to us. 'Hi girls,' she said, 'how was the weekend?'

And I committed the first of many unforgivable acts. I raised my eyes to hers and replied:

'Oh, Jehan killed himself on Thursday, and I was busy with the funeral until yesterday.'

Lissy's face crumpled, her eyes welled up and I stood up and walked away to the assembly hall. The assembly that morning was sombre. Head Miss briefly spoke of Jehan, how much he had been loved by all in Wayland Manor, how much he would be missed. By now, the events of the past four days were common knowledge. The rustle that went along the lines of students made its way among the teachers, until Head Miss asked for a moment's silence. I stared down at my feet, my mind peaceful and blank. Before assembly was done, she came up to me and asked me to meet her in her office.

Her bright, sunny office had always been a place I dreaded entering, even if I was one of her favourite students. Today, I sat there, uncaring, staring out of the window.

Head Miss came in, sat down from across me. 'Tell me everything, Liana.'

I did so mechanically, no tears thankfully in front of this strong woman I idolized. Her response was brief, unsentimental and practical.

'I don't need to remind you, Liana, of the motto of our school... I hope this doesn't mean that you won't be taking part in the concert.'

She expected no less of me as captain now than she had before. I had duties and responsibilities to the school and to my schoolmates, and there would be no shirking these.

'My parents may not like—'

'Absolutely no question—you are Portia and there's no one else better suited to that role, my girl.' It was the lead role and there was no one else at this point who could take it on.

'And if your parents have any objections, well, then I'll speak to them—they know me well enough by now.' This with a grim little laugh.

Head Miss couldn't have been more emphatic—I owed it to the school and, yes, to my parents as well, to play the game. And that was that. I stood up, she shook my hand, and sent me off to class. I wonder if she ever knew how those categorical words of faith in my sense of duty became my personal mantra.

The first week was a blur. I switched off a lot during

classes, though the teachers were particularly gentle with me. Even the mathematics teacher, for whom I was somewhat of a damp squib, merely motioned to Lissy or some other girl to lead me out of class if the tears came. I never broke down noisily, mostly just sat there quietly with tears running down my face. It must have discomfited that prim little man out of his wits. The boys in my class were also really uncomfortable around me. Most of them avoided me altogether. In the course of that week, two of my teachers pulled me aside and broke down while asking me what had happened to their dear Jehan. It had been expressly forbidden by Head Miss to ask me anything, but these two young ladies, both lovely people, simply couldn't bear it, I suppose. I remember awkwardly comforting each of them, one behind the laboratory, the other hidden behind a rain tree.

That Friday, as I was leaving school, Karthik came running up to me.

'Hi,' he said, 'I have an extra ticket for the match this weekend. Do you want to go?'

I stared at him. 'My brother died,' I said a little helplessly. Didn't this great booby know that? What had happened to his suave style just when I could have done with a dose of it?

And he said, very simply, 'I know.'

I knew very little, as it turned out. He had lost an elder brother years earlier to a heart ailment; his home life was not as normal as he would have liked. So, in many ways, he did know.

Amita tried, very hard at first, to get me to talk, to tell her why I was behaving so. I just froze every time she came near me or if I heard her voice on the telephone. She gave up gradually. I missed her tremendously but there came a point in time after which there was nothing I could do. I didn't know how to apologize. How to make amends. I didn't know how to ask her to help me understand the rage I still felt every time I thought of Fali's words. Perversely too, the anger against myself for believing Fali without giving her a chance to clarify the conclusions I'd jumped to. It was easier to just leave things where I had abandoned them. I refused to tell anyone what had happened between Amita and me. I guess Rama Miss comforted her and advised her to leave me alone. And so she did. (I next spoke to her after six years, at a memorial meeting for another friend who died young. We met sometimes at parties or at common friends' homes. I would look through her, much to everyone's discomfort. She never showed how much it hurt and I was grateful to her for that.)

Pia and Nalini were too nervous to make any overtures at all. Luke too in his laconic way tried to get me to talk. I cried when I heard his voice but gently replaced the receiver. The rage I inside me already tempered with longing and subsequent guilt.

And so began my new life. I went to school each morning, daydreaming my way through classes which I was now perilously close to failing. I ate my lunch alone, the days I remembered to eat at all. Or I sat with another group, one that did not include Amita. That was difficult because she was so popular. I started walking endless circles around the school to pass the lunch break. Once or twice, I found myself walking home in the middle of the day. Perhaps the school watchman had instructions to leave me alone because I don't recall anyone stopping me. I would reach home, silent and still in the hot afternoon and wander off to Divya's place to while away the hours until it was time to go home. That evening, a teacher would casually call in on her way home. She would exchange pleasantries with Honey, pass on some unnecessary message to me and leave. But not once was I pulled up in school for playing hooky.

It was one such day when I was walking home, head bent to watch my feet take one step after another, when I heard someone call out my name. I looked up and saw Ravi, sitting perched on the first-floor balcony of his house, one leg slung over the parapet. He was one year behind us in school, a rebel and misfit if ever there was one, even in our school, and he beckoned me to come upstairs, grinning cheekily at me. To my everlasting surprise, I obeyed. We sat slouched on the floor of the balcony, talking of nothing in particular. His mother knew mine, and came up to give me a note and a small book of poetry to pass on to Honey. She didn't ask me any questions either, just placed her hand on my arm and squeezed it. It felt good to have some physical contact with people again. And Ravi was very physical. He was a big bulldog of a boy, thick-necked and with hands like hams. He would become a very good rugby player later on. His way of showing affection was to haul friends into chokeholds. Sometimes, he'd pick me up in his arms and squeeze the air out of my lungs.

'I'm gonna hug you, Miss Chin-Chin-Chinoy and there's nothing you can do to stop me.'

'Ravi, let me down or I'll knee you where it hurts!'

'Ooh, who's been teaching Miss Chinoy about sensitive parts?'

And the silliness would continue. It was completely innocent but we caused a sensation in school: Miss Prim and Proper and the school brat. One day, I was sent out of my classroom with an errand to run. Ravi was kneeling outside the Standard Nine classroom, looking impenitent. I stopped, and he gave me the most beautiful smile. I couldn't help it, I let out a peal of laughter that brought the teacher running out of class. She stared at us grinning at each other and shooed me away. I still don't know why we hit it off. His mother was a bohemian lady, very artistic and sensitive. His twin sister was away at boarding school. I think Ravi had been asked to leave this school for too many contretemps and had washed up in Wayland Manor, like so many of us. His dad was not around. We chattered about music and his string of girlfriends, chomped our way through lots of food in his kitchen. We experimented with flirting but mutually decided that it was a non-starter. I was too frozen with grief and he was too much of everything for me to handle. He knew about Luke; the whole school knew by then that I had a boyfriend who went to the big rough boys' school that shared a wall with ours. The Waylander boys didn't care for this defection, and one day, some of them even held an intervention and told me so. This was in the days before September.

I had laughed at them merrily, saying, 'I'll go out with whomever I like, and you can all suck it!' I had flipped my plait over my shoulder and walked away. Now Ravi began to tease me about Luke mercilessly until one day I couldn't stop the tears. His big honest face became alarmed, and he hauled me into a tight hug.

'Hey, hey, hey, no tears, pretty face!'

He never mentioned it again. He started coming over in the evenings. For all his roughhousing, he had beautiful manners and oodles of charm when he chose to unleash it. We would run up the winding staircase to our terrace, and sit there, watching the sun go down. Sometimes we talked about Jehan, but mostly we let it be. Once, he brought along his Walkman, hooked us up to one earphone each and we slow danced there on my terrace. He was the first of my four musketeers. His rough kindness saved me in those first few months. His undemanding affection was exactly the balm I needed when I had actively rejected any overtures from my own people. We were close friends for a while, then our lives diverged. He came to my wedding, drank a toast to us, but we met only once after that. Still, the affection remains for my bull in the china shop.

Gestation

SEPTEMBER WAS OVER and done with. The struggles with maths continued and it was decided that I would have to take extra tuitions with the maths teacher, who tutored a group of my classmates at one of their houses. Since the group included Pia and Nalini, the decision was a reluctant one on my part. To make the best of a bad job—oh, how the high and mighty top rankers had fallen!—I dressed carefully and dramatically for the first class. I must have looked a right sight as I emerged from my lane that evening, dressed as I was in a black skirt, my favourite black wrap around top and silver bracelets. And who should come sauntering down the road but the school stud, Callum? The same guy who had almost come to blows with an affronted boyfriend at my party so many eons ago.

He loped up to me and said in greeting: 'Wow, you look hot.'

That could be taken literally—I was wearing nylon and wool in the sweltering October heat—but I chose to take it as a compliment. He asked if he could walk me up the road to where I was going. As we walked, we had a real conversation. This was the guy every girl in school had a secret (or not so secret) crush on, and he was actually talking to me, about stuff that couldn't be misconstrued as flirting, not even by a silly fourteen-year-old girl. Though he was insanely popular, Callum was a nice guy who genuinely loved women. He appreciated them and took the time to listen. I had had my first slow dance with him, the perfect gentleman. This was a boy whose mom had brought him up right. Even Jehan had approved of him. That evening, Callum didn't mince words. He bluntly asked me to tell him what had happened with Jehan.

He listened without comment, then said simply, 'Is it okay if I come over and visit you sometimes?'

'Sure,' said I, still a bit dazed that this demigod had deigned to even talk to me.

He was true to his word. We became friends that October. He would come over sometimes, another charmer who knew how to cheer everyone up. Mainly though, he had my back in school. He had always ignored me in previous years when he entered school, the second student to my first. Now he would walk over, exchange a few words before hailing a friend and disappearing. That daily exchange wasn't lost on any of the prospective girlfriends and new vicious rumours began to circulate. I didn't have the energy to react and Callum couldn't care less.

Charmers all.

A third unexpected visitor to my house was Abraham—

Baro, my Paribesa friend, the older man with beautiful light eyes and a laid-back attitude so far removed from my own that we might have had nothing in common if it hadn't been for that night of confessions on my first ever turtle walk. Another listener, another lover of women in the nicest sense possible. One afternoon, I was curled up in my usual position in those listless days—on the sofa, head turned towards the open front door and the garden, blank headed. The gate clicked open and Baro walked in, in his chappals (flip-flops) and loose jeans.

We walked out to the porch to chat and the very first thing he said was, 'You look like you need a hug.'

But this was Bay City of the 1980s, so of course he didn't actually hug me. But his voice was like a hug anyway. If Ravi had skirted the issue, and Callum had been blunt about it, Baro was positively brutal.

'Can't pick up the phone? Trying to ditch me like everyone else or what? Too bad, Chinoy, here I am, and you better start talking!'

And 'What the hell have Luke and Amita done to deserve this freeze?' he'd growl.

'Bitch,' he called me, in the most loving way.

He would drop in unannounced, force me to go walking with him, and insist I talk to him about Jehan. He kept me in touch with the goings on at Paribesa, told me about the gang, news I desperately wanted but didn't have the moral strength to ask for.

Ravi, Callum, Baro: they all rallied around me in those

first months after Jehan. They had offered me their friendship freely and without any expectations at all. As the years passed, I lost touch with Callum and Baro too, as with Ravi. Not so with my fourth musketeer—Paddy Pillai. Paddy was dogged about staying in touch. He came around, with stories from the Snake Park or crocodile bank where he volunteered. Or with tales of his escapades in the National Cadet Corps. He just wouldn't give up, chattering away even as I sat, sometimes in a fog, often looking patently disinterested, basically being a bitch.

Slowly, I began to open up to Paddy. It was awkward at first, confessing my loneliness and conflicted longing for Amita and Luke. He staunchly defended both of them, saying he just wouldn't believe that either of them had played the role that Fali and my imagination accused them of. He didn't mince his words either, often pulling me up for my behaviour. Then he'd make me laugh, call me Chinstrap. (My surname, Chinoy, had long been mangled into all sorts of interpretations: Chin Chin Choo was an obvious one; Chinstrap, as in the penguin, was another.) But he stuck to his guns that I wasn't playing fair with these two people, whom I missed desperately but to whom I no longer had any roadmap to make my way back.

These four boys pulled me back from the brink so many times. I wasn't suicidal, never that. But each time I felt like I was losing my grip on sanity, one of them would be around to remind me that the world was still doing its thing, even though it might seem like it had stopped that September evening long enough for me to get off.

Fali's friend Hari was a support in a more clinical way. He became my de facto therapist, to whom I poured my heart out after making him swear that not a word would be said to Fali. He was possibly the only person who knew what was going on in my family around that time. We walked for hours, just talking about Jehan, my guilt, his guilt, our common grief. Hari listened, counselled, but there was not much more he could do, given my age. All he could advise me was to try and talk things over at home.

I was gradually becoming obsessed with Luke and his tenuous connection with Jehan's last days. That obsession, and being torn between loyalty to dead brother and the living boy I thought I loved, would turn into something horribly unhealthy. It was partly due to my personality. I was like a dog with a bone, and I had no coping mechanisms to deal with the trauma. I spiralled further and further out of control, even as I maintained a façade of being perfectly normal at home—the obedient, studious daughter—and equally successfully kept up the farce of being a bitch to the outside world.

The trigger was definitely that short conversation Zarir and Fali had had with me as Jehan's body cooled in the next room. My mind splintered in those moments. What might have been a sweet and innocent, short-lived love affair, became something far more portentous in my head. Jehan and Luke and I were linked in an obscene triad; the two of us who were left behind fought the attraction, struggled to break away, struggled to be the dominant partner, when, all along, it was the dead who called the shots. Luke was at best a reluctant participant. I don't doubt he loved me inasmuch as an eighteen-year-old boy defines love (Lust? Cure for boredom? Excitement?), but he certainly hadn't bargained for what was to come. We were so radically different that, left to our own devices, we might have lost interest in each other once the physical attraction cooled off.

Did Fali ever imagine what he had unleashed with those words? It had the almost exact opposite effect to what he had hoped to achieve. It was funny how he was left satisfied for having done his bit. In his mind, it probably seemed that he and Zarir had used the right moment to warn me away from these undesirable friends—friends I had made on my own, defying family dictates such as they may have been, flouting Fali's authority in a way. He shouldn't have been that complacent because what that conversation did, in reality, was to set some part of me free. I could be two or even three different people all at once, and there was nothing to stop me. The good little girl at home became a horrible, sarcastic, tongue-lashing bitch with friends, then switched back into the emotionless blank-minded me in private. It wasn't quite schizophrenia, but I came dangerously close to believing that all these personas could co-exist without doing my psyche any harm.

I no longer believed anyone, and particularly Fali. Though I had not questioned his version of the events that took place in the days before Jehan killed himself, I had come to the realization that it was a skewed and exaggerated version, and that events might have unfolded in a far more harmless manner than he had described. Jehan had tried to kill himself three times in the past months, much before my relationship with Luke even had its faltering start. But again, as with Amita, I didn't know how to confront Fali or Luke, or ask for facts. Fali's words had impacted me at the most profound moment of my grief, and it would take years for me to separate the trauma of Jehan's death from that conversation, and to view it in an objective light. One part of me still continued being the docile, quiet younger sister, and I strove for years afterwards, with some success, to be the perfect daughter, but another part of me walked away, did my own thing, chose a direction my family remained unaware of. But that was in an unseen future, and right now, all the grieving and agonizing would have to wait. Fali's wedding was rescheduled for early January, by order of my grandmother—the unspoken command of course was to pretend all was well and normal.

~

How did we get through it? I was barely functioning, but I did have a new routine, one that incorporated crying in secret, long periods of blessed blankness, recurring nightmares where my imagination, never again at rest, placed me right there in the bathroom with him, watching him in pain and agony...or at peace—it was a different dream every night. Sometimes I'd see him in his grave, his face being eaten by worms. I think I must have had a psychotic break with reality in those first months. I had delusional daydreams where I had convinced myself that Jehan was alive, well and happy somewhere far away, and that if I achieved such and such target, he would come home. This usually unachievable target could include counting the crows that flew by my terrace in an evening, or bearing the pain of my nails digging into the palms of my hands for a certain number of minutes. It didn't work of course. Jehan never came back to mock me with that sarcastic smile of his, or to laugh away all the pain as a silly joke.

And what of the rest of the family? Honey stared at me stone-eyed the one time I dared voice my sorrow.

'Not now, Liana. We won't talk about it right now.'

It had taken a lot of nerve to even broach the subject. My heart was beating quicker, my pulse tripping erratically, and the combination of those physical symptoms and her measured refusal to speak of what threatened to overwhelm me, turned the key in the lock. I never spoke of it again to her. Or to Eruch, who went off to work the Monday morning after Jehan's death, and recounted his day to us at the dinner table.

'My colleagues came to my office today, to offer their condolences. I told them then and there, "This is not professional, chaps. I've come to office to work, why don't you all do the same? *Samajyuné?*"'

Perhaps they grieved in private, perhaps they held each other in the night. Perhaps they watched, sorrowing, as their two surviving children drifted far away from them, even as we lived in the same house. But we never spoke of Jehan's death. We were too busy searching for our new normal. Besides, there was a wedding in the family, and life on the surface was busy and happy. The wider I smiled, the louder I laughed, the more it seemed to me that I was gasping for breath. Was I the only one grieving for Jehan? I couldn't articulate the question, so I had no way of knowing. It became embarrassing when everyone else seemed to be getting on with the business of living. I locked my grief deep inside, never letting it out in front of my family. That key was lost and the lock stayed firmly in place until a few years ago.

One evening, Fali sat sprawled on the little sofa. The house was silent, Zarir wasn't around, and no music was playing for a change. I barely noticed his presence. It was unusual for him to be home in the evenings, with the wedding planning on in full swing at his fiancée's home. As I brushed past him, he pulled me onto his lap and cuddled me, while I sat there, tears running down my face. I had mastered the art of crying without movement or sound; sometimes I didn't register that I was crying myself. After a while, my face grew hot and sticky, I shrugged his arms away and left him still sitting there. That is my only memory of Fali and me mourning together. He dealt with his grief in his own reserved way, and this was the only point at which the arcs of our grieving ever met. Perhaps I could have tried harder to say the words: *I miss Jehan so badly. I hurt so much. Do you?* But the words would not come. I was scared I would wail out my grief if I opened my mouth. I was terrified of being pulled under the surface. There would be no emerging, it seemed to me, from that final drowning. So I trod water, I smiled, I laughed and no one ever questioned my normal behaviour.

Cherie, our dachshund, had stopped trying to enter Jehan's bedroom ever since that September evening. She had been brought home as a tiny puppy, soon after our old dog, Tina, passed away.

I had come home from school one day to find Jehan and Honey in a state of high excitement. I was extended an elaborate invitation into that holiest of sanctums, Jehan's bedroom, where, normally, I would be greeted with a shoe thrown with unerring accuracy if I so much as put a toe in through the door. I entered his beautifully appointed room. The curtains were a deep blue, scattered with cheerful lighter blue and yellow daisies, very Seventies. The counterpane on his bed was a matching shade of blue. I coveted those curtains and counterpane, hand-me-downs from the American family we had known in our home by the Arabian Sea.

I didn't notice who was lying on the bed at first. A tiny dark chocolate velvety cushion, set off artistically by the bright blue counterpane and a big red satin bow. Then the cushion unfurled herself and stared up at me with the most melting dark eyes. She was Cherie and I think she felt that Jehan's room was her territory by law of first possession. Vagabond, our house cat, was far too dignified to ever enter a room where a piece of footwear might be chucked at him. Not so Cherie. She kept up her determined forays into Jehan's room, yelping when the shoe found its mark, her love armour enough.

Cherie and Vagabond reacted differently to the death in the house. Vagabond disappeared for some days, then came back, thin and hungry. He remained skittish about entering the house, no matter how much we coaxed him. He ate at the back door hurriedly and then melted away. Cherie moped. She went off her food, hid under furniture or curled up at Honey's feet. She avoided Jehan's room, much like the rest of us, even though the door stayed open. The lock had been broken when Zarir barrelled his way into the room and it would stay that way. None of us had yet worked up the nerve to enter it. In fact, I did not step into his bathroom until just before we fled from that house forever. Even then, almost a year later, my palms were sweaty and my heart racing as I entered and forced myself to look up at the shower pipe.

One morning a few weeks after the funeral, Honey woke up and found Cherie curled up on a pile of Jehan's shoes and boots in the middle of the living room. She had spent the night dragging them out and then lay in this nest until Honey gently routed her out for breakfast. This went on for a few nights until the shoes began to show signs of scuffing and teeth marks. Finally, Eruch gently closed the door that had stayed open all these days and thus ended Cherie's mourning.

Zarir too was changing. He still came home almost every day; he was a rock to four people, each grieving in a private space, and he tried to be there for each one of us.

Our dependence on him was wholly unfair. We should have been helping him come to terms with what he had seen and with what he had had to do. Instead, each of us leant on this twenty-four-year-old for solace and comfort. It would take some time for the trauma to leave its mark on him. I imagine, in those early days, the shock had left him as empty and dazed as I was, and that was the only thing that got us both through the next three months.

~

The ball room at the best hotel in town was booked for Fali and Preeti's wedding reception. Shopping was in full swing, a morning jacket and a three-piece suit were ordered for the bridegroom. Honey and I went looking for saris. This was to be my first official appearance in a sari, complete with a little ceremony to signify my entrance into womanhood, not a very edifying prospect for the shy, self-doubting fifteen-year-old that I was. We ended up with an array of beautiful Kanjeevarams, none of which I could wear, then or again, without swallowing that hitched breath.

I still had two occasions to shine at before the wedding and the first was one I dreaded. It was the school's annual Sports Day. Now I had always been the hopeless, last-to-be-picked non-starter at sports. I couldn't dribble the basketball, I couldn't spike the volleyball, I certainly couldn't throw the throwball and let's not even talk about Rounders or French cricket, that quaint and created-in-hell spawn of cricket and baseball. I was the despair of my house captain, Head Miss had been known to throw her arms in the air and gnash her teeth when I was out on the field, and all my teammates could do was keep me away from the ball and out of harm's way. This was the person who was now expected to carry the school flag and march single file behind Venkatesh, carrying the national flag, leading the rest of the school in the march past. In years past, I had been tucked away in the middle ranks of my house marching team and hadn't really managed to cause any damage. Now it suddenly dawned on Head Miss, the PE staff and to the entire school that their captain was actually a giraffe. I had a terrible co-ordination problem. My brain couldn't comprehend that my left arm had to swing out in unison with my right leg. In my defence, I had started life out ambidextrous, happily switching my pencil from right hand to left hand without a thought. Until, that is, some short-sighted teacher decided this went against all that was holy, and began to rap me on the knuckles if I switched to writing with my left hand. The end result—or at least that's what I always believed had caused it—was a girl with a hilariously uncoordinated left and right side.

While lack of coordination didn't matter on the way in because my arms would be holding the flag, once the flag had been planted, I did have to march smartly away in full view of parents and assorted dignitaries. Head Miss took it as a personal affront to her Australian sporting genes that the captain of her school simply couldn't march. It became the collective effort of the school to teach me marching. Every evening after school, Head Miss would stand, feet planted firmly on her balcony, with arms akimbo, glaring at me down on the football field. The PE sir would strike up a brisk left-right left-right-left on the drum, and while everyone else stood around, clutching their sides or rolling on the ground, I marched up and down. Head Miss stridently pointed out each step I put down wrong:

'Chinoy, head up, stomach in! Chinoy, it's *Left-Right-Left*, girl, not Left-Left-Right!'

'Oh Good Lord, can someone explain to the child she has a right side as well as a left side?'

'LIANA CHINOY, should I get the juniors to demonstrate simple walking to you, dear girl? Here, Bears House juniors, fall in and show your captain how it's done! I need a strong coffee!'

It was great fun for the students. I think the juniormost members of school felt that this had been arranged specially for their entertainment and begged to be allowed to stay behind after school so as not to miss it. That sports day was possibly the most exhilarating and humiliating day of the year for me. Venkatesh was a huge support. He and my house captain, Callum, took me aside just before the whistle blew for the march past to begin and gave me a pep talk.

'You can do it, Liana!' said earnest Venkatesh, helpful as ever. 'Just watch my feet and you'll be fine.'

But Callum was red-faced with the effort of keeping his temper in check. '*Do not*, I mean it, Chinoy, do not screw this up! It's my last year in school and I want the Best House Trophy—what do you say we find you a pair of shorts in blue? Or red?'

'Callum, no, no, she'll be fine in her orange Bears House shorts! Won't you, da?' replied Venkatesh hastily, still helpful but not to the extent of letting his own Lions House (red shorts) down.

'Nobody loves me, everyone hates me, I'm gonna eat some worms,' Karthik chanted mockingly and my heart sank even further.

I made it through the ordeal without too many missteps though. My house even won the shield that year for best house and my cup overflowed with relief. With a B and an E and an A R S, with an H and an O and a U S E, Bears House, Bears House! Victory!

~

The second big day before Christmas holidays was the school's annual concert. It was to be held at the National Theatre, the beautiful circular red stone building next to the matching Museum of Natural History where Luke and I had met for the first time under a snake skin display. The dress rehearsal went well, and then it was the night of the concert. Honey and Eruch had felt unable to come for the concert, so instead, Zarir, Hari and Fali were there to cheer me on. Paddy had warned me that the whole gang would be there, and I was terrified of a confrontation between Fali and Zarir and my friends.

We seniors doubled up as ushers before heading into the green room to change into our costumes. As I walked the wide balcony that wrapped around the hall, lined with the beautiful red stone pillars, Luke came up to me. Naturally, Sunny and the rest of the gang were there too, to give Amita support. I saw them all waiting in a group but none of them approached me, only Luke. It had been three months since we'd met or spoken. The damned tears threatened to spill over so I stared at my feet while Luke made awkward small talk. He may have asked how I was doing. I may have said I was okay. Then, mercifully, Head Miss asked me to escort the chief guests to their seats and I escaped.

As I walked away, I saw Fali and Zarir walk towards Luke and the guys. Then Hari and Joe were separating the two groups and the much-dreaded showdown fizzled out. Somehow, I don't think Fali's heart was in it, not with the formidable Head Miss stalking the corridors, her nerves on edge as they always were before the start of our annual fundraiser concert. She would have given him what for if he had started a rumpus: to her, she was still his principal and he, her student.

The concert was a huge success. Karthik made a very devoted Joseph to Arwa's golden Virgin Mary. He was besotted, and couldn't get over his good luck at being paired with this beautiful, and warm-hearted senior, the best example of a true Wayland Manor product. My Portia went off without a hitch; neither Venkatesh nor I stumbled over the long speeches.

There was a bottleneck at the gate as we left the National Theatre in Zarir's car. I stared out of the window, feeling deflated and strangely euphoric at the same time. Suddenly,

Luke's head was ducking down to the window. He poked his head right in, gave me a cheeky grin, revved his motorbike exaggeratedly and then roared away. Fali and Zarir grumbled about it all the way home, while I sat there, wrapped in the feeling that I wasn't completely friendless. It was a feeling that kept me going for the next six months.

~

The family began arriving for the wedding. The same people who had come for the funeral in September turned around and returned for a wedding, on the insistence of my grandmother who made it clear that an auspicious occasion such as the wedding of her beloved eldest grandson must not be cancelled or postponed any further. I wonder what everyone thought about it in private. New Year's Day was spent in comings and goings from one house to the other, as the engagement ceremonies got under way. There was a party that night at Zarir's house to kick off the celebrations.

I had a ceremony of my own that morning, wearing my first official sari. The photographs show me smiling a little shyly as I was garlanded and made much of by my grandmother and the other ladies of the house. The men hung back. This was a women's celebration.

The next morning, the wedding was held at my sister-in-law's sprawling first-floor flat. Her family, a large and loving collection of aunts, uncles and first cousins tried their best to make it a huge celebration for her sake, because the groom's family were, in all honesty, a little lost and forlorn.

Her parents were very kind to me, proclaiming that I was like their daughter now. Her brothers, sister and sister-in-law tried their best to include me in all the festivities. Again, I found myself enjoying all the attention, the beautiful bride and the gorgeous saris, at one level. The other me hovered somewhere in the corner, wondering how it was possible that everyone seemed to be having the time of their life. Wondering too why I was so out of sync with my family that I just couldn't feel their excitement and energy.

Zarir and I exchanged miserable looks just once; I think Jehan's ghost must have brushed past both of us at the exact same moment. We were remembering him planning this very day with such anticipation, and it just didn't seem right that he wasn't there, the flamboyant master of ceremonies, charming everyone from the staidest aunt to the youngest cousin sister. The ceremony over, lunch over, it was time for the ceremonial bidaai (farewell). Fali and his bride sat in a sedately decorated car, and her brothers and Zarir push started it after some happy goodbyes from her female relations.

The reception that evening was a scintillating affair. I was in a bright yellow Kanjeevaram sari. My hair was pulled up in a rather grown-up bun and I wore Honey's long gold earrings. Zarir, Preeti's younger brother and I hung out in the corridor outside the ballroom, ostensibly to meet and greet guests as they arrived. In reality, we bitched about each guest, steadily getting drunker, on the excitement of feeling very adult in a sari in my case, and on the booze snuck in by the two of them, in theirs. Eruch had decreed a vegetarian menu and no bar. Hence the discreet withdrawal to the corridor, out of sight of Eruch's strict gaze. I can't think of an occasion that warranted a free-flowing supply of hard liquor more than that evening.

When I look back on that day, a wedding album montage runs through the mind. Two families celebrate a happy union. The preparations have been hectic. Sari shops have been raided, jewellery hauled out of bank lockers. Family and friends have come pouring in from all over the country. Wedding songs have been sung in that peculiar nasal tone middle-aged women have. The house has been cleaned, the bedroom meant for the happy couple fitted out with new furniture. Food and drink has been consumed in excess. A fancy reception, family, and friends in their finery, each photograph a masterpiece of happy faces. No bride has ever looked as beautiful and the groom is as all grooms ought to be: disbelieving of his great good fortune. He's cleaned up nicely too. His mother looks radiant; his young sister wears her first sari and soaks up the compliments. His father is the life of the party, playing the perfect host.

Look carefully though. The mother's smile is brittle, the sister looks dazed. The groom won't meet your eyes. The father tries his best to be cheerful for the sake of his surviving son.

The wedding was done. The visiting family departed, the happy couple left for their honeymoon and the little interlude was over. Life hit very hard now. It was lonely at home. Honey and Eruch, while physically present in the same house, had become kind strangers, wrapped in a world I could not follow them to. They behaved normally, were loving and attentive towards me, and yet all I felt was an echo of our former selves. It was now that the enormity of my solitude really hit me. I barely spoke to anyone in school. The rest of the girls in my class had valiantly tried to make up for the loss of my three dearest friends, even though they were torn between sympathy for me and horror at how I had callously discarded my life-long buddies. Karthik and some of the boys kept up the gentle joking and ribbing, raising a smile every now and then. The crying had stopped. Still, going to school was no longer something I looked forward to. The excitement of finally becoming captain of school had evaporated and it was simply another chore that I had to get done with. Returning home was another ordeal. I dreaded bumping into Luke or any of the boys from Boys' Academy. I walked, face down, carefully watching my feet take one step after another, as had become my habit lately.

Home was a strange place these days. We had a new family member who kept our spirits up when she could spare the time from her brand-new husband. Most evenings, they were out, either at her mother's home or with friends. They invited me to go along to parties and picnics some evenings, at Honey's insistence, and I did; it was a relief to delay, at least temporarily, the nightmares that came with monotonous certainty. I should have felt like a third wheel. The truth is,

I didn't feel much of anything at all. Zarir came over less regularly now. His absence at the dining table was felt keenly but it wasn't something any of us had the right to question. The evenings would drag on interminably. My school work was suffering, in spite of those hateful maths tuitions. I wasted most evenings curled up on the sofa, staring out at the garden. No one bothered me; no one asked me why I wasn't sitting with my books in a Board exam year. Seven o' clock was the worst point in the evening. I'd sit there, willing the phone to ring. But it never did. Perhaps Fali and Zarir had got the message across loud and clear. Luke was certainly leaving me alone. Amita, Pia and Nalini seemed to be doing just fine without me too. Talk about cutting off the nose to spite one's face!

My fifteenth birthday came and went. Finally, the waiting took its toll and I called Luke one evening. When he answered, at first I could think of nothing to say. He heard the silence and guessed.

He tried very tentatively: 'Hi, are you okay?'

I blurted out: 'You didn't call on my birthday.'

And he replied, supremely logical to my confused mind: 'You asked me not to call you any more.'

Had I? I couldn't remember if I had actually said those words to him. When did I do that? At the concert? Did I say to him: 'Leave me alone, I want nothing more to do with you'?

On cue, my brain shut down. I listened to the sound of his breathing for a second longer, then I gently replaced the receiver on the hook. I waited for the tears to come, but they seemed to have dried up. I waited for a couple of days for the shock to wear off. This was my grand plan, after all. I had decided in the days after Jehan's suicide to cut all contact with this group of friends, admittedly in the worst of confused states, thinking incoherently. It had seemed the only way to deal with the grief and the rage. I had executed the plan beautifully. It had worked. I should have felt better for its success. So why did I feel rejected and betrayed and lonely?

By the time February rolled around, the prelims were done and we were on study leave. I had failed my maths prelim exam and the finals were looming. In a last-ditch act to salvage my academic grades, I started studying again, trying my best to block out any thoughts or memories of Jehan, only letting them out late at night. Karthik once again reached out, probably goaded by Head Miss, asking tentatively if I wanted to join a group study at his home. Much to his and my own surprise, I went along one afternoon. He lived in a first-floor flat with his parents. Uncle was a retired merchant navy captain, who had suffered a debilitating stroke some years earlier, and had lost a lot of his motor and speech control. Aunty was a petite, beautiful woman, with a backbone of finely tempered steel and a soothing manner. I didn't say much on those first few visits, and I imagine she too was taking my measure. Karthik patiently helped me with maths and physics, going over solved examples and theory with the touch of a born teacher. Our relationship was slowly coalescing into friendship, albeit with much sarcasm dripping off my tongue, and many laughing protestations about his noble intentions in rebuttal.

~

Wayland Manor's centre for the Board exams was a large school, Paddy's alma mater in fact. Three schools sat their exams in the large hall. Two of these schools consisted of serious, extremely studious kids determined to rank high. Us Waylanders were tiny in number, and proceeded to freak them out with our early morning antics on each exam day.

We realized a little late that Head Miss, determinedly teaching us her idea of a balanced Geography curriculum, had completely skipped over key chapters on the Indian monsoon and agriculture. We could reel off every obscure geographical fact about the great continent of Australia, but we couldn't tell you one damned thing about ocean currents and monsoon winds. An emergency and secret meeting was held with the other social studies teachers a couple of days before the examination day. They advised us to forget about learning the myriad facts and concentrate instead on the two or three vital maps that were sure to be part of the paper. We were confronted, for the first time in our school careers, with a life-or-death situation. We had to memorize the complicated maps if we had any hopes of passing the Geography exam.

Everyone panicked. Having been brought up on a steady diet of high ideals and the constant admonition that marks aren't everything, it suddenly dawned on us that real life didn't actually work quite along those lines. Still, we knuckled down and did our collective bit. Our best hope, it was decided, lay with the sole boy in class who took tuitions in Geography, an enterprise fraught with danger, if Head Miss were ever to find out. The fact that his family donated generously every year to the school may have given him a sliver of immunity that the rest of us simply did not have. He had been boning up on all the neglected bits of the syllabus, and he assured us that the maps were engraved on his brain for all time to come. Fortunately, his roll number meant that he sat almost at the beginning of the single row assigned to our class. We worked that morning like a well-oiled machine. Every twenty minutes or so, someone at the rear would raise his hand. As the invigilator was distracted, our friend would raise his map to eye level, examine it carefully for its beautiful rendering of the area of the winter wheat crop or direction of the monsoon trade winds while the rest of us quickly checked our maps to see if we were on the right track. The two kids in front of him would carefully turn around for a split second, yawning and stretching so that they too could have a look at his maps. We all passed Geography with flying colours, I am happy to report. I passed maths too, much to my teacher's and my amazement. This in spite of completely ignoring the Trigonometry section. The invigilator asked me why I had run my pen through that section, and my explanation that I didn't know any of it sent his eyebrows straight into his hairline.

I guess everyone partied the evening the Board exams were done. I wasn't invited and anyway, I had a more urgent appointment. I went with Honey to her beauty parlour and asked a dismayed Freddy, the hair stylist, to chop off my waist-long poker straight hair, the bane of my existence. Honey had tired of having to plait my hair every morning; she'd been doing it for years. She gave in because I can be pretty obdurate when I set my mind on something and this, for me, symbolized the letting go of the old.

I had convinced my parents to let me switch schools, the supposed reason being I needed to move to the state board if I wanted to study medicine. The real reason, left unacknowledged, was that I could no longer bear to stay in Wayland Manor, sitting in the same classroom as Amita, Pia and Nalini, missing them but unable to walk over and say: I'm sorry. I was wrong. I wasn't thinking straight.

When I confessed my decision to Head Miss, she made the rare gesture of clutching my hands.

'Oh, don't, Liana! You'll be miserable in that school—they don't teach; they preach in Prathiman Vidyalaya.'

She was right, as usual, but the deed was done. I had impressed the principal of the new school, dressing in my best, most sophisticated dress, designed by Jehan of course; and Honey had plaited my hair in a high French braid. I was quaking in my shoes as I entered her office, but Wayland Manor's training stood me in good stead. I met her eyes steadily, shook her hand firmly and told her the truth about why I wanted to move from my beloved school: that my brother had died, that I couldn't bear to remain in Wayland Manor, with all its memories and heartaches. She must have had her doubts but she kept them to herself and offered me a seat in standard eleven. One more link to Jehan snapped, it seemed that only my hair was a reminder of my childhood days. It had to go.

Freddy wrung his hands in anguish, pleading, 'Be sensible, dear. People would kill for hair like yours.'

I was rude. 'Freddy, if you don't have the balls to take it off, I'll find someone else.'

Honey hushed me and nodded to him to go ahead. He gave in, inch by inch, trimming away at the ends whilst I insisted he chop it off to shoulder length. Finally, I was left with a shaggy shoulder-length mop, very much in the Eighties mode. My eyes suddenly seemed larger in my face, but that might have been anxiety now that the deed was done. We reached home and confronted Eruch. My dear old-fashioned dad, who loved long hair on women. Eruch, who had sulked more about Honey exchanging her thick long hair for a Swinging Sixties-styled bob when she reached the shores of the land of the free than about her more obvious dereliction of duties. Eruch, who now sat gaping in shock, unable to comprehend how his darling daughter was meting out to him the exact same punishment as her mother had done eighteen years earlier. I felt bad for him but remained unrepentant. As that weight fell away from my head, I had felt a slight surge of excitement. I would never weigh myself down with long hair again, I decided.

That summer was long. Three months of vacations before standard eleven began in my new school. I squashed the misgivings I already felt, telling myself I needed a fresh start. Our family was preparing to move as well, away from this beautiful bungalow now filled with echoes and silences to a brand new apartment. For Eruch, especially, this new home was special for many reasons. It would be the first home he had ever owned. Rent contracts and hassles would now be a thing of the past, thanks to the munificence of his beloved bosses, who had offered to buy flats in a new building for the senior managers of the company. It was really a gift, and for loyal Eruch, who had kept faith since the beginning of his career, this was the ultimate proof that his fealty was fully appreciated. And finally, we were leaving behind the house in which his son had killed himself. This was to be a fresh start for the entire family, which we expected to be as simple to make as turning the key in the new front door. Eruch, his heart and mind in the right place, had it all planned. He hadn't bargained for the complicated members of his family, at least one of whom refused to see this as an opportunity to turn the page and leave Jehan behind in the previous chapter of the book.

~

By early June, I had spent nine months in misery, rage and guilt. Nine months of understanding in great detail how the heart breaks, not in the chest so much as in the pit of the stomach. A hollow feeling that returns after every bout of crying, a shortness of breath that becomes a constant companion. It had been very lonely, very scary, the way I missed my brother in those first few months. I could not articulate all the thoughts raging inside my head, though once again, on the surface, I smiled and talked and giggled like any other fifteen-year-old girl. It was a defence against the emotions that continually threatened to overwhelm me. In those nine months, I talked much but never of the only person that I wanted and needed to talk about—Jehan. My new sister-in-law was more or less a kind and friendly stranger, Fali and she too wrapped up in each other to really impinge on my existence. Eruch and Honey were drifting away too, and I couldn't find a way back to them without Jehan to direct my way.

One morning, I was out walking with Honey, running some errand. We passed by a big, low slung bungalow set in greenery and Honey heard her name being called out. The house belonged to the grande dame of local Parsi society. She and her husband lived in rarefied splendour, and did not, under normal circumstances, deign to take notice of ordinary folk. Still, the watchman came running, asking us to step inside for a moment.

'Mom, no! Let's just go!' I immediately protested.

I didn't want to obey such an ad hoc summons from the old dragon. Her granddaughters were snooty spoilt girls and I didn't want to bump into them either. I articulated all of these reasons for not entering that gate, while Honey feebly pointed out the discourtesy of not doing so. The thing neither one of us dared say was that for the past few months, the only reason people seemed to visit us, or talk to us at all, was to discreetly extract details about Jehan's death. I guess Honey was desperate for some human contact outside of her dysfunctional family, and she overrode me this time. In we went, into a huge split-level living room, done in very modern late 1970s style. And there she was, gliding towards us, beautifully made-up face with the skin of a much younger woman. She nodded to me, then grasped my mother's hands in hers and spoke in low tones with her, drawing us towards a sofa. I felt pretty superfluous but I had already learned that I was unnecessary at every condolence visit. Most people paid scant attention to Fali and me, the searchlight of their sympathy seeking out only Honey and Eruch. If there is no word to describe the agony of bereaved parents, there is not even the concept of it for siblings who have lost one of their own. I lost myself in my usual daydreams while Honey and the old lady had a long chat.

I only remember the lady saying, 'But what could have gone wrong? He seemed such a happy young man.'

And I smothered the snigger bubbling up inside me. When we left, she graciously came up to the door and waved us off. Honey seemed very happy to have met her, and almost became animated as she described this odd little interlude with the high and mighty to Eruch that evening.

~

Late that May, Paddy came home with a verbal invitation. Jay, a common friend, was celebrating his eighteenth birthday and he had asked me to his birthday party. I barely knew Jay, and in the whirling of my mind, it never occurred to me that perhaps he had extended the invitation at someone else's goading. It was a toss-up between Lucas and Paddy—or did both of them suggest the invitation from two very divergent viewpoints? Jay played along, completely oblivious of the tensions. It had been nine months since I had had any face-to-face contact with a group of friends outside of school. My first reaction was complete panic. Following close behind was the greatest urge to just get out of the house and do something normal for a change. I made excuses.

'No one really wants to see me, Paddy. Not after what I did in September.'

Paddy's moustache bristled. 'Don't be silly, Chinstrap,' he snapped. 'Why the hell would you be invited if we didn't want you there?'

The next excuse.

'My brother hasn't been dead a year,' I reminded Paddy.

'So? You're not dead too, are you?' came the even snappier retort.

'I can't ask my mom to—'

Before I could do anything to stop him, he was dragging me inside the house in search of Honey. He was not given to diplomacy or flowery speeches, my friend.

'Aunty,' he said, 'there's a party at Jay's house. Can she go with me?'

Honey gaped at him. I could see her arguing with herself: What will people say? But who would know? And then, a firm voice from behind her made up Honey's mind for her. It was my sister-in-law:

'Of course she can. What time will you pick her up, Paddy?'

And just like that, my nine months of purgatory came to an end. The evening of the party, I found myself unable to take simple wardrobe decisions. The worrying and waiting had reduced me to what Jehan would have scornfully referred to as a puddle. It was Preeti who stepped in, choosing an outfit that didn't look completely monastic, inspecting me critically but being kinder than Jehan would have been. At the last minute, she slipped one of Honey's rings on my finger. Honey smiled faintly to see the old me and forgot to ask what time I might be getting home. By then, my nerves were screaming and my sister-in-law almost pushed me out of the house when Paddy arrived, bouncing on his toes with excitement.

We were early to the party. Jay looked shyly surprised to see me, but ushered me in kindly. Paddy deposited me in one corner of the sofa.

'You're not going to faint, uh, Chinstrap? Or throw up? Damn. Wait, I'll find us something to drink. Sit tight now.' And he went off in search of fortification.

The party swirled around me. People I didn't know came up to me, said hello, smiled kindly and wandered away. Jay poked his head in once or twice in a worried kind of way, but by and large, everyone left me mercifully alone. The rumble of motorbikes sounded in the backyard. I hate to say this, straight out of a trashy romance novel, but the air was simply sucked out of the room.

Luke came in and stood a little to the side so that I could see his form out of my peripheral vision, and said quietly, 'Hi.' He was in shock—it turned out that he hadn't known I would be there.

He dropped down next to me, and nothing in the world could have induced me to look at him. I think back to the fifteen-year-old I was, lacking in confidence and life, and I can bring myself to feel a little pity for that girl. His brother Joe came in, cheerfully making conversation as if we had met just yesterday instead of nine months ago at my brother's funeral. Sunny came in next, took one look at us and spun away. He had always been fiercely protective of Amita, and I understood his anger completely.

Did we eat? Did we dance? I don't remember.

At the end of the evening, in the time-honoured Bay City tradition of ending parties at the beach, any beach, everyone moved off to the bikes and TVS 50s. Joe came up to me and offered me a ride on his Java. We roared away before I had time to think, not that I was doing any thinking at all. I was far too busy concentrating on breathing, and keeping the panic at bay. It was a long ride from Jay's place to the beach, and Joe, never much of a talker, mostly kept silent. I'd always enjoyed riding with him, so I did just that. The beach was dark and silent. We wandered onto the wide stretch of sand, settling down in groups or couples. Someone hummed a song, people laughed.

Luke and I sat, carefully not touching, a little apart from the rest. He began to make polite conversation. And then suddenly, I was in a blazing rage at his seeming indifference. He had no idea what the last nine months had been like for me, and here he was, talking some rubbish about a new music album. My mood quickly turned ugly and I could either unleash the ugliness or dissolve in tears. Of course, I went with turning ugly: that would be my go-to choice for the next several years. I was done with being a coward—it would always be fight over flight from now on. I placed my hand on my bent knee, and his eyes went quickly to the flashy ring I was wearing.

'It's a gift from Zarir. Isn't it gorgeous?' And then I giggled, sounding silly even to myself. Like the ring meant something to me.

He stared at me incredulously but couldn't articulate the obvious question. I had lost my nerve already so I shut my mouth after that one remark. He shook his head as if in disbelief, laughed a little uncertainly and that was the end of the conversation. We sat in uncomfortable silence, and by the time everyone was ready to leave, he was angry. I could feel it in his tightly set jaw and the heat radiating from his body.

I turned to look for Joe, and he clipped out: 'Wait here. I'm taking you home.'

Prudently, I decided not to argue and so we rode home on Joe's bike, the first of many times we borrowed that beautiful bike and left its owner stranded without transportation. Again, the ride was mostly silent. At the end of my lane, we got off; he cut the engine and wheeled the bike in. The lane was silent too, the houses dark. Both our tempers had cooled in the night air and we laughed quietly to be together in this supremely awkward moment. Nothing more was said about our abandoned relationship and it was understood that we were together again. The daily phone call at seven in the evening, the infrequent meetings—all of it fell into place. We stayed that way, loving and resenting each other, fighting bitterly, making up spectacularly, and growing together, for the next three years. I never wore that ring again, though Honey offered it to me on several occasions.

Reprieve

PRATHIMAN VIDYALAYA LOOKED like a prison block. Four or five stories high, the façade of the building facing the road (and the rowdiest boys' college in the city) had a cement grill covering it. It was claustrophobic to look at, and sent a shiver of apprehension up my spine. To add to the jail-like ambience, the students and teachers entered the school through a small opening in the heavy-duty metal shutter that presented a blank face to curious outsiders. One had to actually duck one's head to enter. It was a scene straight out of the movies where the hero or the villain ducks as he exits the jail after his prison time is done. Except this was in reverse. The Rajasthan Association did not take its responsibilities to the care of three thousand girls lightly. Once inside, the bleak compound, treeless, cheerless, stoically stuck to the theme. I tried very hard not to think of Wayland Manor, with the riotous pink bougainvillea draped over the assembly hall roof, the beautiful white colonial bungalows that housed our classrooms, the cheerful green of the football field and tennis courts, and the dull red of the basketball court, offset by the graceful old rain trees.

Hundreds of girls milled about the inadequate compound before classes began or stood along the corridors, leaning down and calling out to friends. The noise was astounding. It was a shrill, high-pitched constant, very different from the deep-throated calls from the boys in Wayland Manor as they played football or the sound of the piano as a class practised its singing lessons with Head Miss. The ethos of the school was completely different as well. There were no hymns or piano accompaniments at assembly, but beautiful bhajans and patriotic songs instead, accompanied by an elderly music master on the harmonium. This was a new way to start the day and not at all objectionable in an otherwise graceless environment. The classrooms were stuffed with fifty or sixty girls, each grade having up to six divisions.

The girls here were far more informal with their teachers than Waylanders, and at the same time, very removed from them, almost on their guard. Again, I tried not to think of my former teachers, crying as they talked about Jehan, or encouraging us to write and dream and sing; or of Head Miss, playing tennis as the sun set behind the white school building.

I was angry at myself for making this decision, and I unfairly took it out on my new school and schoolmates. The first few weeks were made all the harder by my aggressive stance and refusal to conform to anything at all in Prathiman Vidyalaya. When some senior girls pulled me up for wearing a sleeveless top to school one day (my ugly uniforms hadn't arrived from the tailor yet), I sashayed into school the next morning wearing the shortest of Honey's hand-me-down miniskirts, a red tartan kilt that was really a micro-mini by local standards. The word flashed through the grapevine like wildfire, and crowds of girls made their way to my floor to catch a glimpse of this scandalous new student. The teachers refrained from comment. I think word had come from the principal's office that I was to be left alone. She later hinted to me that she had me on a very long leash those first few weeks of school, testing my mettle, so as to speak.

I went my way, oblivious of these undercurrents, and then, surprisingly, found myself coerced into standing for election as vice-captain of my house. I was vocal in my refusal, even sabotaging my own campaign by making the most anti-vote-for-me speech ever, and I still got elected by a fair margin. My house captain, a sweet and mild girl, sat me down and appealed to my better self. She made a case for our house, on a losing streak for the past many years, painting a pitiful picture of the support she needed if we were going to drag this no-good, lazy bunch of shifters away from the bottom of the points table. She knew by then that I would not back down to a challenge such as this. By God, I was going to show them what Waylanders were made of. And so began my love-hate relationship with this new school, my teachers and my fellow students. The ruder and more obnoxious I became, the more they seemed to like me. I refused to budge from my high principles, preaching about integrity and honesty, and though most of them didn't see the point, living in a far more real world than I did, they laughingly allowed me my eccentricities.

One day, about a month after I joined Prathiman, I went back to pay a visit to Wayland Manor. I avoided my classmates but the teachers called me into the staff room. They were agog with curiosity—how had I managed to fit in at my new school?

As I left, Head Miss accosted me outside the standard ten classroom. She grasped my chin, forced me to meet her stern gaze, and simply said:

'You're unhappy. Just come back. There's always a place for you here.'

I couldn't speak. I just nodded my head, mumbled that I had to go, and ran before temptation overtook me.

By the time the first month had passed, I had made a new friend, Meenakshi, another new student. Paddy, who had his eye on her, had described her swaying hips, doe-like eyes and beautiful long hair.

'Can't miss her, Chinstrap, she's sooo sexy!'

I was under stern orders to make friends with this girl and use all my influence to show her what eligible boyfriend material lay behind Paddy's goofy exterior. When Meenakshi came up to me in school, face dimpling into the biggest, most infectious smile I had ever seen, I heaved a little sigh of relief. Here was a quiet rebel, who went her own merry way while projecting the image of the quintessential good girl to the world. She was quite popular already. Her sunny personality ensured she was always surrounded by friends, and slowly I became a part of their group, even though I strenuously resisted attempts to turn any interactions into more meaningful friendships.

Bay City, 1987–1990

ANOTHER PERSON CAME into our lives in August of that year, just a few weeks short of the first anniversary of Jehan's death, a date that I had attached far too much significance to. Earlier in the year, around April or May, Eruch's cousin from Bombay had called one day.

'Their friends' son wants to apply to Bay City University for engineering. They need the forms posted to them,' said Honey and then, casually, 'so, I said, of course, Liana will get them for him—no problem!'

I reluctantly trudged off one morning to the University, in those days, a barren, treeless campus with the longest driveway in the world! Hatless, waterless, I stood in a snaking, somnolent line for a couple of hours and then did something that drew everyone's eyes to me and embarrassed me beyond redemption: I fainted for the first time in my life. When I came round, I was lying on the ground, concerned faces staring down at me, someone forcing me to take a sip of water from who knew where. I couldn't speak the language fluently, even after all those years in Bay City and I fended off those well-meaning strangers as best as I could. Finally, the line moved forward and I reached the blessed cool of the hall. Where I fainted again. There and then, I declared war on this stranger from Bombay who was the direct cause of my shameful collapse.

I slammed home with the application form.

'I never want to meet this guy, mummy! Why do you and dad have to do favours for people we don't even know? I've never been so mortified! I hope he fails! I hope they tear up his damn form and reject him!'

By that evening, Zarir, Preeti, and it seemed everyone I knew, were laughing at my escapade.

My sister-in-law declared that this was the boy for me.

'Just see, mummy, such a good Parsi boy. From Bombay, that too. She's swooning over him and she hasn't even met him. It's a match made in heaven.'

And the family fell about laughing as I sulked and inwardly swore vengeance on this Bombay bawa.

When my old friend Ziya heard the story—I don't even want to know how she found out—she helpfully brought over a clipping from a Bombay newspaper. It announced the retirement from competitive sports of the reigning national champion, Carl Mistry, who was giving up a sparkling sporting career to pursue further studies. Aargh! I was more determined than ever to give this spoilt brat (for what else could a Bombay bawa be?) the short end of my stick, the cold shoulder, anything at all to show my complete and utter disinterest in him and his wily ways.

Then Carl got admission in chemical engineering and my parents agreed to be local guardians to him. The evening that Carl and his mother came over became something of a farce, in the best Parsi natak style. He was not very tall, very broad at the shoulders and very slim at the waist, and burning up with a fever. His mother, not to be outdone, wore a bright ginger skirt and blouse and the whole effect was much too red for my sensibilities.

As they sat, making polite conversation with my parents in the living room, Preeti and I clutched at each other in the dining room, whooping with laughter at the sight. Fali and Zarir tried their best to keep the hilarity down but I'm pretty sure the sounds of our merriment added some more lines to Carl's mother's frowning face.

Carl quickly became a part of Fali and Preeti's social circle. Zarir was a bit standoffish at first, but soon, all the young people, with the sole exception of yours truly, were hanging out together. I stayed out of Fali's way and he, mine. And in the beginning, so did Carl. Once Zarir got married, Carl slowly slipped into his place, eating dinner with us a couple of times a week. He turned out to be a decent guy. A bit too polished and urbane for my liking, but still down-to-earth and solid all around. He never mentioned his sports career. Though Ziya had gleefully shown me that newspaper clipping, I only got to know the full extent of his records and medals from friends later on. I introduced him to my gang and Luke and he didn't get along almost from the start.

'He's too smooth, Liana. All that opening doors for

girls and polite talk. Has he never been out in the sun? He's so white. Your parents must just love him, right? Another Zarir, huh?'

Luke felt threatened but it didn't matter much. Carl was never going to figure in my life other than as a friend of the family.

It was a busy, interesting life. We had moved into our new apartment. I had responsibilities in school, and studies too. So Luke and I met infrequently but we were back to speaking almost every day at seven in the evening. Honey became curious, then upset, when she finally realized who my love interest was. It seemed that even she had heard the sordid story and she was very put out that I would continue my friendship. I began to lie when I was going out with him. But my face was a dead giveaway; Honey knew from the blush creeping up my cheeks each time I told a whopper. I should have known. (My nickname in the gang was Tomato Face: because when I blushed, I looked like one.) But she let my lies pass. Either her child psychology training kicked in, or she simply could not summon up the energy to put an end to it. Or maybe she was glad that there was something bringing me out of the zombie-like state I'd been in since the previous September. Anyway, she kept quiet, only rarely reading me a lecture about 'that boy'. How seriously I took that little rebellion was something I came to terms with many years later, while Honey lay dying. I fought the temptation to tell her then—as I had fought it all along—to crow and gloat to an old woman:

'Look, look, I'm still in touch with Luke—I never stopped. All your dislike, all the ganging up you did with your sons, none of it mattered one little jot. He's more a part of my life than you could ever imagine.'

Of course, I never said those words to her, or to Fali—but in my mind, I paid them back for that evening of Jehan's death each time I spoke to Luke or thought of him or wrote to him. That's unfair, my mind tells me, so unfair to Luke. I really saved the worst part of me for him, and for some reason, he kept coming back for more.

I still avoided any contact with Amita or Sunny, refusing to confront the reasons why. The rest of the gang though began to get in touch, and that awful isolation seemed to be at an end.

All these years later, I think back to my adolescent self. I see now that my anger at Sunny and Amita made no sense. There was no one good reason: my mind seethed with too many half-truths and unsubstantiated accusations. Luke was still comparatively a stranger, but Sunny? He was like family to me. I had slowly opened up to Amita and him over the years. They knew how to tease my reserved, self-conscious self out of my shell, and if there was such a thing as love, I loved these two. And so, even the suggestion that Sunny might have gone behind my back to join Luke in teasing Jehan was too frightening to comprehend. The enormity of that betrayal, if true, left me gasping for air. I felt resentment too, that their family was safe and well, untouched, while mine was torn to shreds. And underlying all these emotions, there was a terrible feeling of guilt. Please bear with me, reader. I've come back to this guilt again and again. But I had dumped Amita along with Luke and Sunny, never giving any of them a chance to explain or to tell me their side of the story. Now here I was, nine months later, back with Luke, meeting the others, and steadfastly keeping only her, and Pia and Nalini at bay. I was guilty because my unexplained anger would not allow me to apologize, and there too was the instinct that she would not forgive my behaviour as easily as it seemed Luke had done. I could lash out at Luke, and he would take it calmly, waiting for the storm of accusations and recriminations to blow over. Amita was a far more emotional animal. I knew that I could never confront her with the question that continued to burn at my insides: Did you know something I didn't about the last days of my brother's life? Did you tell *them* to lay off Jehan, to not tease him?

The words had dried up, shrivelled inside my heart, and there they would stay until the writing of this book. I was recently accused of being a coward, for not confronting Sunny and Amita in all these interminable years and asking them for their side of the story. Fair enough. If my heart still hitches at these words, if the blood still rushes to my head, a coward I must certainly be.

It wasn't the same with Luke, this laconic almost-stranger I happened to be in love with. I asked Luke often enough. Accused him really. 'Did you tease Jehan, the way Fali and Zarir said you did?'

'Liana, we both said some stuff, yeah, my friends got

involved. I'm not denying it. It was just talk—you know how we guys get! But, Dumbo, we didn't push him around. No one touched him. We didn't know he was fighting all those demons, really we didn't. Shit, I'm so sorry, Liana, but it just didn't happen the way you're imagining it.'

It took me more than thirty years to finally believe him and lay that ghost to rest. I imagine now that Jehan, with his flair for the dramatic, and his dislike of Luke's proximity to me, could have easily exaggerated the small incidents. It was equally likely that Fali had used the same small, insignificant incidents to manipulate me out of what he believed were undesirable friendships. My friends too, young, brash eighteen-year-olds, might have downplayed the cruel remarks made by them, most likely about Jehan's effeminacy or his flamboyant clothes, never suspecting the fragile state of his mind.

Those first three years, though, I was fighting a constant battle between the attraction I felt for Luke and the anger I felt at his supposed part in upsetting an increasingly vulnerable Jehan. It only made my guilt more acute. I felt guilty for having been unable to stop Jehan from killing himself, but also that I was happy, in a relationship with Luke, that I was alive and Jehan was not. This did not make for a happy, calm or harmonious relationship. Luke was intense, given to secret brooding. I was dramatic, also given to brooding which would then spill over into a temper tantrum or an icy sulk. I would scream at him, accusing him wildly, then burst into tears. It usually ended with him retreating into his shell and me contrite and apologetic.

The knots in my head kept me tied up for years afterwards. Unravelling them also threatened the memory of Jehan, already starting to fade at the edges, like an old photograph. I held on with all of my heart because I was too frightened to let him go. What if I found that my life until then had all been vignettes starring Jehan or featuring him? What if my life had no meaning without Jehan's memories to sustain it? I gave all my life force to keeping him alive for as long as I could. Luke's presence in my life, and ironically, Amita's absence in it, became increasingly important in order to achieve this.

None of this was of Luke's making. My emotions were sweeping us along, and he was young enough and immature enough to feel flattered by my intensity. In rare moments of clarity, I would tell him to leave while he had the chance; that we were going nowhere; that we were no good for each other. He would laugh these warnings away. It didn't help that he was becoming more insecure about his place in the world as his family's fortunes waned. This became a lifelong chip on his shoulder that weighed on his moods, his actions and reactions to almost everything important. I would sneer at his lack of culture, his laid-back attitude to his education, and his lack of ambition. He would label me a snob who didn't have her feet on the ground, too concerned about what others thought of her and her precious grades. I was the white girl he brought home to a disapproving mother, he was the bad influence my family wanted gone from my life for good. In reality, we were none of these things. We were just two kids in the throes of first love. And when we were alone together, with no one to judge and nothing to prove, we could be sweet to each other, and often loving and kind. We could read each other's thoughts pretty early on, we could laugh over unsaid jokes because we shared the same wicked, slightly sadistic sense of humour.

A memory of an afternoon spent together is very clear. It must have been a couple of years after Jehan died. The gang had been hanging out at the beach and then it was time to go home. Luke wheeled his cycle to the bus depot and I boarded the bus with Paddy. A couple of stops later, I saw him. His home lay in the opposite direction from mine. But there he was, a long stemmed rose dangling from one hand, keeping pace with our bus. At every stop, he drew up alongside my window, smiling up at me.

'Luke, what are you doing? Go home, Dumbo.'

He just smiled and kept up with the bus. The traffic was pretty bad even then, in the late eighties, but he stayed with us all the way from the beach to my stop. Paddy laughed at first, then became increasingly embarrassed by the two of us and finally gave up. We had eyes only for each other.

'Bye, Paddy!' I said to him when we parted.

'Yeah, yeah, crazy kids, no wonder you're moony eyed about each other. Idiots! Bye, you lunatics!'

His shouts floated back to us as the bus pulled away. Luke handed me the poor, wind-battered rose, and we stood smiling at each other, knowing each other. I loved that he had just done this crazy thing but found it hard to say so. He loved that I couldn't stop the blush creeping up my cheeks though I tried so hard to be cool. We walked a meandering route to the gate of my building and then he wheeled off lazily, glancing back once while I stood there, laughing with him.

Another day, we got drenched on a bike ride after giving blank cassettes to Ananth, the owner of Vibes, for taping. In the eighties, that's how we got our fix of music. We saved up to buy blank TDK or Sony audio cassettes, then spent the entire afternoon at a professional recording shop, mulling over the albums for sides A and B, discussing the pros and cons of Rainbow versus Scorpions, or Dire Straits and Eagles. Best of all, carefully selecting the right mix of songs that would fit exactly on a ninety-minute cassette. Mixed cassettes cost more to record than two straight albums but were the most coveted music tapes in our collection. Having spent a happy afternoon at Vibes, the shop with the most clued-in owner and the best equipment in town, we were on our way home when a cloud burst hit us. We were soaked in seconds and it was glorious. Hari was caught in the same shower. I still remember him at the traffic light, shaking his head at the two of us, laughing as we sped away.

But all this could not make up for the one basic thing: we were two very different people. He would never be the man I wanted him to be, and I would never be content to live the life he imagined, in his shadow, like his mom lived in the shade of her husband. Deep down, I was starting to discover that I was a feminist (my mom had been far greater an influence on my psyche than I cared to admit) and he had been brought up in a far more traditional, patriarchal set-up. This was made worse by his keen sense of pride and defensive personality. But at fifteen and eighteen, it was almost impossible to actually say these things to each other. There was only a vague unease. A realization that in spite of the love, the physical attraction, the friendship, there was still something that yawned between us, growing ever wider as we grew older.

The flashpoint of our disagreements was often my mood. I tended to go days, sometimes weeks on an even keel, but then there would be a backlash of grief that bore me away and I had no way to stop myself. I had struggled to come to terms with Jehan's death, and what I saw as his betrayal of our bond, his rejection of my love, and it still felt like a slap in the face each time I forced myself to take out the carefully hoarded memory of that long weekend when nothing more serious than India winning or losing the test match had been predicted in my life. It played in a continuous loop in my head in the first year. Then I forced myself to lock the memories away, only taking them out occasionally (when I couldn't bear the stress of living a seemingly normal life in what were the most abnormal circumstances, or when I was indulging in a bout of self-pity). Unfortunately for Luke, I usually had these flashbacks when we were together. The downward spiral meant I would grasp at straws and lash out at anyone who was willing to be the victim, until the pain subsided.

The other factor that played a part in these showdowns was my need to punish myself. The seeds of that conviction had been planted the evening of Jehan's death. There was an insistent voice inside my head that if I hadn't met these friends of mine, the situations described to me by Fali and Zarir would never have come to pass and Jehan might have been happier in his last days, sardonic grin, drawling voice and all. This same little voice would whisper to me that I didn't deserve to be happy. How could I be happy when my brother had been so sad, so miserable that he saw no other way out but to take his own life? Using *my* skipping rope. When that voice grew strident, once again I would lash out, trying to hurt or goad Luke enough, or even other friends, so that they would see me for the bad person I really was, and run as far and as fast as they could. This voice was my constant companion for years. I had managed to lose Wayland Manor, Amita, Pia and Nalini the first time that voice sounded inside my head. Then it was my own family. I felt myself observing our life from a very great distance, and slowly, the ties that bound us began to dissolve inside my head. I blamed myself for Jehan's death because I was too frightened to blame anyone else, and most of all, I could not bring myself to not blame anyone at all. And now, the next person on that voice's hit list was Luke.

All our major fights seemed to involve my clothes or my ambitions and his lack of it. One day I visited Ziya who lent me a shocking pink clingy vest that she could never have left her own house wearing. I promptly wore it that afternoon.

Luke and I were dropping in on his elder sister who worked at a fancy hotel. His eyes went wide when he saw the top I was wearing. We had a huge fight in the middle of the hotel lobby. He ordered me to go home and change; I refused. I loved the vest, who was he to tell me what or what not to wear?

He turned and left, with me still standing there, still snarling.

He would stand protectively over me in the bus, glaring at any boy or man who gave me the eye. I was blithely indifferent to the lecherous stares which were as much the result of my clothes (usually a miniskirt and a little blouse) as of my light skin. My complexion certainly did single me out for unwanted male attention in the Bay City of the eighties. But he accused me of deliberately flaunting my body. I laughed at that.

I had never been told what I could or could not wear in my own home, and saw no reason why this boy could dictate terms to me. What he could never fully articulate was the intense and insecure possessiveness he felt towards me, my mind, my body, all of it. I felt it, though, in his touch, in the moodiness, in the diktats he tried so hard to lay down. I, too, could never fully articulate my resentment at the intensity, the sense of ownership towards me, the constant feeling of being in a room without any air, if you will. Unlike the first time though, now it was simply suffocating.

All I knew clearly was that I loved him and that should have been enough. And it wasn't. Not for either one of us.

Another time, we had a screaming match in Paddy's bedroom, over my future plans.

'It's mom's alma mater, so I thought I could also apply there for my post-graduation.'

'But that's so far away, some dusty western town! What's wrong with universities in Bay City?'

'Nothing, but this one is ranked higher for genetics and microbiology. And it's my hometown. I could get to know my cousins better. Get away from this dead town!'

'Oh, Miss High and Mighty wants to get away from this loser town, yeah? And her loser boyfriend too, I bet!'

'I didn't say loser, I said dead. Don't you want to get away too, Luke?'

'Hey, I'm happy here. I'm a simple guy, Liana. I don't have all these ambitions like you do. Post-graduation? So posh. Wow, so you've been making all these plans! Was I the last to know? What about us? You and me.'

'What about us, Luke? We fight, we make up, we fight again. What's that got to do with my plans for post-grad?'

'Nothing, nothing at all, Dumbo. Thanks for clarifying—we have no future, that's what you're saying, right?'

'Luke, you're twisting everything again.'

'Who, me? Nah, that's your speciality.'

'I can't help it if my family values education, especially for girls! My mom was a college professor, remember?'

This was meant to sting, because his mother was a far more traditional lady than Honey in every sense of the word. Though his dad was highly educated, we didn't speak much of him, just as we rarely spoke about Eruch. Our mothers were the focal points of our families, and the comparisons were odious but constant. So the fights continued, sporadic at first, then increasing in frequency as I grew older and more confident.

And then Zarir sprang the biggest surprise on us all. Smiling vulpine into his moustache, he announced that his aunt had done some match-making and he was about to host the girl and her parents to dinner the following evening. Please would Fali, my sister-in-law and I keep him company as his side of the family?

Shock and awe. Shock, because though Zarir and we had drifted apart somewhat, he was still very much a part of our lives and we had no inkling that marriage was on his mind. I had goaded him often enough to spend the evening with this or that set of sisters. He did accept a dinner invitation or two, returning with horror stories of their feminine wiles. So to find him announcing his intention to set up hearth and home with a complete stranger was enough to make us all reel.

Of course, we attended the wedding and reception, dressed to the nines—determined to support Zarir and make him proud of his surrogate renegade family. Honey insisted that we three women wear her best garas, the heirloom embroidered saris that each Parsi family cherishes. These saris were originally made in and sourced from China—hence our surname Chinoy, from our ancestors who traded with China. We watched Zarir, his face pink and pleased, as he married his beautiful bride. It was all very heart-warming and lovely, except that I really didn't like her much at all. Sour grapes, a little voice said in my head, and I shrugged it off. I just cared more for Zarir than I had realized up until now, and some instinct warned me about this girl more insistently as time went by.

Soon after his wedding, Zarir simply disappeared from my life. The rumour reached us that his wife had fallen in with the sister acts. She had been swayed by the horror stories of my loose morals and fast reputation and had decided to cut the cord. It was a brutal end to a deep friendship. Later the following year, we heard disturbing stories of how the marriage had fallen apart. She went back to her parents soon after. Honey was furious on Zarir's behalf. She had been very hurt by his sudden disappearance but wouldn't hear a word said against him. To her he would always be the boy who had cradled her dead son in his arms. So now, hearing of the breakdown of his short-lived marriage, she took out all her ire on the unknown people who had so ill-advisedly set up the match. Zarir visited us once or twice afterwards, but his heart and spirit were broken. He had faced far more in his young life than was fair, and this was the final blow. He wouldn't meet our eyes. He seemed unable to talk to me at all. He sold the house, pulled up stakes and left to make a new life in another city.

~

And what of Jehan?

As Luke and I stabilized our new relationship, I was also forging a friendship with Karthik. I introduced Luke to him, they hit it off, and we ended up spending many afternoons and evenings together. Aunty and he became my de facto grief counsellors. The first time I broke down, really broke down and screamed and wept and shivered with the intensity of the grief was in Karthik's bedroom, huddled on the floor. Luke holding on to me, Karthik just sitting there, talking me out of the hole I was in, in his soothing teacher's voice. After I had calmed down, his mother, who had been waiting outside, came in, sat me down next to her, took my hand in her fragile but firm grip and began to talk to me about what I was feeling. After Hari in the early days, this was the first time someone had analysed my grief. But there was a line she could not cross. She knew my family did not talk about Jehan, and there was no way for her to encourage me to get the help I needed. So she continued with her informal therapy, mostly just giving me a safe space to vent my anger and grief, helping me more than she could ever know. I finally had a place to go to, where no one shied away from talking about my brother, if that was what I chose to do that day. Aunty was a lot like the old Honey, headstrong, ruthless and stubborn, but in the nicest way possible. She brooked no nonsense from any of us—though she did not quite approve of our shenanigans, she fed and watered us and gave us pretty much free rein in her house.

Luke became very close to Karthik's dad in those years,

patiently listening to his garbled speech, helping Aunty with the heavy lifting when Uncle simply could not or chose not to bear his own body weight. We were all healing in our own way in those early years. Luke was finding his new normal. The family business had been shut down and the siblings were managing the best that they could. The older two stepped up, holding down jobs and keeping the family finances on a precarious even keel. Luke chipped in, working jobs after college, but still, things were tough for them. For Luke, financial insecurity became a lasting obsession. The cocky young guy, whose father owned three flourishing shops, suddenly had very little spending money and his pride took a beating. Most of our time spent together involved sitting on the beach, or if it was the beginning of the month, a cheap meal I financed. Karthik generously lent us his motorbike, but still, most of our travel involved the bus. Luke's ego hated these obligations he felt he owed us and there was nothing I could say or do to convince him that we were equals in this relationship and that it did not matter who paid for lunch. It mattered a great deal to him.

Meanwhile, Karthik and I became buddies. I called him LP (short for Long Playing record, because he could play his keyboards endlessly for me) and he called me CD (short for Chinoy, Chinoy Darling: his standard way of greeting me). But in spite of outward high jinks, LP's heart marched to the beat of a different drum. For one, he enjoyed his own company and appreciated solitude. He could sit quietly with a book or meditate. And he never once apologized for any of these quirks. He was very self-contained and extremely confident. That came from a fine intellect and a strong relationship with his mom. Luke never quite got him. He, on the other hand, had the full measure of Luke, though he kept his opinions to himself.

But what of Jehan?

I was very angry with him. The hardest thing in the world is to rage against the person you love the most, knowing well that he is impervious to your anger or love. I tried telling myself that he got what he wanted, what he deserved, that he was so selfish he hadn't thought of how it would affect our lives, or that perhaps this was his vengeful way of paying us back for unarticulated hurts. I was bitter with the anger; the night he died, I had said that we'd all now be able to rest in peace. When the words for his tombstone were being decided by the family, I had once again suggested 'Rest in Peace'. Not so much for him, because he was at peace, of that I was certain. I had meant that *we* could, that *I* could finally be at peace, not having to worry about waking up the next morning to an overdose or slit wrists. There was a certain furtive relief that came over me when I saw his dead face. One part of me did actually think: it's finally happened. The thing we had been dreading for the past year had actually come to pass. No more waiting.

I was very angry with my family. That poem on the inside of his cupboard door, it clearly said that he wanted to die. My mother opened that cupboard every day to put away his clothes. How was it possible that she hadn't read those dreadful words? Why had they not done something? Why had they given up before he was even gone? And my brother? My other brother. Old enough to hold down a job, old enough to want to get married and settle down, but not old enough to see the storm that was coming? I was fourteen years old and I had seen the clouds looming as clear as day. And these adults, none of them had done a thing about it. I was always kept out of the loop; I had no clue whether this anger was misplaced or not. Nothing was discussed in my presence and I was left to put the pieces of the puzzle together myself.

I remember an incident maybe six weeks before the last day. Just as he had done two days before he died, Jehan came home from college complaining of a terrible pain in his abdomen. By the time forty-eight hours had passed, he could barely stand upright. Honey and Eruch tried their best to persuade him to see a doctor but Jehan became hysterical. He accused them of tricking him into seeing a psychiatrist. Zarir tried persuading him, so did Hari, but he wouldn't budge. He became so worked up that Honey and Eruch backed off, gave him some painkillers and the matter ended there. Was Jehan convinced in his mind that he would be admitted into a psychiatric ward? That he would be given shock therapy which was the rumoured treatment for suicidal persons in the eighties. Wasn't that even more reason to get him some urgent help? The fear of what people would say, the overriding need to supress our nasty little family secret, the desire to appear normal and happy, seemed to trump the almost certain fear that these cries for help, if left unheeded, were not going to end well.

My mind whirled with questions. And no answers, except the ones I was forced to design for myself in order to get some rest. I began to treat myself and my feelings, a form of self-therapy, if you will, and each time in the next thirty years when the doubts surfaced, I rationalized my lack of interest in professional help with my ego: I was intelligent and well-read. I had figured this out without help from my family, and some help from friends. I had got a handle on these fears and doubts and the hollowness in my stomach and the breath I was never able to catch.

I was essentially living two lives. In one, I was happy, outgoing, successful, ambitious, the girl who didn't give a damn about other people's opinions (except for her immediate family, where all that turned upside down and I concentrated on being the perfect daughter and sister—meek, obedient, studious). In my other life, I was a mess. I was punishing myself on a daily basis. I tended to self-destruct every time the happiness became too guilt-ridden. I made excuses for picking fights with lovers and friends. I lived almost exclusively in the past, and still managed to hide this fact from everyone. I became a damned fine actress, so much so that I could fool myself most of the time.

One factor, which definitely had an effect on my behaviour, went unnoticed at the time. I was experiencing severe premenstrual syndrome, and in hindsight, each of my decisions to end something that brought me happiness coincided with the onset of the symptoms. A short visit to a doctor would have red-flagged this pattern but I wasn't unwell so I never had a reason to visit a doctor, leave alone a psychiatrist. Honey and Eruch were of the school of thought that talking about your mental health, family problems and emotional issues were for weak, self-pitying people. They certainly did not believe that any good could come of airing dirty laundry in public. A stiff upper lip was the lesson that was indirectly taught to us. Honey especially, in spite of all her education and worldly ways, was particularly stubborn about her pride and honour. Any announcement from her daughter, after the enormous betrayal her son had dealt to family honour, that a second child of hers needed help, would not have gone down well, of that I was convinced. So the PMS-driven mood swings continued, again for years, until my gynaecologist diagnosed the imbalance during my second pregnancy and put me on some herbal medication to even out the hormonal surges.

A part of me stayed an adolescent well into my thirties—acting out, rebelling in small, sneaky ways, fighting against conformity, more often than not losing that battle. There were days when my fourteen-year-old son took more mature decisions than his forty-year-old mother.

~

The distant trauma, the repression, the mood swings—these forced another part of me to grow older in strange ways. Death was no longer an unknown entity and I lost respect and fear for it. I used to have the strangest desire to laugh out loud at funerals, seeing the survivors grieving. Wake up, I'd feel like shouting at them, this is only the beginning. This is the easy part, the funeral and the rituals. You have no idea what's coming next. But I clenched my jaw to stop that crazed laughter from erupting, and after a while, stopped going to funerals altogether. Love was harder to anticipate as a given, when loss was its constant threat.

But everything was not a dead loss. I found my own unique perspective on the world and life. I know that sounds pompous! Though I never could joke about suicide or homosexuality ever again, once the initial years of anger, insecurity and acting out the bitch were past, I was thankful to have retained a sense of humour and empathy. But I'm ahead of my story.

Back in 1987, the new apartment was terribly bright and hot. In a misguided fit of superiority, Eruch, a cardiac disease patient, had insisted on choosing a flat on the third floor of a three-storey building, so that there would be no one living over his head. We were thus happily situated under an open terrace that baked to a crisp by noon on approximately three hundred and fifty days of the year. The electricity failed at regular intervals too, prompting darkling looks from Honey as Eruch huffed and puffed his way up and down three flights of stairs. Honey was obsessed was her husband's health, or the lack of it. She had convinced herself that the new flat was meagre compensation for the stress Eruch was under at work, in her opinion, unfairly so. Apparently, his neglect of exercise and a disregard for a healthy diet had nothing to do with cholesterol levels and blocked arteries. Nor did his son's suicide play any role whatsoever in Eruch's deteriorating health. In Honey's mind, it was work stress, and that alone, which had affected her husband's health so adversely. She moved into her new home, the first one she had ever owned, in the manner of a queen granted her tribute. I missed the bungalow and its cool shady garden, but it was good to get away from the memories.

The real victim of the move became, sadly enough, our dachshund Cherie. She was suddenly transplanted from the only home she had ever known, a place of mysterious smells, and muddy spots to roll in, a home inhabited by squirrels to chase and her faithful feline companions, to a boxed-in flat home with no garden, perched high above the earth, surrounded by concrete on all sides, and windows so high that she could not even easily look outside. She was bewildered and lost without Vagabond, the gentleman tomcat who had been her devoted mentor, guide and companion since the day she had come into our home. Vagabond had sensed our move even before the packers came in. He had taken to disappearing for longer periods of time, until, on the day that we finally fled our bungalow, he was nowhere to be found. A cat stays with the territory he stalks, and that is something a dog can never comprehend, tied as she is to her humans. Cherie went into decline in the new flat. She moped around, went off her food, and became so dispirited that Honey became alarmed for her life.

Finally, the gut-wrenching decision was taken to give Cherie away, ironically to a lady who also lived in a flat, but who had other dogs to keep her company. It was hoped that this would help Cherie adjust to her new family. I try not to think of the confusion and distress she must have felt when we left her behind in a strange new place. Our family's history of abandonment had reached its nadir. I still carry the guilt of abandoning Cherie, which is one reason I never brought home a dog again. Honey, true to form, refused to speak of her. We didn't seem to possess a single photograph of Vagabond or Cherie in our meagre collection, and it was as if she had never existed.

Again, the pattern repeats itself. Honey warned me that I was never to try and visit Cherie ever again. But I did go, just once though. Luke waited downstairs while I went up to the flat. The lady was kind enough, but she didn't approve either, for Cherie's sake. Cherie hesitatingly wagged her stump of a tail, but would not venture close enough to be patted. I was selfish, but not completely heartless. I left in tears and that was the end of the bitterest fallout of Jehan's death.

'Did he stop and think of the animals who loved him?' I raged to Luke. 'Did he care about that little puppy he had brought home all those years ago, or was she the last thing on his mind when he slung my skipping rope over the shower pipe?'

As you can see, I milked as much drama out of every occasion as I could get away with.

The two years at Prathiman Vidyalaya were coming to an end. There were days when I would bunk afternoon school and ride off with Luke, still wearing my uniform. But those were rare. I managed to get my act together, and even enjoy my time in prison. I lost touch with Waylanders, except for LP, and the gang was also evolving.

Then Luke's grandfather died, and he had to go away to his little hometown in the hinterland. Coincidentally, that was the same weekend that I was alone at home, left in nominal charge of Preeti's parents while Honey and Eruch went away for a rare holiday together. Fali and Preeti had moved to another city by then, and so, for the first time in my life, I was without family, and frustratingly, without a boyfriend. Luke and I could have used the time together without constantly looking over our shoulders for Honey or Fali frowning disapprovingly at us. If he had been in town, I think we would have gone all the way in those few days. Instead, he was away and I became irrationally angry with him, though of course, he wasn't off on some jaunt.

I decided that this was the best time to play the field a little. I chose to have a fling with, of all unsuitable people, a friend's boyfriend. They were on a break. A more unlikely candidate for a wild weekend could hardly be found for love or money. He was sweet, but out of shape and mild—not the combination I was usually attracted to. He danced well so I suppose he wasn't a complete loss. Still, we got hot and heavy enough over the weekend for me to tearfully break it off with my bereaved boyfriend as soon as he came back from the funeral, tonsured and shaken.

Instead of reacting as I wanted, Luke withdrew into his shell and left me gnashing my teeth as he refused to discuss my perfidy and thrash out each and every detail of my infidelity. His silence presented me with a fait accompli. What to do? I crept back quietly, tail tucked firmly between my legs.

LP laughed at my discomfort. 'Serves you right, CD. You can't be playing the guy false whilst he's away at his granddad's funeral. Good grief.'

But it had given me a taste of what was to come. That weekend, I grew up some more, and further away from this boy I had loved for such a long time. I had tested his resolve, and perversely found him wanting when he didn't blame me or walk away. All I could do was to warn him that I might repeat the escapade again, and that he still had time to leave, no questions asked. Of course he didn't, and we carried on. As an aside, the boyfriend ran back to my friend, who later became his wife, and who can't stand to look at me to this day.

~

College was everything I'd dreamt of, and then some. It was a beautiful campus of stately whitewashed buildings dreaming under the hot blue sky, of a little clock tower dwarfed by ancient trees. Each morning, as I walked down the long driveway, a wonderful fragrance filled my senses—a mix of damp earth, the spores from the venerable cycas trees lining the Science Block, and the unpleasant yet sensual aroma of the cannonball tree in full bloom.

Annie entered my life around this time. She and I emerged from the same building and walked on opposite sides of the street to the same bus stop, where we clambered onto the same bus, got down at the bus stop outside college and sheepishly entered the college gates together. This went on for a few days.

Then one morning, I heard an abrupt voice behind me.

'Same college?'

We grinned ruefully at each other and became fast friends. Annie and her family had recently moved into our apartment building, she on the ground floor directly under us three floors above. We hit it off because under her conservative exterior, she was a true rebel and open to wild adventures, as long as her parents never got wind of these. She was impatient and abrupt, hiding a very soft heart behind the prickly exterior.

'Liana? Too long, too romantic. I'll call you Li.'

And Li I was to Annie forever after. She educated me about feminist literature and poetry. ('What's all this sappy stuff you read? Here, read Kamla Das. Here, try this—it's Pablo Neruda.') I took it upon myself to introduce her to rock music.

Growing up, I had been lucky enough to appreciate almost every genre of music produced—in our home, the day could begin with Bismillah Khan's shehnai or Ravi Shankar, as Honey sipped her first cup of tea. Breakfast meant a change of pace, and depending on who got to the record player first, our eggs were accompanied by Eagles or Dire Straits, Cream or Boney M or Vivaldi. After we had left for office, school and college, Honey continued listening to music all day, humming or whistling to Hindi film music, Paul Mauriat, Jagjit Singh or James Last. Back home in the afternoon, we'd crank up the volume, and Genesis, Alan Parson's Project and Rainbow would tell everyone in the neighbourhood that we were here. Eruch claimed rights over the music system later in the evening, and our day wound down to Beethoven, opera or jolly polka music. We had an array of music equipment, ranging from Eruch's beloved Sony Spool Player, gifted to him by his Mama, to the turntable they had brought home from Europe, from all manners of cassette players to the brand new Sony sound system that had drowned out the sound of Jehan's death, the only comfort being that he must have heard music in his final moments.

From the age of fourteen, my musical tastes had emerged from my family's shadow and veered off on an unexpected discovery of hard rock and heavy metal music, thanks mainly to Joe, who was slightly evangelical about Iron Maiden and Rainbow. I resisted Iron Maiden, partly to annoy Lucas, whose musical journey basically began and ended with their oeuvre, but happily became a fan of Richie Blackmore's guitar, the Scorpions and other assorted hard rock acts. And now the time had come to pass on the music.

Annie and I spent many hours in my bedroom, listening to Pink Floyd, Eric Clapton and especially Def Leppard's *Hysteria* album, our absolute favourite. Our very conservative neighbour on the second floor complained repeatedly to my parents about the obscene caterwauling, as he termed our off-key but impassioned accompaniment to 'Pour Some Sugar on Me'. Eruch half-heartedly admonished us, while serving Annie a second helping of his world-famous akoori. Honey scoffed at the complaints, and defiantly whistled (on pitch and in tune) to 'Armageddon It'. Our neighbour's young son didn't seem to mind as much, as I gleefully pointed out to Annie every evening on the building terrace.

'You know, he likes you, Annie. Blushes every time he catches your eye. Like a to-mah-to.'

'Li, he doesn't, ya. You're just imagining things.'

'So why are you blushing, Annie my love?'

'Tch, I'm not, I'm *not*!'

'Methinks the lady doth protest...ow, ow, Annie, stop!'

Annie was steeped in the world of literature, her mother being a well-established journalist and writer. I had meandered away from the dream of medicine, bypassed Genetics and ended up in the Zoology department. The studies came easily enough, and my ego could always do with the boost that topping the class produced on a gratifyingly regular basis. Somewhere along the way, I had stopped being neurotic about examinations. This was a big improvement in someone who had fallen ill with a raging temperature the night before her Sanskrit exam in standard Three, and who had a miserable career in cheating up until Standard Eight, the fear of not being the best in the only thing I was halfway good at overriding all morals and principles.

It never occurred to me that I was not really cut out to go down the path laid out by Honey. All the signs were there. I just refused to acknowledge that my career was more naturally veering towards writing and literature. Honey and I were too blinded by her own academic frustrations and my desire to make up for her loss of career and child. We were in complete agreement that if not medicine, it would still have to be a science subject that I graduated in. I chose Zoology and marched into college, determined to be a stellar zoologist. A more boring course of study I could not have chosen, if I had tried. But college opened up other opportunities—I wrote fiercely in the General English class, making enough of a nuisance of myself to come to the attention of the Literature department faculty. That led to writing for the college magazine, and an optional course in creative writing. I began to spend most of my free time in the Literature department, prompting an interaction with the head of my own department.

'Now, Liana, I just want to remind you that you are studying for a degree in Zoology, not English. Try not to spend so much time there, all right, otherwise I may have to ask you to switch departments altogether.'

She had no intention of letting her star student go, and would have been horrified if she'd known that I was actually toying with the idea of switching departments.

The thought of Honey's dismay pulled me up short. To have all three children defect to Literature would have been the final blow to her aspirations and dreams. So I continued in the Zoology department, managing to top all three years. But my heart was given to Literature's safekeeping, and

Annie became my conduit to the literati. We hung out in college, though she was a year ahead of me, and all the time outside of it. I confided in her about Jehan and Luke, and her no-nonsense practical take on the drama in my life helped to rationalize it somewhat and even brought an outsider's perspective to something that had become increasingly secret and personal.

The faculty of my department didn't quite know what to make of me. I was simultaneously the rebel and the good girl, the one who wore tight, frayed jeans and took on class assignments with a bravado none of my classmates had yet displayed. I spoke my mind, politely and often, scandalizing the good ladies in the staff room but earning some reluctant points for my recklessness. The straitlaced head of the department and the junior teachers had decided early on that I was a hellion bent on spoiling the good name and reputation of their department. But at the same time, I happened to be involved in an array of campus activities, dramatics, environmental conservation and Western music clubs, and this they liked. I was the face of the department, but they didn't approve of anything else—not my clothes or my attitude, nor the fact that some boy, and not always the same one, often picked me up from outside college. But the seniormost professor, Dr Joel, took a shine to me. She became my defender and champion, though I never figured out why. She taught the genetics course and was a fine teacher. She would defend me vociferously in front of her colleagues then pull me aside to reprimand me in turn for riling them all up. The stern face was always betrayed by the devilish twinkle in her eyes. I wish I had told her just how much I appreciated her, one more in the long line of teachers I was fortunate to have had. But I think she knew anyway.

One morning, as I walked into college, a hostellite came running up to me and said she had been sent to wait for me. The message she delivered was short: Puppies behind banyan tree. Sure enough, there were two puppies, eyes still to open, mewling and crawling around at the base of the giant banyan near the front gate. The watchman said that he hadn't seen the mother for a couple of days. I went straight to Dr Joel. These puppies would die, we agreed.

'I could take them to the Blue Cross Society,' I suggested.

Her gaze was penetrating but I managed to keep a straight face. She and I both knew this was a fabulous excuse to bunk college for the day.

'How will you go?' was her next question.

The Blue Cross Society was pretty far from college. I decided honesty was the best policy.

'My boyfriend is at his computer course next door,' I said. 'I could go and ask him to pick the puppies and me up from college.'

Her expressive eyebrows said it all. Then she shrugged and said, 'Okay. Let me see.'

We hustled to the head's office and got that poor simple lady so confused with facts and fiction that she gave in after a few minutes of our combined haranguing. No boyfriend was mentioned. I ran to NIIT next door, and waited till

Luke emerged from his computer programming class. After we spoke, he went to borrow LP's bike, and I headed back to college to pick up a get-out-of-jail pass and the puppies. I remember I was wearing my favourite ganji that day, layered with Luke's shirt that he'd lent to me because I loved it so much. I nestled the puppies inside the roomy shirt and we headed off to the Blue Cross shelter near the beach. Puppies carefully handed over, we suddenly had a whole day to ourselves. We parked at the beach, fooled around in an abandoned shed, ate some lunch and Dr Joel was forgotten. The next day, she called me to her office and read me the riot act.

'Liana Chinoy,' she said sternly, 'no more of this foolishness, my girl.'

This act of rebellion on my part and collusion on hers was never to be repeated. I agreed readily but the wide grin on my face must have given away the pleasure of yesterday's memory. Dear Dr Joel.

~

LP and I had become closer than ever. I nagged him mercilessly, calling him overgrown and a giraffe, and he called me Dr Frankenstein, because we both agreed that he was a monster of my making. I had bullied him into a different kind of confidence, haranguing him into believing he was a catch any girl would want to find in her net. Unfortunately, when he did find girlfriends—which he did with great regularity—not one came up to scratch in my book. I could only disparage every candidate as they came and went, also with monotonous regularity. No one was good enough for LP, in my considered opinion. When Paddy and Meenakshi broke up with great drama, I took along a heartbroken girl to LP's house one day. The tiny bombshell and the overgrown giraffe took one look at each other and the deal was sealed. She was the only one of LP's girlfriends who met with my whole and unqualified approval.

Years later, LP's prospective mother-in-law quizzed me about our relationship. She pointedly asked if we had had anything between us ever. I snorted with laughter at the very idea and tried to explain to her what it meant to have a rakhi brother and a friend like LP. He had stood by me through the very worst of times; we loved each other dearly, but there was never anything remotely romantic in our relationship.

LP's dad died one cool, misty morning. Luke and I had been to the plant nursery opposite my place to pick up a little potted plant for Aunty. I can't remember what the occasion was, maybe there was none. Maybe I had some money to spend and we just wanted her to know how much we—two rude, cranky and disturbed teenagers—loved her. We walked from the bus stop to his house, happy to be with each other, not bickering for once.

As we approached his house, we yelled out, 'Hey, LP, LP darling!' wanting him to help us smuggle the plant upstairs to surprise Aunty.

Instead, he came out on the veranda and hushed us. 'My father died this morning,' he said.

We spent the rest of the day just hanging around his place, trying not to be in the way. In the evening, Aunty came and sat down with us at their small dining table. She reached out, held our hands in her elegant ones.

'Thank you for being here, you are my dear children.' That's all. And it meant the world to both of us.

Luke was particularly upset over Uncle's death. It had been a release from years of frustration and suffering, not just for Uncle but for Aunty and LP too. They seemed calm and composed, while Luke grew very angry for a while. It was almost as if he had lost his own father, though he could never express those deeply buried emotions to me or anyone else.

It brought us very close, that loss.

We were happiest when we were alone together, which happened rarely. We had our special places. A road that led past the TV tower along the river to the Exhibition Grounds, where the city held its book fairs and SPIC MACAY their concerts. We'd walk its length slowly. It was private and secluded and I wasn't constantly worrying about Fali or Honey spotting us. The bylanes meandering past the beach, with a broken bridge at one end—this was the place where we had met for the second time, again at a Paribesa meeting, very different from the gloomy museum hall of our first encounter. Here, the air was clean and the sun shone on our faces, the breeze blowing my hair back. He reminded me in a telephone conversation a few years ago that I had carried along homemade macaroons for everyone to snack on at that long-ago Paribesa meeting.

Things were very different in company. We were best friends in private and bitter enemies in front of almost everyone else. We loved each other very much, we just didn't like each other a whole lot. If I had backed down, given in, been meek and non-argumentative, we might still have made it. If he had been mature, secure in himself and his circumstances, not afraid to give it back as good as he got, we might have still made it. I read this, and I think how unfair I am being to him even now. All the faults were his, if I am to be believed. All the virtues were mine. Well, it was no such thing. He hung on, gave me room, put up with my bad behaviour when almost anyone else would have walked away and never looked back. The only real truth was that I did love him very deeply, and if that had been enough, we might still have made it, in spite of all our differences. But the fifteen-year-old I had been, needy, desperate, devastated, was not the seventeen-year-old I was now.

~

I was faithful to Luke, except for that one weekend fling, and deeply in love with him, until the day that I wasn't. The last time I remember defying my parents over him was when I went away for the weekend to surprise him at a concert they were booked to play in Bangalore. The gang had turned out in full support of Dragonsmoke, as the band was called—Joe on lead, Luke on bass, Keecha on rhythm, LP on drums and keyboards and a floating population of lead vocalists. Of course, Honey and Eruch wouldn't hear of me going to Bangalore for the weekend, Honey more so because she knew exactly what I was up to by then. I had more or less given up on lying about Luke to her, but by tacit agreement, we had decided this was not something to trouble Eruch with, or Fali for that matter.

Fali and Preeti had returned to Bay City after a year away. They moved out into their own little apartment, one street away from where I spent each afternoon, at LP's place. Yet, I saw them infrequently. They had their own life and friends, as did I. My only concern was that they shouldn't catch me with Luke, and though on a couple of occasions, Hari and Sid had encountered us at traffic signals, they had seemingly not ratted me out to Fali. So the weekend seemed impossible, until LP stepped in.

'Aunty, I'll watch her every move,' he said convincingly.

Since LP's word was gold at home, things quickly fell into place. Luke and the others had gone on ahead, Karthik and I followed on the morning of the concert. In those pre-cell phone and internet days, no one in Bangalore knew about the change of plans. An elderly couple mistook us for a newly married one on the train, and there ensued a hilarious comedy of errors that kept us all entertained for the few hours it took to reach Bangalore.

'I say, listen here,' he'd coo, batting his eyelashes at me.

'What is it? Where's my breakfast?' I'd snap back, in complete role reversal.

'Here, dear, is the coffee hot enough?'

LP acted coy, I played the brazen bride and we stepped

off that train leaving the good folk gaping at us and shaking their heads over the younger generation. LP was going to milk the drama for all that it was worth. He kept me well hidden behind his gigantic frame, waited until Luke hailed him and then watched gleefully as the look of absolute delight and amazement spread across Luke's face. I think I loved LP more in that moment than ever before. This guy had my back then and he always would.

It was an amazing weekend. We were together for almost forty-eight hours, a first in our relationship. The concert was a hit and miss affair as the vocalist got cold feet and messed up the lyrics to 'Paranoid', the one song every collegian in the eighties knew by heart. I think he was high because why else would he have substituted the words from an Emami Cold Cream tub label for the lyrics of Ozzy's biggest song? The reaction from the college crowd was unsurprisingly unpleasant. Short of throwing stuff at us, they indicated their disapproval very clearly, booing the singer off the stage, until Joe pacified them with some fine guitar playing. There was a definite surreal feeling to the weekend. That night, we all crashed out in a dirty little flat, as basic as they come. Luke and I snuck off for some time alone, but it was all very furtive and hurried, with half a dozen boys snoring in the next room. Oh, the throes of teenage love! Luke and I never did get the virginity thing out of the way but we experimented in all ways possible and our physical relationship was by far the most satisfying, grouse-free aspect of our relationship. I think it was lack of privacy and some vague instinct of what was to come that stopped us each time from going all the way.

The two of us travelled back by bus the next day, feeding each other grapes, scandalizing the other travellers, reaching Bay City dehydrated but in a euphoric mood.

The thing that Luke kept repeating to me that weekend, in a stunned kind of way, was, 'You're here. You're actually here.' It would take a girl made of sterner stuff than me not to feel absolutely loved in those moments.

Honey rarely allowed me to go out with Luke in the evenings. Once, I had lied that I was out with Karthik, and managed a more conventional date, consisting of a French mimicry show at the University, followed by dinner at our favourite (and cheap) Chinese restaurant and ending up parked in a deserted lane. This was the most memorable date in our on–off four years together. The rest of the time, it was always as part of a group—once a particularly awkward Christmas Eve out with his family. In deference to my white girl North Indian ways, we had gone out to dinner to a Mughlai restaurant, before heading to the church for a magical candlelit midnight mass. I remember over-dressing in a pale grey sari and a shocking pink blouse, the red poinsettias and gold ribbon decorating the church, the dark blue ceiling of the dome shimmering with little gold stars so that it felt we were celebrating midnight mass under the vault of the heavens. His mom barely spoke to me right through the evening, partly because she was not comfortable with English, partly because I was the white girl who had led her darling son into temptation and away from the straight and narrow path of her religion. His siblings rushed in to fill the awkward gaps in the lagging conversation. And Luke? Oh, he was a huge support—he stayed out of the conversation entirely, steadily eating his way through the extensive menu.

One afternoon, I landed up unannounced at his house. His uncle was visiting—a big shot in some religious organization. To say I was inappropriately dressed would be no exaggeration. Once again, I had on my favourite miniskirt, the red Scottish tartan kilt, cheeky and sexy as most of Honey's hand-me-downs were, and a singlet. The air was frigid and condescending, and the man made a few disparaging remarks about my clothes and my shocking lack of decorum in visiting a male friend at his own residence. My back was up, the temper and independence I had inherited from Honey blazing forth. I was determined not to let this austere man or his fawning family members cow me down. Perhaps I engaged him in a debate about the existence of God. Luke had a fine old time explaining me away after I had left.

The sum total of our evenings out alone could therefore be counted on the fingers of one hand, thumb not required. Of course, we had parties to look forward to (and since I didn't own a lot of party clothes, I'd usually end up in the same red dress, the one Luke liked, and which always prompted the designated DJ for the evening to play 'Lady in Red'). Like that memorable night when someone inadvertently locked the host's parents into their own bedroom, and no one heard their cries for help because the music was so loud. We only realized the next morning, and they stumbled out, half-angry, half-amused, to find that we had all crashed there overnight. Or the one where a couple wandered into my parents' bedroom and emerged after some hot and heavy minutes, wearing each other's jeans. One evening, everything cooked tasted of petrol fumes because we used fuel from one of the bikes to light the barbeque pit. The reckless mixing of the punch would always ensure all of us got good and giggly. No party was complete without that, or the usual ride to the beach, our beach, to wind down after we were done.

Carl

ONE EVENING, DINNER done, Carl rolled his head back lazily on the sofa and asked:

'Seen *Flashdance*?'

'No,' I said.

'So...wanna go for the night show?'

'Nice try,' I laughed. 'No way I'll be allowed out.'

Carl turned to Eruch: 'Can I take Liana out for a movie, Uncle?'

Eruch didn't even glance away from the news on the television. 'Of course, beta, do you want to take the car?'

I don't know which unnerved me more—the readily given permission or the offer of taking out Eruch's most precious darling, his car. It also escaped me completely that Carl was interested in me romantically. He was just another friend, and I had many male friends, a disproportionate number actually, none of whom had ever shown the slightest interest in me.

The only person who immediately and vociferously protested was my boyfriend. All his insecurities, the chip on his shoulder about his precarious financial status, came roaring back and he demanded that I never go out on a date with Carl again. Since I didn't think of it as a date, it was as if he was asking me to stop going out with LP or Paddy. It was completely ludicrous and I first laughed at him, then grew angry and dug my heels in. I would go out whenever I liked with whomever I liked, and Luke could just stuff it.

Carl became my de facto night show guy—I was seeing more movies than I'd ever seen before. The whole arrangement was very cool. There was never the slightest hint of anything more than two friends (and that too was surprising—after almost two years, we had finally become friends, listening to music, talking about college plans for him and for me, a topic that was taboo for Luke) hanging out together. The more time we spent together, the more we found things in common, and it occurred to me that I had ignored a really nice guy for almost two years for no good reason except that he was a Parsi and I had declared too often that, of all Parsis, the worst ones were from South Bombay—snobbish, entitled, full of airs. Carl turned out to be none of those things—well, maybe he was far more polished than any of my friends, with superb manners and not embarrassed to act the perfect gentleman. I liked that he could talk about all manner of things, from Pink Floyd's breakup to which college I could apply to in the US for post-graduate studies to whether Bombay had better street food than Bay City. I had always imagined a Bombay bawa to be a spoilt mama's boy, spineless and namby-pamby. Carl proved to be the antithesis of all those labels. He was physically the strongest boy I had ever met, his years of training having given him the kind of muscle no amount of gym time could define. He was casually confident about his prowess in sports, and very quiet about his achievements. I think that's what I liked best (that, and his sexy smile...). You could never draw him out to boast about his glory days. It's true that I began an unfair comparison between Luke, who went on for days if he had skulled one length of the river or played one game of football, and Carl, whose career as a national level sportsman might have gone completely under the radar, if he had his way.

And while Luke was failing his semesters in college, Carl was topping his class. He never complained about working hard (in fact he seemed to thrive on it, a lifelong habit, I suppose, formed juggling training and school), or living in horrific conditions in a Bay City University hostel. And there was one other thing—Carl simply never put me down. Ever. We disagreed vociferously, but neither of us saw the need to tear each other to bits. Odious, unfair comparisons, and I knew it. Still, I started inviting him to parties. He enjoyed dancing, he was easy-going and friendly. LP liked him and he liked hanging with us. The only hitch was Luke's refusal to be polite to him. He glowered and groused, and made it plain that he did not want this guy anywhere near me. Carl and his college friends started coming around to our place more often, and with Annie from downstairs and sometimes LP, we formed a little group completely separate from the gang.

It became a pattern. The fighting with one, the confiding in the other until a time came when I admitted to myself that the fighting was not winning over the confiding.

Bay City/Bombay, 1990–2008

THE THIRD SEMESTER of college was drawing to a close when Carl suggested I accompany him on the Diwali holidays to Bombay. I was always criticizing his city.

'C'mon, I dare you. Come with me and I'll show you what a nice place it is! It'll be a fun holiday.'

By now, I knew that there would be no objection from the family to any such suggestion. It was entirely up to me.

I had to tell Luke of course. He took it badly, almost tearing up.

'If you go, you'll never come back to me.'

He sensed this was the beginning of the end. I reassured him as best as I could.

'It's only a holiday,' I kept saying. 'I'm not stupid. I'll just see another city and then I'll be back.'

I went on that holiday to Bombay with every good intention, but then I got to see where Carl and I stood, away from the emotions swirling back home. I wrote every day to Luke, much to the disapproval of the family friend at whose home I was living. Like almost everyone else, she thought the world of Carl, and couldn't understand how I'd come on a holiday with him, but still had an unsuitable boyfriend back home. It seemed to everyone, except me, that I had to choose. And I never did. After losing Jehan, I was determined to never lose anyone again if it was within my control. There was no doubt in my mind that I could, and would love Luke forever, even long after I had fallen out of love with him. So I wrote letters to him, bought him presents, knowing full well that there would be no going back to the way we had been before this trip. We were friends—in my mind, that took priority over the romance which we both knew could not be sustained. I had hopes for our friendship though, that we would ride out whatever storm was coming and emerge, battered but still friends. Naïve to the end.

Carl introduced me to his friends from school and college, took me out to dinner, and to a party at a friend's house. Our family friend's daughter discovered to her horror that I had no appropriate clothes for a dance party we were invited to, my red dress being deemed too old fashioned for Bombay. She persuaded me to wear one of her own dresses, and I went off to the party feeling a bit like Cinderella. The change in Carl's behaviour had been subtle but unmistakable. I could no longer misunderstand that he was very interested in taking our relationship further. I was furious at myself for letting him think that there was any chance, but still, it felt good to be with someone who didn't fight and squabble with me all the time. We returned to Bay City, matters finally coming to a head on the train journey back.

I spent more time defending Luke than in confessing that I did indeed have more than platonic feelings for Carl. He was blunt.

'Liana, I'm sorry,' he said after we kissed.

'Stop apologizing, you fool, and kiss me again,' was my bravura reply.

'Look, if you need to use me as an excuse to get out of your relationship, I don't mind. It's still new for you but I've had feelings for you for a long time. I can wait.'

I took him up on his offer. But my brain felt the need to clarify one important point.

'I'll always love Luke, you know. He has a special place in my heart. That will never change.'

Carl replied, 'As long as you're with me and in love with me.'

I was never sure if he understood that I meant every word I said. The issue here had never been about loyalty. I had always been a one-man woman, and I was loyal in every way to Carl once I was committed, but I knew that there were places in my heart for Jehan and Luke and even LP, and these were sacrosanct. Recovering from Jehan's death had taken a collective effort. Luke, LP and I had suffered my rage and grief together, and for that reason, they were forever associated in my mind with Jehan. Luke was the last person left in my world who had known Jehan, who had known the old me before September 1986, who dared say Jehan's name to me. Even if the love died, faded, withered away, this link to my past, the past in which I was convinced I had led a charmed life, was too important to throw away. Falling in love with Carl, and being in love with him all these years hasn't changed that. What I hadn't bargained for, such was my hubris born out of my inflated sense of my own trauma, was that neither Luke nor Carl would feel the same way. Luke, especially, never understood the delineation in my mind between lover and friend, boyfriend and the deeper role of support he had unwittingly played. He insisted for years to come that he wanted all or nothing.

I sat up all night, staring out of the dirty second A/C compartment window, knowing that I had done Luke a huge wrong but sure that it was the right thing to do. I worried, too, that I didn't love Carl. Not just yet. Not the way I loved Luke. Certainly not as much as Carl obviously loved me. The train drew into Bay City Central Station without any resolution of these doubts, just a growing dread of the phone call I knew would come that evening, as it had done for the past few years.

Luke called from a mall, where he and the guys had gone to see a rock show.

'Hi, Dumbo, you're back?'

'It's over, Luke.'

Silence.

'Is it Carl?' he asked.

'No, it's us. We're done.'

We were both crying when I hung up. Later, LP told me the bare details of the long night, all of them getting drunk and keeping watch over Luke. I wandered out of the room in tears, and for once, Honey was there to ask what had happened.

'I broke up with Luke.'

Unpredictable Honey, maverick to the end, was shocked.

'You've lied and cheated to be with him all these years, and now you're breaking up with him? Liana, are you sure?'

'I'm with Carl now,' I confessed.

She just patted my head and said nothing. I knew the new development made her happy but she was still taken aback at the sheer ruthlessness of my decision, my brutality, I think. Perhaps she saw, for the first time, a reflection of herself in my set face.

I'd asked Carl to give me a few days in which to lay my old relationship to rest, to say goodbye, close one chapter before starting another. This was mostly so that I could pretend to ignore the facts: I'd left Luke, much as I had predicted I would, every time we fought about Jehan's death and its aftermath. I had left him at a time when he was struggling, among other things, with a huge backlog of college work. Nothing I said or did would take away my bad girl status now. I was the bitch who had ditched a guy who had never swerved from our relationship. I was cut out of the gang. Except LP, everyone else was firmly on Luke's side. After all, I had a brand new boyfriend. I had my life all sorted. So naturally, they rallied around Luke. The first few days passed in a blur of emotional phone calls and meetings.

The morning after we broke up, Luke called.

'I'll be waiting at the park.'

I walked over to the neighbourhood park. It was raining, a steady drip-drip, clammy and grey. He hadn't slept the night before, I had cried all night, he was hung over and we both behaved very badly. I cried again, and so did he.

'Please, just come back,' he pleaded.

I refused to reconsider.

'It's too late. It's over.' I kept repeating like a mantra.

He dropped me off to college, still weeping, the rain still washing down, so that I was alternately comforting him and worrying whether he would be all right. I made him promise to call me in the evening and headed into college a mess. Annie caught up with me as I wandered in, dazed and upset.

'Hey, Li, what's up? Missed the bus?'

I cried all over again as I told her what I had done.

'Wow, Li. Wow,' was all she could say in response. She hugged me tightly and we went off to the canteen, to drown my sorrows in a cup of coffee.

The phone rang that afternoon. It was Luke, calling from LP's room.

'Why did you write all those letters?' he asked sadly. 'You didn't say a word about this.'

'But you knew, anyway, didn't you? Even before I left. Going to Bombay didn't end us, Luke. We were done before I left.'

'Easy for you to say. You came back with a brand new boyfriend. You couldn't resist how rich he is, all the fancy cars and stuff he can buy for you?'

I protested that it wasn't about the money. That we fought all the time. I had to get out.

'We were happy, Liana. We were fine until this guy, this Carl, decided he wanted you for himself.'

'Go to hell, Luke, no one decides for me.'

I slammed the phone down, only for it to ring again five minutes later.

'Please, Dumbo, come back. Let's just forget this happened.'

'I can't, Luke. It's too late. I got a present for you though—a backpack. Let's meet. I want us to be friends, Dumbo.'

'Go to hell, Liana.'

His contention that Carl had tempted me with a taste of the so-called high life was rubbish. Carl had tempted me but with the finer things—the offer of an equal relationship, with no insecurities and angst, the promise of respect for my intellect and ambition. Luke refused to see this, and he was the wronged person here, so I left it alone.

I met him at LP's house a couple of days later, where we both behaved badly again. At one point, he had me pinned to the floor, desperately trying to get me to kiss him. I was scared and angry and guilty so I of course did the unforgivable thing—I laughed in his face and dared him to get a response from me. This only enraged him further, and he shouted at me for the first and only time in our years together.

'Don't you ever laugh at me! You, you...' and the word he bit off hung in the air after I struggled out of his arms and left the room.

A few friends tried to talk to me, to tell me that there

was still time, that I could stop this, go back. We were after all the golden couple, the two who had been through hell and back together.

'You guys made the temperature shoot up, you know, when you entered a room,' mused LP. 'Are you sure you want this, Liana?'

All I could tell him was that I still loved Luke, but that I had to leave. And Carl was offering me a way out.

I was sure I wanted that but I might not have been if I'd seen the future, one in which Luke dropped out of my life completely. I had imagined we would cry together about our lost romance, then shake it off and go back to being there for each other. I marvel now at my selfishness. I broke his heart and expected that he would still be my friend forever? I had made him my whole world, but equally, he had done the same for me. Now there was Carl and me, and he was alone.

Oddly enough, I was drawn to Carl for the same reason that I wanted to hold on to Luke. Carl had absolutely no connection to my past; the word Jehan meant nothing to him. He was confident, looking forward to a great future, with seemingly no conflicts at all. The only thing he didn't have to spare was time. He was heading off to graduate school the coming summer and leaving Bay City in the next few months, four years of college behind him. He left me alone for the first couple of months but then firmly made his position clear. It was now or never. Either I was in this relationship or I wasn't.

For the first time since the age of fifteen, I had to weigh

the pros and cons on my own. So I did it. I made the decision for all three of us.

And never regretted it.

Not even years later, when Luke and I realized how long we had waited for the other to come back. A friend who suggested that Carl and I could have our fling and then I would naturally return to Luke, found himself cut off abruptly from my life for the next several years. I heard of another dear friend who had joked about my loose morals, and that since I was now putting out for one and all, perhaps he stood a chance with me after Carl was done. I did not waste another thought on him, and he remains dead to me.

It was hard, but it must have been much harder for Luke. I sent back all his cards and presents, all the little reminders of the last four years. He sent back equally meticulously all the gifts and cards I had given him. I returned his shirt, he returned the backpack. Some people took delight in feeding me little bits of gossip: that he had called me a bitch, that he was eyeing a friend's sister, who bore some resemblance to me, other hurtful stuff. I didn't know what to believe so I believed the worst. Unthinkingly, I had finally closed the circle from September 1986. I had walked out on him and hurt him dreadfully—in payment for the words in my brother's suicide letter. By leaving him, I had meted out a final punishment on myself as well. That old obsession was back. How could I be in love and happy? How could I be alive when Jehan was dead? And yet, I did not have the courage to take this reasoning to its logical conclusion. I was weak enough to need love, and companionship, just not Luke's. I would settle for less. I would compromise. At that time, I didn't know I had done myself and him the most enormous favour of all by breaking things off. He admitted this to me many years later—it kindled some gut impulse inside him as well, the need to prove himself, to make a success of his life.

What I thought I was settling for, compromising with, turned out to be the love of my life—not the high drama, high intensity, lightning bolt first love I was still getting over, but a steady, stable and secure love that shone in my darkest places like the searching beam of a lighthouse. Carl did not treat me like some special goddess who deigned to shower her favours on him. He wasn't insecure about what he was bringing to the relationship. And he was candid about his needs and desires, fully expecting that I would meet him halfway and as an equal partner.

While Carl was still in town, I didn't have the time to miss Jehan or Luke. He made me so happy, and the last six months of his college passed quickly. Before he returned to Bombay, I had a farewell party for Carl at my place and the surprise guest was Luke. I asked him to dance, and he agreed for the first time in my memory. We danced for only a few seconds, me smiling brightly, him refusing to meet my eye, before he abruptly turned away and left me stranded on the dance floor.

Carl swung me into his arms, muttering, 'Forget it, he's just upset,' and the momentary hurt passed.

I was in a completely different place now, very happy

and discovering a new side of my personality—a confident person who thrived on Carl's encouragement to be free, independent and even ambitious. We had much in common and many things we didn't see eye to eye on, like any couple. But there was no sulking, no screaming, just lots of lively discussion and argument that never descended into fights. Carl was inherently optimistic and realistic; he was driven though admittedly with no real experience of a hard-knock life. He did not believe in overthinking situations and preferred to let bygones be bygones. He looked to our shared future ahead even as I clung to my past. In the end, it was his relentless, unwavering belief in that future that pulled me out of the dark place I had been in since Jehan's death.

But before that, it was time for Carl to leave for college, and so it was that months after the breakup, I found myself back in my dark place without Luke. And I was completely unprepared for the sense of loss that hit me. I realized too late that he really was my best friend first—we knew every little bit of each other's hopes and fears and dirty secrets. And now, with a snap of my fingers, he was gone. All my stupid selfish dreams of us picking up the pieces as friends for life went with him. There was no one to lash out at, to scream at when the floodtide came rushing in, no one who could speak Jehan's name to my face without flinching. I began to be frightened. Without him, I was going to lose what was left of Jehan. Already, four short years later, I could not recollect the timbre of his voice, the things he said, in his own peculiar way, the way he held his body, loose-limbed and guarded all at once.

With Carl half a world away in Kentucky, working on a master's degree, and LP studying away from home as well, I began a new conversation. With Luke, the one I alluded to before—inside my head. About everything that I could not share with anyone else. I asked him what to do about my night terrors and my day dreams. I imagined what he might have replied: 'Dumbo, stop feeling sorry for yourself.' Or 'Jehan had his demons—you have to let him go.' Or even just the familiar half-groan half-snarl of frustration after we had gone round and round in circles, snapping at each other. Sometimes, I shared happy news with him, laughed with him, commemorated five years, ten years, fifteen of Jehan's passing with him.

Once, the same year that Carl left, at a New Year's Eve party, we—the real Luke and I—got drunk, and it led to some canoodling on the dance floor, and later that night, in my building lift. I confessed to Carl on our next phone call and we both chose to forget about it. Luke and I met only a couple of times after that party. Once at a memorial service for a close friend. We wept together and he held me tight. That day, I stepped into Amita's home for the first time since Jehan's death. Rama Miss reminisced about Jehan to me, calling him her lemming for some strange reason. This only made me even more hysterical. A few days later, I lent Luke my notebooks, the ones in which I wrote my stories and poems and journal. I had written a poem about our late friend and he had wanted to read it. I never saw my books again. Luke made excuses for not returning them to me until

I got tired of asking for them. I had stopped writing anyway. A lifetime later, he confessed that the notebooks had moved around with him until in one move, he had lost them. I even forgave him for that loss.

We met again, later that year, at a beautiful hill station wedding of some friends, and I made him promise that he would be there at my wedding. He moved to the US soon after and we lost touch.

Carl and I weathered a four-year long-distance relationship: first while he was away in the US, and I was finishing college and a disastrous attempt at a master's in Microbiology back in my hometown, then while he was back in Bombay and starting his career and I was finishing up a master's degree (successfully this time) in Pune. We got married the week after my exams were done.

Luke married an American girl in 1997. Ironically, when he first moved to the US, he ended up in the same university town that Carl had just left after two years. Carl and Luke's wife had even known each other very casually. He did send me a wedding invitation but I didn't attend, based as I was in Bombay.

The next time we met was in 2008, at LP's wedding.

USA/Bombay, 2008–2018

KARTHIK CALLED ONE morning, a strange note of suppressed excitement in his voice:

'CD! I'm in love! I'm getting married!'

'LP, slow down,' I stuttered. 'Who? What? When? You ass, didn't think to run it by me?'

'Ah, CD, I'm all grown up now, I don't need your help any more. I found a beautiful girl all on my own and she loves *me* and wants to marry *me*!'

We laughed together and agreed that this was the best news ever.

'But, CD, I need you there, okay? I can't get married without all you guys with me—Dr Frankenstein slash thangachi (younger sister) has to give me away!'

Of course, I'd be there. I had spent too much energy and time polishing up this diamond to miss out on his big day. It was only later that it dawned on me that it was turning into quite the reunion—Luke and Joe, their two sisters, LP, me, with a supporting cast of Fali and Preeti, Carl and Luke's wife, and of course the beautiful bride. And a passel of children. We were all going to be together after almost eighteen years. A month before the wedding, I got an email from Luke.

It'll be good to catch up, it said.

I had spent years imagining this reunion, but now that it was round the corner, I could not admit to myself the deep emotional heft this meeting carried, for me at least. I kept telling myself that we were different people now, with families of our own, and wildly different lives. It was going to be just fine. There would be no fallout, no repercussions from this one meeting. Would there?

The evening we reached Fali's home (LP's bride was from the same city in the US where Fali and Preeti had settled), the phone rang. It was a very drunk and very happy Luke. LP and his fiancée were out at a bar with him and a few others.

'Hey, Chinoy, are you sulking? After all these years? We should be partying tonight, Dumbo!' he blurted out.

'Hi, Luke, listen, the kids are tired, and we came in only this afternoon. We'll meet tomorrow?'

'I was looking forward to seeing you tonight! Silly woman...okay, I'm gonna paaarrrtyyy!' he said, as if we had spoken last only yesterday, instead of years ago.

The next day, Luke came over to Fali's house to deliver some wedding paraphernalia from LP's fiancée. Everyone stood around politely making conversation in the kitchen while I locked myself in the bedroom upstairs and wept. I wept because Fali and Luke and Carl were outdoing themselves with good manners and friendly banter. My heart was beating out of my chest just listening to their voices. It was a scene straight out of some long-forgotten nightmare, the setting as surreal as they come. I wanted to scream at Luke—why was he not in my corner? After everything was weighed and balanced, we should have been in the same corner. Why was it so easy for him to switch sides, to casually chat with Fali and try his best to impress Preeti, to speak with Carl as if they were long-lost buddies, while my voice died in my throat and it felt like I was having a cardiac arrest, just listening to his voice through the door?

The plan that May morning was to meet outside LP's fiancée's home, and then about ten of us in the bridal party were heading to the sky-diving school to watch while LP and a few others attempted a supremely foolhardy first-time skydive, just one day before his thirty-sixth birthday and three days before the wedding! As the best man didn't seem to be bothered that this wedding was in some danger of never really taking off, I took LP aside and gave him some pointed notes on crazy Americans, impulsive actions and the like.

He simply beamed and said, 'I love her and she wants me to do it.'

No arguing with a besotted man, I thought. Anyway, they were soon waving to us, climbing aboard that tiny plane, headed out for the wild blue yonder.

The exercise consisted of climbing into a jumpsuit, then into a toy plane without doors, then up 14,000 feet and into a harness attached to a sky-diving instructor, and then, after all that climbing was done, throwing oneself into space and free-falling for about 4,000 feet before pulling open a parachute and floating gently back to Earth. It was simply terrifying. At least that was how I initially convinced myself it to be. I tried ignoring the faint voice inside my head that whispered, 'Chicken liver, you'd love to do this, but you're too scared!'

I tried arguing back: 'I have a husband and two kids to worry about. Besides, that plane doesn't look in very great shape *and* it's a rather expensive way to kill yourself!'

But that whisper became a shout, and before I knew it, I was telling a reluctant husband that I loved him but I wanted to do this desperately, and calling my kids to tell them I loved them too (just in case!).

Then I was off, with this short little instructor—I'll just call him Asterix—climbing into the plane with ten huge paratroopers who were also diving out of it. We climbed almost vertically, and then, at 14,000 feet, the paratroopers gave me a thumbs-up and casually stepped out of that plane, as if they were stepping into the next room. Finally, it was just Asterix and myself.

We crawled on our hands and knees to the door, tightly harnessed together, so tightly, in fact, that he quipped, 'Don't worry; I'm a happily married man!'

So, of course, not to be outdone, I shouted back, 'And I'm a happily married woman!'

Joking over, he shouted to me that he was going to gently rock us back and forth, and when I was ready to jump, I only had to say so.

At the door, for the first time, I felt a little thrill. For the first time in thirty-six years, I was about to do the kind of crazy, irresponsible thing I'd always dreamt of doing, letting go of years of inhibition and self-doubt, risking a life that had been overly-protected up until... '*Now!*' I shouted, and we were streaking through cold cloud, falling so fast I forgot to breathe!

I tried to scream, but there was no air in my lungs, my cheeks were actually flapping against the little wind there was. Asterix was shouting in my ears, 'Breathe, enjoy this, it's your first jump!'

And then it began. That rush of pure adrenaline. It was as if every cell in my body was jump-started during that initial free fall. Just as I was beginning to get used to the wind roaring in my ears, my instructor hauled on the parachute and suddenly we were at a standstill in the middle of the sky, and everything around me became so quiet, so peaceful, that all I could think was, 'Oh wow, oh wow!' I know that's not very articulate, but getting a bird's eye view of the world for the first time can have that effect—it can make you incapable of coherent thought.

We floated on the thermals for what seemed like a small eternity. If I were religious, or sentimental even, I'd have had a prayer of thanks on my lips or tears in my eyes. All I experienced that afternoon, however, was a sense of peace that had escaped me for over twenty-odd years.

When we finally floated down, making a clumsy landing, I hugged my husband, the instructor, and anyone else within huggable distance. I felt the rage from earlier that morning slowly fade, leaving behind a calmer woman, ready to take a deep breath and face the next few days with some equanimity. Ready to face Luke, without the threat of an imminent meltdown.

The next day, Luke and LP swung by to pick me up for the wedding rehearsal. I was determined to show him that I was totally unaffected by our meeting. I did a fine job, teasing him about needing LP for protection, touching his arm casually, watching him blink in dismay. He certainly never forgot that afternoon—the sari I was wearing, the conversation in the chapel ('Are you happy?'), while LP wandered the grounds, giving us some space. He could have stuck around for we barely paid him any notice. I was happily married, but bored and stupid. He was unhappily married, bored and reckless. We had two boys apiece, no little girl that we had dreamt of. The setting of the wedding in a romantic woodland chapel, the bride's dad mistaking us for husband and wife (we were both in the wedding party), LP's mom making sure we sat apart in separate pews—it all added up to a flood of nostalgia. We were overwhelmed, that's for sure. There was so much to catch up on, an entire lifetime to share with an old friend. For me, all the years of hoping and waiting for just such a meeting were finally over.

We stayed in touch sporadically for the ten years after LP's wedding. We spoke rarely, usually while he was driving home late at night from work. After the initial 'Did you know?'s and 'Oh my God, really?'s our conversations became more reflective, introspective, personal. That was when we reluctantly realized how far we had wandered away from each other. He was a workaholic, rarely seeing his children awake during the week. He once told me that the one piece of advice he would give his teenagers was never to commit to a steady relationship, to play the field, to keep things light, to not give their hearts away like he'd done. That cut very close to the bone. He liked his alcohol a bit too much for my peace of mind. That was all he allowed me to see; he was still hiding.

In contrast, I was an open book, happily sharing stories of my family and a devoted husband who came home at six each evening, and was a major part of our children's lives. I had given up hiding long ago, and I worked very hard to stay as honest as I could with myself and the people I loved. Sometimes, our conversations would bring the old feelings of sorrow and guilt rushing back, and sometimes I was foolish enough to think that he was ready for an equal friendship, when in reality, he just needed a diversion from the unhappy situation at home. I had waited years to be his friend again, and I walked back into a familiar situation without any resistance. In this well-played-out scenario, he could be defensive, hide behind walls and still expect me to be there waiting when he needed a friend. In the end, what had been barely enough for seventeen-year-old me fell woefully short for the forty-year-old. I demanded give and take, a real friendship, and he simply did not have the resources for that, dealing as he was with his own personal issues. It was inevitable that most of the conversations were sentimental and foolish, collapsing into blazing rows—we still couldn't agree on almost anything. Still, we were speaking. Him in riddles, me in angry exclamations. And slowly, without ever being aware of it, we were making our way through the stages of grief, as we mourned our youth and the love we had abandoned so abruptly. I am so grateful for those couple of calls annually, sometimes angry, often sad, and always frustrating. My accusations that he hadn't kept up his end of our understanding met with incredulous anger, the bitterness in his voice often silencing me.

'Hey, you left me, or don't you remember?'

'I waited, Liana, I waited seven years, for you to come back.'

'You just waltz back into my life and expect me to open up? To you? You want me to say I've been lonely without you? Is that it? You wanna gloat?'

'Forget it, Liana, it's not going to happen.'

We argued over all this until we were both exhausted. Then we talked some more. I once even told him about the conversations I used to have with him.

'What conversations?' he asked.

'Inside my head. Secret ones. For years and years.'

'You're kidding, right?'

'I used to tell you almost everything that happened in my life. The day my kids were born, when I was happy or sad...'

'Stop it now, this is weird.'

'Yeah, I know. But it didn't seem right that you didn't know, so I'm telling you.'

He laughed incredulously, convinced that I was making it all up. He was embarrassed at my intensity, when all those years ago, it was his intense nature that sent us careering down a dead end.

'What do you mean, you still love me? How can you? You're with someone else! You're happy!'

'It's not love like romantic love, Luke. It's like there's a connection—shit, I don't know how to explain it.'

'No, because there's no such thing. Love is love—romantic, sexual, whatever. Anything else isn't love, not to me, not the way I define it, anyway.'

'Well, it is to me. I don't want to be with you, I don't even like you most of the time. You're such an asshole. But I love you like I love LP...no, in a different way. Like soulmates?'

'Don't believe in that, Liana. Never have, never will.'

I gave up trying to explain. The only thing we agreed upon was that we would have made each other miserable if we'd stayed together. I understood with renewed gratitude just how lucky I was to have found Carl, listening to this stranger who I had once imagined was to be my forever. Luke and I had grown into two vastly different individuals; our younger selves would not have given each other a second glance. At the very heart of the relationship, a bond remained, but not much else. To paraphrase Rumi, our hearts were old friends.

Each time we met, or spoke, we unravelled one more knot in our long and complicated association. I resisted this at first, haunted by the resurgent fear that letting go of Luke, now that we had found each other again, would sound the death knell for my fragile memories of Jehan. Then I would take a step back, remind myself that we hadn't been in touch for over a decade, and Jehan was as alive in my memory as he had ever been, perhaps a little worse for wear. The realization made the unravelling that much easier. I had held on for so long and so tightly to my past—to the people in it, dead and alive, present and absent. Now, the learning was in the letting go.

And then, one day in 2017, our conversation suddenly turned into something very different. It had been some months since we last spoke, and as usual, after about twenty minutes, I said:

'It's late. Don't you need to go into the house?'

He replied: 'Are you sitting down? I have something to tell you.'

My first response was, 'Are the kids okay?'

And he laughed and said, 'Yeah. I moved out a few months ago. I'm getting a divorce.'

That day, we spoke for over two hours, trying to bridge the gaps of the last twenty-five years. He finally told me the story of the years he went missing. From the time he disappeared after our breakup right up to the time he got married. He made me cry that day, the hope and innocence creeping back into his voice after years of bluster and fake laughter. He told me of his first job, teaching a class full of standard twelve teenagers, and advising them on careers in computers, when he himself had only recently been catching up on semesters at college.

'Can you imagine me, *me*, teaching a class of teenagers? Hell, I didn't feel much older than them, and there I was, giving these kids career advice.'

We laughed at the disbelief in his voice all those years later.

'But I was a good teacher. The kids loved me.'

It made me so proud to hear of that distant achievement. It's hard to describe what I felt during that phone call, really. It's not as if I reached some instant magical resolution, or that my old ghosts were suddenly ordered to their rest. But we were finally talking truthfully, positively, about the missing parts of our lives. I think we made peace with each other and ourselves that day.

The realization that I could finally lay my burden of guilt down was a long time coming. He was not responsible for Jehan's death in any way. No one was. I was not a bad person for falling in and then out of love with him. It happened. It was good, even great while it lasted, and then it was over. He had been unhappy for a long time, but now at last, he was free and happy. I heard it in his voice, in his laughter that day, in the way he opened up secret places for me to walk through. The sound of that clear laugh, it was a sigh that went through my mind, cleaning old wounds, clearing out the cobwebs and darkness, as it were. I had spent years feeling responsible for his anger, his pain and guilty because once again, a person I loved was unhappy and I couldn't say with certainty if it was my fault or not. But that day in 2017, I began to acknowledge that I was no longer responsible for his happiness and well-being. I was only responsible for my own peace of mind, and if by letting him go in the best sense of the word, I could achieve that for the both of us, then I was finally ready to step up. This was the truth that I finally acknowledged and accepted twenty-eight years after we broke up, thirty-two years after my brother killed himself because of untreated manic depression. The truth set us both free.

And so, I let my best friend go. I gave Luke his own place in my mind and in my heart, and gave Jehan his separate place there as well. Letting go of Luke could no longer take away Jehan's memories. I said goodbye to Honey the following year, and in the grief of that farewell, I said goodbye to Jehan too. I found my writing in the grieving, and a part of myself that had been lost for so long.

Bombay, 2018...

FALI AND I were just getting to know each other when Jehan died. Our tentative connection was lost as we stumbled away in the dark, and drifted apart. Fali and Honey were more alike than he cared to admit. They set their faces and moved on—not for them the shameful flood of tears and regret, not for them the family grieving. The years of silence on my part were compounded by my adult perception that neither of them would welcome any attempt by me to sit down, talk about Jehan, his unhappiness, our helplessness, his death. That is, if I could have mustered up the courage. The very thought of broaching this subject frightened me then (frightens me now)—the blank stare that could reduce me to incoherence, the wall of silence that effortlessly shut me out. Just a word from either of them was enough—if Fali's casual threat to 'rave at me' left me speechless, Honey's quietly said, '*Bas* (Enough), Liana, not now,' had much the same effect. Eruch followed Honey's example, and declared that it upset him too much to talk of Jehan. His hand would creep to the general environs of his famously faulty heart and that was that.

At the time of my marriage, Fali and I were polite, formal siblings with nothing in common and very little to say to one another. He had moved with his family to greener pastures the year before. Our lives had always been absent of each other, and this was no different. It didn't matter whether Fali lived in the same city as I did, or whether he lived half a world away. In the nine years between Jehan's suicide and my wedding, I could count the number of occasions on which Fali and I had spoken about something significant—never. Jehan was a subject that I had not dared to broach, and one that Fali never mentioned, and I imagined that his happy marriage, his wife and children had erased the unsavoury memory of a flawed brother. I had kept my distance. As much as I trusted my deepest feelings and emotions to LP and Luke, literally spending my adolescence in LP's home, one street away from Fali and Preeti's flat, I found it almost impossible to share memories, grieve or mourn Jehan in front of my own brother.

Once Zarir disappeared from our lives, the family stopped talking to each other completely. At least Zarir had goaded us to talk a little about old times, about Jehan. Now we all retreated: Eruch and Honey into their bedroom, I to LP's home or into my room, the one I was finally sole owner of after Fali and Preeti moved to a separate flat and drifted away into their own world. A world of which Carl was very much a part. Preeti and he enjoyed each other's company, she treating him as she would her own younger brother.

So when Carl and I announced our wedding plans, Fali

and Preeti were almost as delighted as Eruch and Honey. Perhaps they felt that at last I would become fully a part of their world, of their lives, as Carl was. They returned home for my wedding, laden with gifts and gestures of love and affection. Though it took me by surprise, I was desperate enough for a fairy-tale start to my marriage to be swayed by all the glitz and glamour, to be enticed by this stranger who now behaved like the model older brother. I could have anything at all, Fali would proudly proclaim in the years that followed. He showered us with gifts, spoiling my kids silly. He insisted on splurging on amazing holidays for both families, refusing to accept our share of the cost from Carl.

'If I want to give my sister and my nephews a holiday, that's my right.'

They threw lavish parties when we visited them in their beautiful home, introducing me to his many friends as *his* sister. To say I was flattered into loving him would be an understatement. I was swept away by this outpouring of affection from a brother who had so far been kind but distant, very much a stranger. I chose to ignore that, in spite of all the love and affection, there was still no real relationship between us. My age-old fear of bringing up the topic of Jehan was only matched by Fali's effortless and often unconscious ability to put me in my place—the baby of the family, the one who still froze if Fali raised his eyebrows at me and said: 'Enough, Liana.'

In the years that followed my wedding, I moved away from home, found a new life with Carl and we started our own family. The four of us were now scattered physically: Eruch and Honey in Bay City, Fali abroad and I in Bombay. We spoke on the phone, once a week to the parents and once a month to Fali. I was happy to share all the minutiae of our lives over these long phone calls, except that it was usually Preeti who listened, advised and commented. I remember that we laughed a lot.

Fali rarely said anything beyond a 'Hi, all okay? Good. Here's Preeti.'

And there was no question of reciprocating—their lives, their children, their careers, these subjects were all off-limits beyond the merely conversational. There was only so far we could go while talking to or about his kids. Our relationships were superficial, revolving around holidays and shopping. It was clear that many topics were taboo—his childhood, his separation from us, and especially Jehan's life and death.

Fali was the exemplary husband, father and son-in-law. He made sure that Eruch, Honey and I saw the pride he felt in this new and normal family he had created for himself. The comparisons were obvious. This was what he had deserved all along, not the flawed and dysfunctional family he had been born into. His family adored him and for all the right reasons: he was loyal, loving and faithful to the three of them. He worked very hard to give them the lifestyle he felt they deserved. There was nothing he wouldn't do for them. In short, he was everything to his kids that he'd been denied as a child himself. He was always there for his children, barely letting them out of his sight while they were growing up.

He protected them fiercely from the ugliness of his past life and by extension from the three members of his birth family.

I remained blithely oblivious to this undercurrent for many years, content to bask in the attention and love lavished on me by this suddenly perfect brother. I condoned his reluctance to discuss our past, happy or otherwise, as just another quirk in a brother I loved. But there were two occasions when my gut instinct sounded warning bells, and these I ignored as symbols of my past paranoia. The first time that I was reminded that something was not quite right about our happy family, that we were still that dysfunctional group of strangers bound by blood, was during a summer holiday. We were visiting them, and as always, a huge party had been organized. We were lounging around listening to music after the barbecue.

I was a little drunk on all the attention and alcohol by then, so when 'Hotel California' began to play, I cheerfully said, 'Oh, Jehan used to bring the house down when he sang this!'

Fali stiffened in one corner of the room, but I barely noticed.

One of his friends turned to me and asked, 'Who is Jehan?'

And before my brain could stop my tongue, I replied, 'Jehan? He's my other brother!'

There was silence as the entire group of Fali and Preeti's friends became quiet.

And then, seemingly unstoppable, I said, 'But he died many years ago.'

In that second between my two utterances, some instinct had kicked in and I didn't articulate how he had died. It took me a couple of days to register that Fali may have chosen never to tell his new friends in his new home about Jehan. Jehan was dead, buried. Was he also forgotten? No answer, because I still could not bring myself to ask Fali. Fali never mentioned my faux pas, and if Preeti had a steely look in her eyes when she stared at me, I was too frightened to wonder why. Still, I went prowling around their great big house the next time everyone else was out. I wandered into the sacred spaces: their bedroom and Fali's study. I knew what I was looking for and I didn't find it there. I looked into the formal dining room and the parlour. Nothing. I went down the steep flight of stairs to the cavernous basement. In the game room, nothing. Then, tucked away in a dark corner of a disused book case, I found it—a photograph of Jehan. Forever out of the limelight, our rock star brother, smiling his mocking smile at me. There were no other photographs scattered around their pristine home either, but it hurt all the same.

The second time was soon after, when my teenaged niece stood in front of Jehan's photograph on my piano and asked me, in her sweet, Southern accent: 'How did Jehan Mama die?'

This time, I knew better than to babble. I said to her, fully aware of two pairs of ears straining to hear my reply, and of two parents primed to jump in and recue their innocent child, 'That's something you should ask your dad.'

As with all else about their lives, I don't know if and when Fali and Preeti shared the story of Jehan's life and death with their children. It is clearly none of my business. And anyway, who am I, with my screwed-up worldview, to judge their parenting?

I am the mother who refused to have locks put on the doors in my kids' bedroom; who planned emergency entrances instead of exits so that I would never have to break down a door. I am the parent who broke down upon being told that my younger son had been born with a hole in the heart, not because it threatened his life in any way, but because I was sure I would have to plan his funeral one day soon. No doctor or scan, or even the happy healthy child himself, could convince me otherwise for the longest time. It was only slowly, as with each panic attack, that the absurdity of the fear struck me and it subsided.

As my older son became a teenager, I watched him, hawk-like, for signs of...anything at all. I hovered about him, I obsessed, I imagined each flaw in Jehan's personality magnified hundred-fold in my child. It got unbearable for him and for me. Finally, his dad, in a rare moment of intervention, asked me why I was behaving so badly. I broke down and explained that I was frightened that the genes I had passed on might flare up like some dormant creature in my son's mind. Once again, Carl only pointed out the simple truth:

'He has my genes too.'

And I could lay to rest one more demon of my own creation.

I am the mother who, once, in the middle of a screaming match with my thirteen-year-old son, accused him of not caring enough about his little brother.

'Are you waiting for him to die before you realize you love him? Or miss him?'

And howled on another occasion, when the kids had shouted to each other to 'DIE! Just DIE', and 'I'M GONNA KILL YOU':

'You don't know anything about dying! My brother died! He died and I could do nothing about it! Stop talking about dying and killing each other—you little brats have *no* idea what it means!'

That phase thankfully passed but the damage had been done to my relationship with my older son. He bore the brunt of my inability to deal with this grief, every time I lashed out at him or forced him to live up to unreasonably high standards. All because I was convinced for many years that my brother had been spoilt rotten by my parents. His demands were always met and they were ultimately helpless against his many threats of suicide, paralysed with fear really, finally leading to his death. So I set out to be the opposite kind of parent. Strict, loving but demanding, never showering my kids with gifts, making them wait for and earn every reward.

My son, all credit to him, weathered these stormy years by sensibly distancing himself from his mom, and getting on with his own life as best as he could. We both grew up in those years. When my kids were fifteen and seventeen, a famous musician whose music they loved, took his own life. My younger son, especially, was distraught.

'But, mom, he was so happy. He posted a video just two days ago playing with his kids. Why did he kill himself?'

Mom had no answers. It seemed like an appropriate time to tell them about Jehan, all of it. I had made an uneasy peace with myself and I had never been ashamed of him, his life or his death: I told them so. They were cool.

'Oh, yeah, we always knew.'

'How? I never said a word to you guys.'

Eye-rolling ensued.

'Yeah, of course. I mean, duh! Jehan Mama was gay and he probably killed himself.'

'Chill, mom, I won't kill myself, if that's what you're worried about.'

And, 'You were so paranoid, mom—we couldn't ever joke about suicide or gays. So we figured it out.'

That laid to rest a troubled motherhood, and years of worrying about hereditary traits and locked doors and whether I would have to one day attend one of my children's funerals.

I understood that I was in great need of professional help, but I had spent too many years being self-sufficient and dealing with the guilt and anger on my own, guarding my grief jealously. To let it out would cause great pain to the ones who did not deserve any more, I felt. I had become my own therapist. I read obsessively about homosexuality, and AIDS, about depression and suicide, until I truly thought I had managed the trauma of a lifetime. I had never been short on pride and it kept telling me I could handle this too on my own terms.

When my older son went away to college, our equation changed, became more peaceable. Life was happy. There were months that went by without thinking of the past. I thought I was finally done with my brother's death. I felt the time had come to reach out to others, share my story and my brother's story, perhaps do my bit towards preventing another death by suicide.

So some years ago, I applied to the Human Library Project and was accepted as a book. This involved telling my story to groups of strangers. The first session, when I laid down my history, was frightening. I had imagined I might break down, but instead, I found myself smiling and laughing. It unnerved my audience at first but we reached a tacit understanding that the relief of finally talking about Jehan was so great I couldn't help the unconventional behaviour. Any panic I had felt initially slowly subsided.

The Human Library was as much therapy for me as it was a means to share Jehan's life and death with others. I was wary at first of the tears these strangers cried, the hugs they offered, the grief that spilt out of their own stories. I was taken aback at their reactions—everyone had a story to share, it seemed. Sure, some older folk disapproved of what I was trying to achieve.

'You need to see a psychiatrist. You are deeply troubled.' 'How can you smile while taking about your brother? For heaven's sake, he killed himself.' And on and on.

The younger readers had a different perspective and they saved me.

'Thank you for doing this. I don't know who to talk to—my cousin/friend/mom/sister have tried to kill themselves.' 'Thank you for sharing your story. It's a relief to know there are others out there going through what I'm going through.'

All I could do was accept the hugs, urge them to find professional help and then repeat this story of mine for the next group who wandered in. I felt good about this new phase of my life. I was making a small difference. Jehan's life was making the difference. I still kept quiet about what I was doing of course. It's not as if I told Honey or Eruch or Fali about this new-found storyteller avatar of mine—I was feeling good, not reckless.

~

Honey died in 2018, after many years of debilitating blindness, and a second-round battle with breast cancer. She won round one, had three peaceful years and then the cancer came back, viciously and mischievously attacking the only faculty she still possessed in spades: her mind and intellect. She and Eruch had enjoyed the birth and babyhood of their four grandchildren, Honey doting especially on her eldest grandchild, Fali's daughter. That little baby was a grown woman of twenty-eight the year Honey died, and Honey had only seen her through a growing haze for the last twenty of those years. As her eyesight began to trouble her, and progressively deteriorated, Honey changed from the independent, outgoing mother I had known, to a nervous, obstinate and frightened woman. Eruch bore the brunt of her changed personality, and their loving relationship, always dominated by Honey, deteriorated into a series of toddler tantrums.

She insisted that he and only he could look after all of her many and exhaustingly endless needs. The moment he sat down, there would come a quavery: 'Eruch?' And he would sigh, and get up to fetch her a drink of water, or a hanky, or turn on the fan, or whatever she needed to reassure her of his presence. Everything that could possibly go wrong with her eyes had gone wrong—cataracts, detachment of the retina, a botched glaucoma treatment in one eye, and finally, cruelly, macular degeneration in the other eye. All her pleasures in life—reading, embroidery, painting, gardening, were lost to her. Her formidable intellect proved to be best friend and at the same time her worst enemy. She honed all her other senses to a sharp edge, listening intently to every murmured conversation, every nuance in voices around her, and drew her own conclusions and judgements from these. Stubbornly refusing to accept her blindness, she left audiobooks unheard, abandoned her precious books and switched her loyalty to the television. She took out all her anger on poor Eruch, who blamed himself for the botched glaucoma treatment. The doctors at the best eye institute in the country had given her a course of ophthalmic steroids and advised him to bring her back after three weeks of the treatment, even though he had wanted to bring her in every other day for monitoring the eye pressure. They overruled his worries, and diligent Eruch faithfully administered the high dose of steroids until the eye pressure rose to unmanageable limits and she lost sight in that eye. I think she secretly blamed him too: for his diligence? His faithfulness?

But it wasn't just her eyes: in her last years, she had battled a broken hip that had to be reset twice surgically, breast cancer and a mastectomy, and the loss of her confidence.

Eruch and I confessed to each other, only once, sitting in a bank of all places, that we both hoped that she would go first, because if she survived him, I would have to look after her, and no one except Eruch could really handle her eccentricities, plain pig-headedness and anger. But she was a formidable woman to the last. Whether it was because of a lust for life and an innate tenacity for dealing with its pains and sorrows, or from a debilitating fear of ever becoming more of a burden on anyone than she was already, she remained game for adventure till the end. She travelled, never refused a holiday or an outing. Only when the eyesight went completely, a week before she was leaving with Eruch for what was meant to be their last trip abroad, did she panic.

'I don't want to go,' the trembling voice came over the phone. 'I won't come back if I do. I'm frightened.'

And I said, 'Don't be silly, mom. Go and have a good time. The tickets are bought; you can't cancel now.' I am ashamed that I disregarded her very real fears that day.

Honey was right. A woman did return from a truncated holiday in the physical form but Honey herself never came back home. The cancer returned on that holiday after three years of remission, frightening in its aggression, and made its way to her brain. As the tumour grew, so did her ramblings, her outbursts at long-forgotten or imagined hurts and grievances. Eruch and I tried our best to hide these accusations and confessions from each other. She accused me of trying to murder her for her fabulous wealth: my mother, who owned almost nothing of monetary value. She threatened to call the cops and have me thrown in jail. The creative ways in which I was supposed to be trying to kill her off impressed even me. One morning, she gifted apartments to anyone who came rambling through her mind, very much in a grande dame manner. The only hitch was that those apartments belonged to Eruch's boss, the man her husband worshipped, causing Honey fits of jealousy no woman had ever aroused in her.

In that time between her diagnosis and her death, it often seemed to me that the real Honey had finally broken free of the shackles of social propriety. Her alter ego, the evil step sister, the scheming, conniving money-obsessed person she had valiantly kept hidden away, now burst forth. Friends and family remembered her generosity, her open-handedness. We saw her greed, her need for the material wealth that she felt her father had carelessly squandered away in his youth. They enjoyed her sense of humour, we felt the lash of her sarcasm, the finely honed sliver of steel she had passed down two generations—my own son could often reduce me to tears with his cruel words, just as Jehan had done. They remembered her fierce loyalty, we cringed under the intense hatred she bore for so many people. I learnt of a whole new person who lived behind my mother's face, and I did not like her at all. I comforted myself that it was the tumour talking, but really, the tumour was not to blame—it had only unleashed her innermost self. I couldn't have borne it for too long, that steady stream of vitriol. And through the haze, Honey knew this. She measured out her pain and anger in full, leaving me with a fresh perspective on this complex, complicated and confusing entity I called mom. Then she lay down, ordered her heart to stop beating, and brought her life to an end one short month after the tumour came calling.

The nursing staff at home were polite but one of the nurses couldn't help but ask:

'Mummy is asking for her son—he is coming, isn't he? The son should be there to feed her the last mouthful of food.'

I had no answer. The son Honey was asking for, recalled from ancient memory, was long dead. It was the son her mind no longer remembered couldn't be there.

I reflected on the irony of being a daughter when apparently only a son would do, even as I fed Honey a small bowl of aamras and a piece of fresh mango cake, both of which she lapped up like a kitten. Those were the last foods she ate. Neither one of her sons were at her bedside.

She lay there that afternoon, breathing shallow breaths. I stood by her bed, stroking her soft white hair that had been crawling with lice the day before. I had cleaned out each nit, revolted by the sight and determined to rid her of every last one of them. Now, as I stroked her hair, the nurse gestured to me not to touch the top of her head—the local custom dictated that the soul should have no hindrance as it left through the skull. Eruch wasn't in the room. I was alone with her when she took one, two, three breaths and then just stopped. Honey wasn't going to let a paltry end-stage malignant tumour have the final say in a lifetime spent relishing the last laugh, the cold revenge, the clinical response to grief and sorrow even. She went quietly at the end, having let me in on some of her secrets but without the solace of explanation. This too was so much in character I couldn't complain. Enigmatic, alone and contained, even as her heart gave out and her organs shut down.

~

Honey's death left me relieved at first—she had gone with minimal suffering and lying peacefully in bed at home. Then the anger erupted. At first, I didn't know where this was coming from. I would find myself trembling with rage without any reason. The months passed and the anger grew. It was as if Honey's death set me free to give vent to years of suppressed feelings. These, well-hidden and tamped down, came roaring out of me with an intensity that overwhelmed me. I stopped functioning, and allowed my mind to rage without any checks over imagined hurts, real betrayals and all the memories in between. Jehan's life, Jehan's death, Fali's visceral dislike and distrust of Honey, Honey's mind games, Eruch's pacifist nature, our family's uncanny ability to gloss over all the yawning cracks and pretend life was perfect—and most of all, my inability to speak out, to speak up. I raged against the too successful façade I portrayed to the world, while inside I lived in a vacuum. I was in free fall, and there was no one to pull open a parachute or offer a soft landing this time.

What came next was in some ways far worse than the rage. As the uncontrolled emotion receded, and it did, I found I had nothing left to say. No loyalties. Nor any feelings at all. Not for Fali, nor for Honey. And just as well. It took months of therapy to understand that I was no one special, no Sister with a capital S or Darling Daughter. I was just one of a broken, dysfunctional family obsessed with showing a happy and united front to the world.

A few days before Honey died, I was asked to speak to the children of my son's class about suicide, and the lasting effects (edited heavily) on the family and friends left behind. One of their classmates had killed herself and it was fresh in all of our minds. These were a bunch of bright sixteen-year-olds, and they heard me out with all the scepticism of their years. It was a short session and honestly amateurish. I was very nervous of leaving them with a wrong impression in any way, and so I was stilted and edgy. I didn't know it then, but this short session was the first step towards healing the anger that would threaten to overwhelm me after Honey's death. But that was in the future. For now, in the days following Honey's funeral, I spent my time alternately raging, then sobbing with sorrow, then swearing revenge and hell fire, until the endless cycle of grief had exhausted my family. My kids were stellar—quietly hugging me when I raged, helping at their grandmother's funeral, and staying out of my way when things got too stormy.

Honey died in my home in June of 2018. It was hard, mostly because I had imagined that Death had no hold over me any more, that all the tears I had cried gave me some immunity to fresh grief. I had lost a brother and two friends too young—the death of an old woman who had lived a life, mostly happy, shouldn't have affected me as much as it did. She died quietly, no fuss, an empty husk of a vibrant, fun-loving, generous, intelligent human being. But still I struggled.

At some point in time, after the stages of outward rage and grief and inner emptiness had passed, a small realization took root: I had spent years living in a cobwebbed mind, living two lives, living in silence. I had imprisoned myself over the years. Now, Honey had set me free. Dutiful daughter, compensator of loss, replacement for her favourite child—all these self-imposed duties fell away with her passing. I didn't have to stay silent about Jehan, in deference to her wishes. Not even Fali had the power to stop my words. Not without her tacit support. The lock placed around my grief was broken; I didn't even need a key.

~

I sat down one September morning, and wrote about Jehan. I had written about him on several occasions before, but no one, not even Carl, had been given a glimpse into my writing. This time, I sent it out into the internet for the world to read. It was my declaration of freedom from my past, and it was an ode to my brother.

September 5, 2018

Today is a happy day. My brother Jehan is no longer a criminal in his own country. Or at least, he wouldn't be one if he were still alive. 32 years ago, September 18, 1986, my 22-year-old rock star brother killed himself. He was gay, frightened, manic depressive, had too many demons to deal with and no real support.

Today, with the Supreme Court of India reading down Section 377 which had criminalized homosexuality, it felt like Jehan was for a brief moment and in an alternate universe, alive again. 54 years old, stylish, successful (possibly an interior designer or chef), happily or dramatically living in with a partner, spoiling his nephews, still bullying me about my fashion sense. Enjoying my older son's sarcasm, so like his own. Delighting in my younger son's wry humour. Holding my mother close, loving her as she lay dying, something I was incapable of doing and cursed myself for. I felt his loss most keenly while dealing with the loss of my mom.

So today is a happy day. One step forward towards a world where 22-year-olds easily and fearlessly accept themselves, and everyone around them accepts them for what they are—brown, pale, gay, hetero, undecided, driven, laid-back. In fact, no labels. Just be.

The sharing of this piece brought back a flood of emotion. Friends and family wrote back to say that they missed Jehan still, that they had hesitated to talk about him in the face of my silence. They shared with me their memories, happy and sad, their feelings of grief at his passing that they hadn't dared to share with me at the time. It was an overwhelming wave of love and support.

September is a cruel month though. It took Jehan in 1986, and suddenly, thirty-two years later, in 2018, a young cousin. This loss, coming a few months after Honey, hit all the harder because of his youth. But I was now finally free of the code of silence I had imposed upon myself for so many years, I finally stopped hugging my words and my thoughts to myself. I gave myself the permission to write and to talk again—to say Jehan's name out loud, to write about him, to acknowledge that he had been alive for twenty-two years—this boy, almost a man.

But the universe wasn't done with September yet.

~

Do you know that scene in a movie when a person lies on a hospital bed or operating table, surrounded by a team desperately working to revive her, while her ghost hovers somewhere near the ceiling, watching the goings on with a stunned expression? A large part of my life was suspended in moments like these. One part of me, the rational, intelligent, empathetic me, watched incredulously as the other me, raging, venomous and hurting, lashed out at people I loved, or any people actually, who simply didn't deserve this treatment. Sometimes the two switched sides. But always, these two parts of a whole, strangers to each other, were surrounded by people who could not understand the dichotomy or were unaware of its existence. Most people had been carefully allowed to see only one of the twins.

I felt lonely. But there also seemed to be a misplaced sense of superiority in me. I know I pitied many of my peers who had never yet faced the loss of a loved one. What did they know of real life? We'll talk when you have lived through trauma as deep-rooted as mine, I seemed to be telling them. Most people never made the mark. My closest friends had all faced loss early on. Father, brother, sometimes both, attempted suicides, suicides masquerading as accidents, depression, overdoses, divorce, even bankruptcy, all figured in our group's dynamic. The knowledge held us fast. This was our shared history. But most of us had never brought up these events in years. It was not something we discussed.

I had always known that I needed help. There were years when I didn't know how to ask for it, and years when I was filled with a hubris born of my self-designed therapy. Years of numbing out the grief blending into years of acting out and lashing out... Thirty-two years in all.

Recently though, I had begun to doubt my sanity on those nights when I woke up sweating after a dream of the night my brother killed himself. I doubted my character. Was I self-seeking? Narcissistic? Needy? Was I drawing attention to myself by refusing to let go? Worst of all, was I using Jehan's death to win friends and influence people? And most urgently, was I the only one who had been clinging so hard to the trauma and grief while others apparently had made their peace and moved on?

It was in September 2018 that I came across an article in the newspaper about a support group for people who had lost someone to suicide. I went with great trepidation to my first meeting. It was heart wrenching and brutal. I felt very old, rehashing decades old memories to people dealing with loss from a couple of years to a couple of months ago. But I found myself going back regularly.

The support group met once a month. It had a floating population. Sometimes we were four, sometimes eight. It was a new and rewarding experience for me. After thirty-two years of hardly ever talking about my brother's suicide, to be in a roomful of women who bared their lives to each other and shared thoughts about heartbreakingly similar feelings and experiences and broken relationships was cathartic. Suddenly, years of questions were answered. And no, I was not, and am not, the only one who couldn't let go.

We're mostly women. We grieve together, wipe away tears, hug and mourn our lost ones. We listen to the strangest stories. We hash and rehash old emotions, feelings of betrayal, anger, trust. We rage against the unfairness of it all, the waste of young lives. We wonder at the strange common threads in many of our stories. We share our relief that we aren't crazy or selfish or alone.

Most of our lost souls are men. Fathers, husbands, sons, brothers. The similarity does not end there. We are all dealing as well with the loss of the men who are still alive. The ones coping with grief through anti-depressant medication and alcohol and denial, who refuse to give us a chance to talk together and heal together.

So, sadly, a lot of our anger is directed towards the men in our lives. The ones who died, as well as the ones who live in isolation. The men we love but have drifted far away from. Brothers, husbands, fathers.

One day in my support group, we celebrated a birthday and a pregnancy. For the first time, we laughed together instead of crying together. Actually, we did both.

It feels like family. Not the one I was born into, but one I've chosen to be a part of. A family for the other me still hovering like a ghost in the corner. The nightmares continue and the doubts still linger. But I know the first Tuesday of the month will come again. Someone will offer a hug and unconditional understanding. We will smile through our tears and try to work out a new way to be. Surprisingly, it seems possible now. It's been a long, long time coming.

I also found a therapist to talk to. It was finally Carl, scientific tempered and rational, who quietly scoffed at New Age healing, who held me close one evening and suggested: 'I think you need to find someone to talk to about this anger you're feeling.'

The rage and grief I felt after my mother's illness and death had frightened me. My friends, like Carl, were concerned, and one of them inspired me with her courageous attempts to heal herself after a tragedy in her life. I was exhausted, mentally and emotionally, and that probably made it harder to convince myself that I didn't need help this time around. In truth, there had rarely been a time when I needed help more. Carl had held me and comforted me, but it was his acknowledgement that I needed professional help that ultimately changed my mind.

The body and mind heal at different speeds and in different ways. For me, talking to my therapist and writing were the tools I learnt to use, at first reluctantly, then with greater confidence.

One afternoon, an old friend and I exchanged notes on healing. Both of us had lost a sibling, she only a few years ago, me an eternity now. We spoke of carrying a weight, of grief and pain. We mused about the healing—the when and if of it. She signed off with a wonderful thought: we didn't come into the world bearing this pain, but we might still be able to put it behind us and move on.

My friend and I are dealing with loss in our own ways. Though we have experienced it at different stages in our lives, it is still all encompassing and overwhelming in its intensity. She is so much more emotionally intelligent than I am though. She realizes the pain is something to be dealt with, and that one day she will leave it behind. I wish for you, my friend, a healing that leaves you whole, changed but unbroken. I wish it for myself too. For the confused fifteen-year-old I was, for the young adult who lost out on love and then found it again, for the young mother who almost lost her son, caught up in her own grief, and for the woman I am today, learning a little later than most what it is to come out on the other side of loss.

I know many people in my life quietly feel that this grieving has gone on long enough. I think so too. The years have passed. I have a happy life. I am lucky in my friends, my family and increasingly grateful for the choices that have brought me to this point. In some ways, I am the person I know today because of my loss. It changed everything for me. I don't feel grateful for it but there's no escaping its reality. A person I loved died. That reshaped me in the most visceral ways.

Every now and then, the grief returns. Once, I used to drown in it. Now, I keep my head above water. Surely, there is a point in my future, I tell myself, when I will swim against the tide and into calmer waters. This my friend has taught me to hope for with her example. We smile for each other though neither of us allows the mask to drop completely. I know she hurts for me just as my heart aches for her. We listen to each other's words, offer tough love, try to stay positive and bolster each other. What else can friends do?

The loss of a loved one is not a rare occurrence. Death is not in the business of bargaining or negotiating. The aftermath of death is still an isolating existence. Invisible lines stretch between each of us who have lost someone, which can and do offer solace and comfort. But no one's grief can compare to your own. It is truly something that is yours alone.

There are no words to describe the loss of a young friend to an overdose, or a bright, beautiful sister to cancer, or a child to heart disease. Language literally has no word for a parent who has lost a child, or for people like my friend and I, who lost a sibling we hoped to tease and irritate into old age. I can tell you about the horrible aftermath of such loss. We the surviving siblings constantly underplay our loss, because really, how can it compare to the loss our parents are dealing with? How can anything we do compensate for their loss? The rest of our lives could easily be about making up for it, giving them the comfort and support they need or that we imagine they need. Our own sorrow is subsumed by theirs. And things can appear to stay that way for a very long time. Three decades in my case and counting.

A wonderful lady I loved showed me another way of dealing with loss and grief. She was the warmest, most elegant older friend I had. She had lost her two children, one as a child, the other a troubled teenager. In the face of this, and here I find any word inadequate (tragedy, loss—pale imitations of the reality), her lined beautiful face was never glum, her serene smile always lit up the world. Her immense dignity was like a guiding light. She chose silence but not coldness, a smiling face and a gentle heart without outward anger. Her grieving was private and personal and I had the greatest respect for her choices. I never dared intrude on her privacy in all the years I knew her, never asked her how she had come out on the other side, as if through a wall of fire, her spirit burnished and strong and so very beautiful. Our friendship was about the small things—potted plants that we exchanged, little gifts of food, and most of all, the respect I had for her, the smiles she left me as a keepsake.

One morning, she called me to her home. She was dying. Her face was pinched and drawn, her elegant hands like claws. I could feel the fever raging through her skin as she gently held my hands. Our unspoken history washed over me like a balm. She smiled her beautiful smile and handed me a package—it contained a gift that she said she wanted me to have now, not after she was gone.

Tears welled up in my eyes but all she said was: 'I have no regrets, Liana. I am ready to go.' She died a few days later.

My grief, in comparison, still feels messy and noisy, young and raw, while hers was, at least in my eyes, a grief grown venerable because of her dignity in dealing with it. I admired her but I'm not her. I've said it before: there is nothing more personal than grief. And I have chosen to deal with it by writing about it. Sharing it. Not locking it in any longer to fester at my core.

This healing is a soul-wrenching experience and a life-changing one. Painful, and in its own way, as overwhelming as any other experience we have known. But it comes to each of us, through unlikely agencies and in surprising forms. To some, it comes early. Others wait for a lifetime. It's a matter of recognizing it. Letting it in. Letting go of the addiction that grief can become.

Letting ourselves love again, letting ourselves believe again. Believe in love. Believe that we are not just made up of anger and grief, but of softer emotions as well.

I spent too many years doling out love in miserly portions. Consequently, I was often and accurately termed a bitch. Friends, lovers, family shared the common and unpleasant experience of the sharp edge of my tongue. I thought nothing of hurting people's feelings, as long as it meant my defences were up, the barricade unbreached, and the walls unscaled.

Love, though. It is relentless. The more you push it away, the higher the wave that rushes you off your feet. Maybe this is menopausal talk but my forties have been such a revelation when it comes to love. It's getting easier all the time. To say words of love to the people who matter. To show love to them and to the world around me too. To learn the hard lessons of kindness and gentleness. To love myself a little better than before, give myself a break. I'm still aggressive and abrasive and not everyone's cup of tea. But this love business is a process of evolution. I'm hopeful of the results. Like the MRI I spent weeks dreading and obsessing over, and which turned out to be a calm and peaceful experience, I see now that I wasted too many years worrying about the fallout of bringing the old barriers down. Now that they are gone for good, I can laugh at my silly fears.

There is irony in this la-la land though. Not everyone wants this love apparently. The more I reach out, the harder I try, the farther away they retreat. I haven't given up yet but I can see that day in the near future when I stop flogging dead emotions and make my peace with the absence of some love from my life. A day when I let it go. Leave it behind. Let it be. This too is love. Once the heartbreak is done, the passion wasted and the resignation overcome, this too is a measure of love. Learning to let go of the ones who are going anyway. Holding on with light hands and a light heart to the ones who choose to stay.

Of the people I love most in the world, two are dead. Honey and Jehan. One, Luke, I had to let go of, for his sake as well as mine. There's my family—Eruch, Carl and my kids, and my best friend, Karthik. And finally—and I fought it forever—me. It is tough love; I don't know any other kind I would trust around myself. But it's progress. Learning to go a little easy on myself. The willingness to look myself in the eye and to like who I see most of the time. These are small but hard won victories. A grand love for the ages may be what the poets dream about. As for me, I'll take the peace that this small world of love brings me every day.

As a child, I entertained superstitions and improbable beliefs dependent on phenomena beyond my control. If I left my footwear upside down, I'd quarrel with my brothers. If I tied a rakhi on their wrists every Raksha Bandhan, they'd rescue me in times of trouble. Or that the new moon looked like my face, which is why my mother had to look at me and kiss my forehead as soon as she spotted the thin sliver in the sky. I stopped believing, the year Jehan died.

I could have believed in God. I almost did, for a time in my very early years. It's an inviting and tantalizing prospect: to hand over your hopes and dreams and thoughts to an obscure, erratic entity who may or may not listen to your prayers. But death intervened. It has a way of erasing lightly held beliefs. God was dispensed with along with skipping ropes and innocence.

What I do believe in are the simple, everyday things. Nothing that may influence the world or its future, no great philosophical truth in them, just my personal keys to living each day the best I can.

Birdsong on a silent morning. Just before the city hums to life. The greens and browns of my backyard, never bare, always changing, the trees I love.

The smell of rain hanging in the cool air. The grey monsoon sky and the crisp blue of a windy February morning. The ocean.

The hug, bristly, brief and sleepy, of a sixteen-year-old.

Music. All kinds. Shehnai and sitar and the heavy beat of drums and bass guitar. Ghazals and pop, heavy metal and disco and Bollywood. Classic rock. The effortless voice of Karen Carpenter. Kishore Kumar and RD, Dio and Freddie, Jagjit Singh and Kishori Amonkar. Lata and Asha. Tina and Sheena and Gloria. Armstrong's trumpet and Blackmore's guitar.

Old friends. The ones who remember you from nightmarish days and dream-like nights, who know your pretence and artifice and hypocrisy. Who take you as you are and call you out on all of your nonsense. Your comrades of the heart and partners in crime.

The smell of onions and garlic and carrots roasting in the oven. Or bread baking. Or the taste of hot khichdi with a dollop of ghee. Three meals a day. A full pantry. So much to be grateful for.

The 8 am and 6 pm hug and kiss. Like a cool breeze and a hot sun. Reassurance, relief, respite, reason for life.

A book so beautifully written that the urge to read faster and internalize it rages against the need to slow down, savour it, never let it end. A full book cupboard.

My cross-stitch projects. A retreat into solitude. The act

of stitching in step with my breath, each stitch a song or a curse. Every finished square a moment of unthought, just the needle and me and the thread.

And once again, my writing.

These are the things I believe in.

Some people go from a fearless youth to a frightened old age. My life went down the opposite track. I was frightened away from happiness early on. Now the fear has receded. The worst, I dare to believe, has come and gone. What need, then, of prayer and ritual? These were of little use when I was young and running scared. I'm older now, maybe not wiser. The simple things are enough to believe in. They make for an unremarkably happy life.

Acknowledgements

Thank you, Vaishnavi, Sunitha, Jerry, Veena and Mala. I couldn't have written this book without you. You made me the writer I am.

Thank you to the team at Speaking Tiger Books for taking my baby on board: Ravi, Nazeef, Maithili and Rajinder.

Thank you to the readers of the first draft, the friends and family who patiently listened to late-night doubts and first-time writing jitters. You made me a kinder writer.

Thank you to the critics, the sceptics and the gaslighters. You made me a stronger writer.

ALSO FROM SPEAKING TIGER

A BOOK OF LIGHT

When a Loved One Has a Different Mind

Edited by Jerry Pinto

'[*A Book of Light*] reminds us why we need more art and literature around the subject of mental illness...it is a book we must all read.' —*Scroll.in*

In 2012, Jerry Pinto published his debut novel, *Em and the Big Hoom*, which drew upon his experience of living with a mother who was bipolar. It touched thousands of readers, among them many who also had a loved one afflicted with a mental illness or infirmity. Some of these readers shared their stories with Jerry, and agreed to share them with the world. *A Book of Light* collects these harrowing yet moving, even empowering, stories—about the fragility and immense strength of the human mind; the bleakness and unexpected grace of life; the terror and majesty of love. It has now become a book that many people with psychological challenges, and their friends and family, turn to for insight and solace—and to feel less invisible and alone.